The New Observer's Book of Cricket

About the Book

Few sports have undergone such momentous changes, and the *New Observer's Book of Cricket* traces its history and evolution since those formative years when only two stumps were used and players bowled under-arm. Each of the Test-playing countries is comprehensively reviewed and a special section is devoted to the 17 English first-class counties, listing their development and principal achievements. But its pages offer much more, including the various competitions played in the United Kingdom and in many other lands; the growth of women's cricket and the thriving Northern League game.

Who scored two double centuries in the same first-class match? Who hit the most first-class hundreds in his career? Who completed 1000 runs and 100 wickets in a season on most occasions? The answers to these and a myriad of other fascinating facts can be found in the many pages of statistics. Nor are the greatest stars of cricket overlooked. Their prodigious feats which made them household names are recorded in a series of easy-to-read biographies.

Ian Botham, whose exciting all-round talents have made such an impact on domestic and world circuits, introduces this compact and informative work.

About the Author

Reginald James Hayter has been closely involved in cricket since his days as captain of the St Marylebone Grammar School eleven. He helped compile *Wisden Cricketers' Almanack* both before the Second World War and afterwards; reported Test and county cricket for Britain's leading agency, The Press Association, and visited Australia, South Africa and the West Indies as cricket correspondent of Reuters. During the war he was joint founder of the British Empire XI which raised £100,000 for the Red Cross.

He edited *The Cricketer International* magazine during three of its most successful years and is proprietor of a Fleet Street freelance sports agency which he began in 1955. He is also the author of several books and a member of the MCC.

The New Observer's Book of

Cricket

by Reg Hayter

Frederick Warne

Published by Frederick Warne (Publishers) Ltd, London
Copyright © Frederick Warne & Co. Ltd, 1983

First published 1973
Revised edition 1976
Second revised edition 1979
Third revised edition 1983

Photographic acknowledgements

Sport & General Press Agency: Keith Miller and Godfrey Evans,
Len Hutton, Jack Hobbs, Wes Hall, Don Bradman, Denis
Compton, Gary Sobers, Fred Trueman, Frank Worrell; All-Sport
Photographic: Bob Willis, Clive Lloyd, Dennis Lillee, David
Gower, Imran Khan, Kapil Dev and Ian Botham

Originally published as The Observer's Book of Cricket in small
hardback format.

Library of Congress Catalog Card no 73-75026
ISBN 0 7232 1644 4

Typeset by CCC, printed and bound in
Great Britain by William Clowes (Beccles) Limited,
Beccles and London

Contents

Foreword
by Ian Botham
(*England & Somerset All-Rounder*)

Ever since my boyhood days when I played in the school teams at Milford School and Buckler's Mead in Yeovil, the first weeks of a fresh cricket season have always excited me.

The activity at any county ground, as staff prepare for the summer, and the general air of expectancy about the places, never ceases to fill me with optimism.

I start each summer thinking to myself: England are going to win all the Test matches; Somerset are powerful enough to pick up any of the various domestic prizes and, for my part, I expect to score lots of runs, take a crop of wickets and, of course, hold some spectacular catches, mostly in the slip area.

If that sounds cocky and brash, I make no apologies. To succeed in life you must adopt a positive attitude to whatever you undertake.

I go out to win every match. It has been that way from the time I haunted the local recreation ground as a nine year-old, carrying my kit, ready and eager to play for any side that happened to be short of a player. Not only did I want to be a part of that sporting scene, I wanted to help my team to succeed. I hated the thought of failure. I still do.

I soon discovered that confidence in one's ability is essential, whether you happen to be a Test cricketer or someone seeking to establish himself in a school, club or village eleven.

No player should give less than 100 per cent, and that is especially important when form suddenly deserts him.

I still recall, with agonising clarity, how depressed I felt after being *twice* dismissed for a 'duck' against the Australians in the second Test at Lord's during the 1981 series.

I knew then it was time for me to relinquish the captaincy and concentrate all my energies on atoning for those twin failures. The Aussies were one up as we went to Headingley for the third Test. What happened there, and in the subsequent Tests at Edgbaston and Old Trafford where we retained the Ashes, is now part of cricket's history. Suffice for me to say how thrilled I was to play a part in those successes.

That series provided the perfect illustration of how swiftly playing fortunes can change. So my advice to every sports-conscious youngster is not to despair if you begin to believe your bat has a permanent hole in it, or that your bowling arm is being guided by a malevolent force. Keep on trying and I am sure it will all come right in the end.

One of the fascinations of this marvellous game of cricket is its very uncertainty. I have known days when everything clicks. You strike the ball sweetly; the catches stick and life is great. Another day and, for some inexplicable reason, you down an absolute 'sitter' and get carted all over the field, probably by somebody who is not a recognised batsman!

Obviously, the bad days cannot be enjoyed but at least do your best not to let them affect your enthusiasm. After all, other players in the team depend upon you to keep going in difficult times. That is a mark of your character. They will not thank you if they sense a lack of effort simply because you have not had a successful day.

Cricket has taken me all over the world, from the great arenas of Australia to the astonishing synthetic grass surface of the Sharjah stadium in the United Arab Emirates. I have marvelled at such sights as the Baroda ground where the Maharajah's palace peeps over the trees, and the vast crowds which fill every corner of Eden Gardens, Calcutta, on Test match occasions. I have shared the uninhibited joy of West Indies fans and their steel bands in the Caribbean and savoured the unique rural charm of the game played on a typical English village green.

Yes, cricket has been good to me. I hope it will be for you, too, whether as a participant or onlooker.

Certainly, its worldwide appeal is splendidly conveyed in this informative book, which traces the game's phenomenal growth to the present era of enthralling one-day and international competitions.

I know some people regret the introduction of what is called 'instant' cricket. Yet the thousands attracted to the one-day game are proof, surely, that it is here to stay.

In this highly competitive marketing age, a winning business formula cannot easily be dismissed. As I have said, I enjoy winning and am all for introducing any idea which will strengthen cricket's hold on its public.

History of the Game

Cricket has passed the years of reluctance and has marched firmly into a new era—an age of sponsorship and mass appeal.

Gillette first breached the game's independence on a large scale with the introduction of their knockout cup in 1963. Since then, Benson and Hedges, John Player, Schweppes, Prudential, Cornhill, NatWest bank and many other companies have given financial support on varying scales.

Since 1972 many county grounds have housed betting marquees for spectators—another innovation that brought wide-eyed surprise from the traditionalists. But in fact all this is nothing new.

Cricket took healthy root in England and grew in popularity largely through the support it received from gamblers and sponsorship—in the form of patronage by some of the more wealthy families in the country—when the game was adopted as a leisure-time pursuit by members of the more privileged classes during the early 18th century.

Rules and regulations acceptable to all came much later. In those early days of the 1700s the rules varied from match to match, the conditions of play often depending on the terms of the wager struck between the opposing sides, but the broad outlines of the game bore a striking resemblance to cricket today.

For many years before, however, a simplified version of cricket—far removed from the game known today—had been played in England, although years of research by historians and scholars have failed to establish exactly how and when the game started.

There are several early references in various writings to people playing 'Creag', which is thought to be a rough form of cricket.

Such a reference appears in the household accounts of King Edward I, around 1300, concerning the Prince of Wales—the Prince of Wales feathers are used as the Surrey emblem—and there seems no doubt that 'crickett' was played by boys at the Free School of Guildford about 1550.

Cricket is again thought to have been associated with royalty in 1666 in St Albans. There is a reference to the St Albans Club having been formed in that year. It is said that King Charles II and his court, having been forced to move out of London by the flames of the great fire of London, were kept amused by the local inhabitants playing cricket.

Ten years later it is known that Englishmen started spreading the gospel of cricket around the world, for a group of sailors from the Royal Navy landed at Antioch in the Middle East and played cricket at Aleppo.

What seems certain from these rather vague and sparse references to the game is that the south-east of England was the early home of cricket and where it was later encouraged by the noblemen. The early references also show that no stumps were used, but the bowler was required to get the ball past the striker and land it in a hole. Later that hole was marked by a piece of wood, which led to the introduction of stumps.

In the early 1700s two stumps were used, widely spaced with a bail across the top. If the ball went between the stumps the batsman was not out. The bats were curled more in the manner of today's hockey stick to cope better with the under-arm bowling and enable the batsman to sweep the ball away on the rather crudely made pitches.

There is little known about the rules of the game in those days, but there must have been a fairly common code of conduct, for the first so-called inter-county match took place in 1719 between Kent and London in Lamb's Conduit Fields situated near present-day Bloomsbury.

Much of the credit for the establishment of the rules probably belongs to the gentlemen of the small Hampshire village of Hambledon and in particular to Richard Nyren, the landlord of the Bat and Ball Inn. He did much to inspire and encourage the formation of the Hambledon Club whose events were dutifully noted down by Richard Nyren's son, John. It was the Hambledon Club, for instance, who pioneered the use of the third stump in 1775, one year after the first set of widely accepted rules had been drawn up.

These were framed at a meeting of the Star and Garter Club in Pall Mall early in 1774, 30 years after a group of Noblemen and Gentlemen from London's Artillery Club completed the first known code. Although the Laws of Cricket have been taken out and revised from time to time, with various notes added to cover all eventualities, they still bear a striking resemblance to those worked out 200 years ago.

The one stipulation missing in 1774 was the number of players on each side, which was not specified until 1884 when a complete revision of the rules was undertaken. Until that time it was generally accepted that there should be 11 or 12 players on each side, but against some of the All England teams the opposition would field as many as 22!

At the time the Hambledon Club was becoming recognized as the leading influence on the growth of the game, the White Conduit Club was being formed, playing matches in what is now Islington. Out of the White Conduit Club came the Marylebone Cricket Club and the Lord's Cricket Ground, both of which were in existence in 1787.

The first Lord's Cricket Ground was not on the present site. It was named after a Yorkshireman, Thomas Lord, a member of the White Conduit Club, who was asked to start a new ground when their old ground was threatened by the expansion of London; he would be financially supported by members of the club.

His first ground, close to Marylebone Station, was opened in 1787—the same year the Marylebone Cricket Club was formed—and cricket was played there until the lease expired 23 years later.

The next ground was opened within three-quarters of a mile, but Lord was soon forced to move again when it was decided to build the Regent's Canal through his ground. This time he selected the site on which the present Lord's Cricket Ground stands. It was threatened once more when Lord retired and was given building permission for part of the area. He was persuaded to sell the land for £5000, however, to another player, William Ward, and it was not until 1866 that the ground was purchased by the Marylebone Cricket Club for £18,000. A year later they paid a similar amount to take over a neighbouring flower and fruit garden known today as the Nursery End.

Over the years cricket has found itself engaged in numerous controversies. One of the first major rows was brewing nicely about the time cricket was first played on the present Lord's site in 1814. This concerned the use of round-arm bowling instead of the gentle under-arm lob.

Under-arm bowling had proved efficient enough during the early days of cricket when the wickets were pitched on rough turf. Often the ball would bounce and deviate awkwardly for the batsmen—the reason for the curved bat. As the wickets improved and more care was taken over their selection and preparation, so the odds begin to swing in favour of the batsmen. The art of bowling began to change.

During the days of the Hambledon Club some players had attempted to use round-arm bowling, but its use was frowned upon by the majority of the players and under-arm bowling was still in common practice. From time to time bowlers still attempted to introduce round-arm bowling and in 1816 the Marylebone Cricket Club—now recognized as the senior authority on the game in settling disputes and responsible for alterations in the laws—sat in judgement and announced that all bowling must be under-arm. Any ball delivered with the arm horizontal would be illegal.

One of the most stubborn characters on the question of round-arm bowling was a John Willes of Kent who was determined throughout his cricketing life to use the round-arm method. It is believed that the idea came to him when his sister Christina was bowling to him at his home. As a result of the crinoline fashion worn by the ladies of that time, which consisted of a hooped petticoat to make the dress stand out from the waist downwards, Christina found difficulty in bowling the normal under-arm delivery. She solved it by bowling with a more horizontal arm and Willes was immediately struck by the awkwardness of playing a higher type of delivery that lifted after pitching, and adopted it in his own attack.

Round-arm bowling was finally legalized in 1835 and it was not long before cricket was engaged in another controversy. Bowlers began delivering from higher than the shoulder and, after a long dispute, over-arm bowling became accepted in 1864.

Other parts of the laws framed in 1774 were being overhauled gradually, although the weight of the ball of between $5\frac{1}{2}$ and $5\frac{3}{4}$ oz stood the test of time. In 1774 the over consisted of four balls and it was kept at this number for more than 100 years before the five-ball over was introduced in this country, the Australians going a stage further by making it a six-ball over. The number was increased to six balls in England in 1900, the Australians favouring the eight-ball over system after the First World War. Throughout this time the height of the stumps was gradually being increased from 22 in. in 1774 and 6 in. wide until they reached the present size of 28 in. and 9 in. wide which was agreed in 1931.

In the early 19th century cricket was gaining in popularity

throughout the country, helped by a number of touring All England teams. One of the most famous was organized by a William Clarke who married the owner of the Trent Bridge Inn, a widow, in 1837 and turned the neighbouring field into a cricket ground, the present site of the Trent Bridge ground and the home of Nottinghamshire.

About this time cricketers were looking for a larger identity than their own local clubs, and county associations were becoming organized on proper lines. Kent, Sussex and Hampshire were already well advanced and by 1850 most of the sides in the present championship were in the process of being launched.

The spread of cricket to other parts of the world was already well advanced by this time, the Army and the Royal Navy taking much of the credit. Wherever the Army pitched camp or the Navy docked, matches were organised between themselves and the game was taken up by the local inhabitants who were helped, in most cases, by having a suitable climate for the game. Sailors spread cricket to Australia, New Zealand and South Africa, the Army in the sub-continent of India and businessmen in South America.

Cricket was also being played in Canada and North America and it was to these countries that the first tour was undertaken under the captaincy of another famous Nottinghamshire cricketer, George Parr, in 1859. Cricket is still played in Canada. MCC send out teams every so often but the climatic conditions, coupled with the influence of the French have resulted in this being one corner of the former British Empire where the game has not become a leading national sport.

When the Australians heard about the tour to Canada and America they quickly arranged for a side to visit 'down under'. A Melbourne firm of caterers, Spiers and Pond, provided the financial backing—another early form of sponsorship—and in 1861–62 a touring side went out. Visits to South Africa, West Indies and New Zealand were made before the end of the century and teams from Australia and South Africa made reciprocal trips to England.

Although tours were becoming quite fashionable after that first visit to Australia in 1861 the Test series between England and Australia did not really get under way until the 1876–77 tour, the first Test between the two countries being staged at Melbourne in the March of 1877, Australia winning by 45 runs. England won the second Test, also at Melbourne, by four wickets, to level the series. The first Test in England was not until 1880 when England won the only game played at the Oval.

In those pioneering days some of the best players were often missing from the England and Australian sides, the authorities of the ground staging the Test match being responsible for the 'host' team. Not until 1899 was an England Selection Committee formed, a year after a Board of Control for Test Cricket had been set up.

Ten years earlier in 1888–89 the first England side had gone to South Africa and played a 'test' series, although the strength of the South Africans was poor. For some time this series and the three following tours by England sides were not counted in the first-class figures and it was not until the 1905–6 visit by a touring side to South Africa that real Tests are considered to have started between the two countries. Nevertheless the previous tours remain in the official statistics.

The first Test series against the West Indies was not until 1928 in England. The series against New Zealand began in 1929–30 and against India in 1932. The latest countries to gain Test status were Pakistan, following partition, and Sri Lanka, in 1981.

On the domestic front the County Championship—the senior and most prized tournament in English cricket—was first organized on a proper footing in 1895, although for a number of years before this inter-country matches were played. There was no organized county championship table, the press nominating their own champions at the end of the cricket season largely based on the number of matches lost, and the list of championship winners dates back to 1873 when Derbyshire, Gloucestershire, Kent, Lancashire, Middlesex, Nottinghamshire, Surrey, Sussex and Yorkshire took part.

Somerset joined in 1891, Essex, Hampshire, Leicestershire and Warwickshire entered in 1895 and Worcestershire four years later. In 1905 Northamptonshire was admitted and the total was increased to the present 17 when Glamorgan became 'first class' in 1921.

The rules for deciding the championship have varied greatly over the years, starting with the first system when the championship was unofficial. The title then went to the county with the 'least matches lost', which was an unsatisfactory system because not every county played the same number of matches.

13

This system was in operation for 13 years until 1887 when a win counted as one point and a draw half a point. The procedure lasted three seasons and from 1890 to 1909 the number of points gained was decided by deducting losses from wins. This was still an unsatisfactory method because of the difference in the matches played by each county. A much fairer method was introduced in 1910 when the result was decided by a percentage of matches won to matches played.

The following year first-innings points were added for the first time and in 1957 bonus points were awarded to the side scoring at the faster rate measured in runs per over when first-innings lead was taken. There was another small alteration in 1960 when some county sides played 32 matches and others 28, and it was decided that the championship should be gauged by the number of points gained, divided by the number of matches played.

This continued until 1963 when the championship was standardized to 28 matches, and in 1966 the first innings was limited to 65 overs, but that lasted for just one summer.

There was another change in 1969 when bonus points were re-introduced, points for first-innings lead being dropped. One point was awarded for every 25 runs scored over 150 by the batting side in the first 85 overs of the first innings, and the bowling side was awarded one point for every two wickets captured in the first 85 overs.

Then in 1974, by which time each county was playing just 20 Championship fixtures, came the most recent change. The first two innings were limited to 200 overs, with the side batting first confined to 100, and a new ball was made available after 100 overs in each innings instead of 85. The bonus points system was also altered.

For more than a decade, the championship game, the real backbone of English cricket, has suffered from a comparison with the flourishing limited-over variety. The arrival of the Gillette Cup in 1963 heralded the birth of a new world for players and a new breed of spectators.

The major advantage from the spectators' point of view was that they could see a result in one day, provided there was no rain interference. The knock-out element also attracted people who found the three-day championship game difficult to follow and who demanded runs quickly scored however crudely. Quarter-final rounds played in mid-week often draw near 'ground-full' crowds.

The formula was so successful that tobacco companies looked to cricket as a means of advertising when they were banned from advertising cigarettes on television, and this led to the introduction of the John Player League in 1969. Matches are played on a Sunday, limited to 40 overs and run on a league basis with points awarded for victory.

A further competition was added in 1972, the Benson and Hedges Cup. The first section is run on a league basis with the country split into four zones. The first two in each zone go into the draw for the quarter-finals and the competition finishes on a knock-out basis. It was in order to make room for this competition that the county championship programme was reduced to 20 matches.

Prudential, whose cricket involvement had previously been confined to the sponsorship of several one-day internationals, launched the sport's first World Cup in 1975 and NatWest took over from Gillette in 1981.

Each of the major Test-playing countries with the exception of South Africa, plus East Africa and Sri Lanka, participated in the event, which was staged in England over a 15-day period blessed with almost incessant sunshine. West Indies became the first holders by beating Australia in an emotional final before a Lord's full house.

Other Test-playing countries have their own domestic competition. In Australia it is called the Sheffield Shield, in New Zealand the Shell series, the Shell Shield in the West Indies and the Currie Cup in South Africa; the main competition in India is the Ranji Trophy, and in Pakistan they have both the Quaid-e-Azam and the Patron Trophies.

One other change forced on cricket in recent years was the renaming of the Imperial Cricket Conference. This body, with representatives from all cricket-playing countries, meets once a year at Lord's to make sure there is uniformity in the interpretation of the rules. They also discuss possible amendments and arrange future tours. The name was changed following the decision of South Africa to withdraw from the Commonwealth, and it is now known as the International Cricket Conference, countries outside the Commonwealth being permitted to send representatives.

As a result of the South African apartheid policy there has never been a full Test-playing programme. South Africa have not met West Indies, Pakistan or India at Test level and their international programme has been confined to matches against England, Australia and New Zealand. These were interrupted in 1968 when the South African Government found the presence of Basil D'Oliveira, England and Worcestershire all-rounder who was born in Cape Town of Cape Coloured parents, 'unacceptable' in the MCC side to tour the country in 1968–69. The MCC had little alternative but to cancel their tour—visiting Pakistan instead—and were finally forced to cancel the proposed South African visit to this country in 1970 when anti-apartheid bodies threatened to disrupt all the games involving South Africa.

A visit by South Africa to Australia in 1971–72 was cancelled for a similar reason. In both instances the South African 'Test' fixtures were completed by sides drawn from players from the Rest of the World, with South Africans playing alongside West Indian, Indian and Pakistan players.

In 1970 the MCC decided they would not accept another invitation to tour South Africa until they were satisfied that steps were taken which would lead towards cricket in the country being played on a non-racial basis.

In 1977 World Series Cricket Pty Ltd, a company run by Mr Kerry Packer, an Australian businessman, successfully won a law suit against the International Cricket Conference and the Test and County Cricket Board who wanted to ban World Series players from Test and other first-class cricket following the WSC decision to stage their own series of international matches. Mr Justice Slade ruled that it would be an unnecessary restraint of trade. Many of the world's leading players signed for Mr Packer and the ramifications were widespread. Some English first-class counties offered only one-year contracts in 1978 to those who had joined WSC. In 1979 the major Test playing nations, plus 15 of the 17 Associate members of the ICC, took part in the second Prudential World Cup tournament in England.

Sri Lanka were admitted to full membership of the International Cricket Conference in 1981 and England won the inaugural Test between the countries by seven wickets at Colombo in February, 1982.

Cricket in England and Wales

The County Championship

As with the early beginnings of cricket, the first years of the county championship are partly clouded in uncertainty and conflicting information. Official recognition can be traced to 1895 when MCC first became responsible for naming the winners. Other chroniclers still insist that the competition should be recognized from 1887 when a points scoring method came into operation, and a further body of opinion maintains that the first winners go back to 1864.

For most record purposes, however, the championship is considered to have started in 1873, following a meeting of county representatives in the previous year when a start was made on establishing rules for the formation of the county sides playing at the time.

Yorkshire dominated the competition in the period between the two world wars and again during the 1960s. Surrey have been the next most successful county. They set a record in the 1950s when they won the title seven years in succession, and are followed by Nottinghamshire whose record of 14 outright championship titles plus a share of the prize on five other occasions was largely gathered in the early years of the competition. They shared the championship in 1873 with Gloucestershire when nine counties took part, Yorkshire, Surrey, Derbyshire, Kent, Lancashire, Middlesex and Sussex making up the number.

Derbyshire

Formed: 1870

The County Ground, Nottingham Road,
Derby DE2 6DA. Tel: Derby 44849

Throughout their first-class cricketing life Derbyshire have had
to struggle to remain a consistent force in the county championship. Yet over the years few counties have produced a finer
array of fast-bowling talent. The red-haired Bill Copson, George
Pope, Les Jackson, Cliff Gladwin, Harold Rhodes and, more
recently, Alan Ward and Mike Hendrick, are among those who
have opened England's attack. In many instances recognition
has proved brief. Jackson, for example, made two appearances
for England, the first in 1949 and the second 12 years later in
1961, though few understood why this splendid bowler was
ignored for so long by the selectors.

The early history of Derbyshire belongs to the determined
band of enthusiasts who strove to convince people both inside
and outside the county that the club deserved first-class status.
Formed in 1870, Derbyshire was one of nine first-class playing
county sides in 1873 when championship-qualification rules
were first agreed.

After early successes, which according to some historians
included winning the championship in 1874, Derbyshire began
to tumble and in 1887 lost their first-class status after only one
victory in the previous four seasons.

Seven years elapsed before they were accepted again by their
rivals as worthy first-class opposition. They had been assisted
during this period by that fine Australian fast bowler Frederick
Spofforth who married a local girl and captained the side for a
season. His reputation and personality helped awaken interest
in the team's activities.

There was, too, a memorable occasion in 1910 when J.
Chapman (165) and A. R. Warren (123) put on 283 for the ninth
wicket against Warwickshire at Blackwell, which remains a
world record.

Nevertheless, Derbyshire's struggles were far from over and
10 years later they lost all 17 matches. Happily for them, the
county at last began to find a succession of captains with
outstanding leadership qualities; men capable of moulding the
side into a fighting unit and making the maximum use of the
talent available. The first was G. M. Buckston in 1921 who
successfully wiped away the bitter memories of that previous

summer. Next came G. R. Jackson a year later, and A. W. Richardson, who took over in 1931, led the county to their championship success in 1936 after they had finished sixth, third and second in the previous three seasons.

The side at that period contained some of the outstanding individuals in the club's history, including Stan Worthington who toured Australia with MCC in 1936–37 under G. O. Allen and the left-handed Denis Smith who played twice against South Africa in 1935. Les Townsend proved a reliable batsman as well as a useful bowler, but the bowling honours were shared between leg-spinner Tommy Mitchell who still holds the Derbyshire record for wickets in a season of 168 in 1935, and Bill Copson. All five played for England in the 1930s.

Derbyshire came close to repeating their title success the following season, but rain interfered with their programme, and both Copson and Mitchell missed matches because of injury.

After some unrewarding seasons the county made another positive challenge for the championship in 1954, this time under the leadership of G. L. Willatt, but were edged out by Surrey and Yorkshire.

Twelve months later Donald Carr accepted the captaincy and his appointment marked the start of one of Derbyshire's most consistent playing periods for a number of years. Indeed, only once in the eight years under his leadership did the team finish in the bottom half of the table. Carr himself proved a reliable batsman and in 1959 became the first player to score more than 2000 runs for the club in a season.

In 1982 Peter Kirsten, a South African-born batsman, hit eight championship centuries, and John Wright, a New Zealander, hit seven, each beating the previous county record. The previous year, led by Barry Wood, formerly of Lancashire, Derbyshire became first holder of the NatWest Bank Trophy.

In addition to producing fast bowlers Derbyshire have a reputation for finding wicket-keepers of the highest standard. Four have kept wicket for England—W. Storer in 1897, J. Humphries 10 years later, H. Elliott in the 1920s and, more recently, Bob Taylor who has dismissed more batsmen than anyone in the game's history.

Best in County Championship: Winners 1874, 1936. **Best in Gillette Cup:** Finalists 1969. **Best in NatWest Trophy:** Winners 1981. **Best in John Player League:** Third 1970. **Best in Benson and Hedges Cup:** Finalists 1978.

Essex   Formed 1876

The County Ground, New Writtle Street,
Chelmsford, Essex. Tel: Chelmsford 354533

Even today when financial rewards have put a higher premium
on success and induced a more cautious approach Essex still
look as if they are *enjoying* the game and there is no more
popular side in the country.

This spirit has been a feature of their play over the years. In
fact, the character of their cricket has enabled Essex to
overcome serious financial problems and also the handicap of
being a rural county with limited population from which to draw
players and supporters.

Despite winning the title only once, Essex have produced
numerous personalities and many England players. Minimal
reserve strength, especially when players are away on Test duty,
probably accounts for the rather switchback course run by the
county in their final placings since joining the championship in
1895.

One of the earliest personalities was Charles Kortright,
undoubtedly the fastest bowler of his day and a player who
refused to be weighed down with theory. His one object was to
bowl as fast as he could and as straight as he could. Two-thirds
of his victims were clean bowled, which makes it all the more
remarkable that he never played for England. Essex possessed
two other bowlers in that period who made Test appearances
against Australia in 1899, Walter Mead, the first Essex player to
take 100 wickets with his spin bowling, and left-arm bowler
'Sailor' Young.

Another player whose outstanding ability as a county player
was not rewarded by an England cap was Percy Perrin whose
343 not out against Derbyshire at Chesterfield in 1904 still
stands as the highest individual score by an Essex player.

A contemporary of Perrin was C. P. McGahey who played
twice for England and led the county for three seasons until
handing over to one of their most notable all-rounders—Johnny
Douglas. This outstanding fast medium bowler and solid
batsman played 23 times for England, twice leading them on
tours of Australia and also in South Africa. He captained Essex
from 1911 until 1928 and his name still figures prominently in
the county record books. F. L. Fane and A. C. Russell were two
other batsmen who achieved considerable success for Essex in

the first 30 years of the county's championship life, both playing for England. Russell was the first England batsman to score two separate hundreds in a Test.

Essex were then approaching one of their most consistent periods in the championship. From 1933 to the outbreak of the Second World War they were never lower than ninth.

In these years Tom Pearce first made his influence felt throughout the county, both as a batsman and a captain. He shared the leadership with D. R. Wilcox until the war and was solely in charge for the four years immediately afterwards.

Essex had at their command probably the best opening attack of the day, consisting of 6 ft 5 in. Kenneth Farnes, a fearsome fast bowler who played 15 times for England, H. D. 'Hopper' Read, supported by Col. Jack Stephenson, Ray Smith and all-rounder Morris Nichols, plus the leg-spin of Peter Smith. Pearce was a force in the batting, together with Nichols and Jack O'Connor, another England player, who scored 1000 runs in 15 successive seasons.

In the postwar years Essex were splendidly served by the batting combination of 'Sonny' Avery and Dicky Dodds, the latter a fine player of fast bowling; the unorthodox but effective middle-order belligerence of Doug Insole—later to become chairman of England's selectors in the 1960s; and the all-round strength of Trevor Bailey who played 61 times for England.

Under Insole and the first few years of Bailey's command Essex threatened to challenge for the championship, but lack of adequate replacements when leading players were not available for one reason or another, resulted in their faltering in vital matches.

Under the enthusiastic captaincy of wicket-keeper Brian Taylor, they became a strength in the one-day competitions. When England batsman Keith Fletcher succeeded Taylor, the cultured batting of Graham Gooch and the accurate seam bowling of John Lever served both county and England well during the 1970s. In 1979 Essex won the Championship, Fletcher, who led them, also captained England in India in 1981–82.

Best in County Championship: Winners 1979. **Best in Gillette Cup:** Semi-final 1978. **Best in NatWest Trophy:** Semi-final 1981. **Best in John Player League:** Winners 1981. **Best in Benson and Hedges Cup.** Finalists 1980.

Glamorgan

Formed: 1888

Sophia Gardens, 6 High Street, Cardiff.
Tel: Cardiff 29956

By far the youngest of the first-class counties—they were not admitted to the county championship until 1921—Glamorgan have achieved more success than a number of older rivals. Twice they have taken the title outside England, in 1948 and 1969, and each time the feat has been greeted by scenes of unparalleled enthusiasm from their supporters.

To a large extent the story of Glamorgan cricket is dominated by three personalities, Maurice Turnbull, Johnny Clay and Wilfred Wooller. This triumvirate was dedicated to spreading the gospel of cricket throughout Wales and encouraging the provision of facilities for the future. All three served England as selectors.

For the first few years after admission to the championship Glamorgan faced a struggle to gain acceptance as worthwhile first-class opponents and to convince their competitors that cricket was worth watching in the break between the rugby seasons.

The one occasion in the season when they seldom lacked support was for the match against the touring side. Welshmen viewed this game more as an international than a friendly fixture, in which national pride was at stake. This is partly why Glamorgan can point to such an outstanding record against touring sides, having beaten every test-playing country.

The turning point in their fight to be established came with the appointment of Turnbull as captain in 1930. He was a strong disciplinarian, a positive thinker and a man capable of organization as well as leadership. Turnbull captained the side until the Second World War, and while their final positions in the championship were not impressive, the county was to benefit in the long run from his shrewd handling of affairs both on and off the field.

From their first year in the championship until the competition was suspended after the 1939 season, Glamorgan regularly finished in the last four. There were two exceptions. In 1926, when Clay was leading the side, they finished eighth and in 1937 they were seventh under Turnbull. Throughout Turnbull's reign he was fortunate to have Clay's off-spin bowling to call upon as well as his advice.

Turnbull became the first Glamorgan player to be capped by

England when he appeared against New Zealand at Christchurch in 1929, and the following winter toured South Africa with MCC. Clay became an England player in the 1930s. Another stalwart of these times was Emrys Davies, the regular opening batsman who, in 1935, became the first Glamorgan player to achieve the 'double'. These three were the main heroes in Glamorgan's best pre-war season of 1937 when Clay took 176 wickets with his off-spin.

After all the work Clay put in for the club it was appropriate that he should have another fine season in 1948 when Glamorgan, under the captaincy of Wooller, won the championship for the first time.

They clinched the title against Hampshire at Bournemouth in Clay's final match. He was then aged 48. In that season Wooller was helped by the off-spin bowling of Len Muncer, recruited from Middlesex to assist Clay, the all-round batting and left-arm medium-paced bowling of Allan Watkins (who was to open the England attack that year against Don Bradman's all-conquering Australian side), Gilbert Parkhouse, a fine batsman who played for England in the 1950s and Haydn Davies, a wicket-keeper whose talents were sometimes underrated outside his native Wales.

Perhaps the main reason for their capture of the title that season was the splendid close-to-the-wicket catching, particularly on the leg side. This has been a feature of Glamorgan's play in recent years and was clearly in evidence in 1969 when the Welsh county took the title again, this time captained by Tony Lewis. Three years after this triumph, Lewis was appointed captain of MCC for their winter tour to India and Pakistan. He retired from first-class cricket at the close of the 1974 season, leaving the county captaincy in the hands of Pakistan batsman Majid Khan. Alan Jones, who has scored more runs for the county than any other player, led them to the 1977 Gillette Cup final when they lost to Middlesex. Another loyal servant was Don Shepherd who, in 1969, became the first Glamorgan bowler to take 2000 wickets.

Best in County Championship: Winners 1948, 1969. **Best in Gillette Cup:** Finalist 1977. **Best in NatWest Trophy:** Second round 1981, 1982. **Best in John Player League:** 8th 1977. **Best in Benson and Hedges Cup:** Quarter-finalists 1972, 1973.

Gloucestershire

Formed: 1871

The County Ground, Nevil Road, Bristol.
Tel: Bristol 45216

Twice in recent years Gloucestershire entered the last month of the season well placed to carry off the championship. On each occasion, however, their batting let them down. In 1969 they were overhauled by Glamorgan, and in 1972 they bowed to the strength of Warwickshire.

How ironic it is that Gloucestershire should falter in this manner, for the county has a tradition for producing powerful stroke-makers and none more famous than William Gilbert Grace, who dominated cricket in this country in the late 1880s, and Walter Hammond, the outstanding all-round cricketer of his day.

Before the county championship began on a regular and acceptable basis in 1873 Gloucestershire were already a formidable side. The most influential figure in those early days was Dr H. M. Grace, a Bristol man who showed a deep love for the game and gave it his five sons, three of them, Edward, W. G. and Fred all going on to play for England in the first Test held in this country against Australia at the Oval in 1880.

The three brothers were all in the Gloucestershire side during their first season of championship cricket when they were unbeaten and shared the title with Nottinghamshire. They won the championship outright in 1874, 1876 and 1877.

W. G. Grace captained Gloucestershire for 29 seasons until a disagreement with the committee in 1899 resulted in his resigning, and settling in London. He continued to play cricket although he was then 51, but he never played for Gloucestershire again.

Towards the end of Grace's career two other players were beginning to establish themselves. One was C. L. Townsend, a fine left-hand bat and one of the first in a long line of famous Gloucestershire spin bowlers.

The other was Gilbert Jessop, among the mightiest hitters the game has known. Whenever he was at the wicket for a long innings he would score at the rate of 100 runs an hour. He was also a brilliant fielder in the covers and a medium-paced bowler good enough to open for England. He took over the captaincy from W. G. Grace in 1900 and held it for 12 years during which time he played regularly for England and toured Australia.

During his captaincy reign Jessop saw the start of the career of perhaps the county's finest bowler, Charles Parker, whose near medium-paced left-arm spin bowling brought him 3278 wickets.

Towards the end of his career Parker was partnered by Tom Goddard who had the physique of a fast bowler and, indeed, started his career as one until switching to off-spin. The career figures of the two are similar. Goddard took 2979 wickets in his first-class games. Like Parker he achieved the hat-trick on six occasions and took 100 wickets in a season 16 times.

Perhaps the most famous name in the Gloucestershire side during the time Parker and Goddard were in harness was that of Walter Hammond who as a batsman ranks with the greatest names of cricket. He also possessed the additional qualities of being an outstanding fielder, particularly at slip, a gifted opening bowler of just above medium pace, and a leader of England Test teams.

Reg Sinfield, steady batsman and off-spinner, Charlie Barnett, an aggressive batsman, Jack Crapp and George Emmett made Gloucestershire a thrilling side to watch in the 1930s, especially with the adventurous B. H. Lyon as skipper, yet the championship eluded them. After the war came Tom Graveney, one of the most elegant batsmen of the last 20 years, to maintain their reputation of producing exciting stroke-makers. Arthur Milton provided the steadying influence through 30,000 runs, while Sam Cook, John Mortimore and David Allen were top of their class as spinners. In addition to their 'near misses' in 1969 and 1972, Gloucestershire were runners-up in the championships of 1930, 1931, 1947 and 1959.

The county's first 20th-century triumph came in 1973, when magnificent performances from long-serving skipper Tony Brown and South African Mike Procter gained victory over Sussex in the Gillette Cup Final. It was generally through these two players, aided by Pakistan Test stars Sadiq Mohammad and Zaheer Abbas, that Gloucestershire gleaned some success in the 1970s.

Best in County Championship: Winners 1874, 1876, 1877 (Shared title in 1873). **Best in Gillette Cup:** Winners 1973. **Best in NatWest Trophy:** Quarter-final 1982. **Best in John Player League:** Sixth 1969, 1973, 1977. **Best in Benson and Hedges Cup:** Winners 1977.

Hampshire

Formed: 1863

The County Ground, Banister Park,
Northlands Road, Southampton.
Tel: Southampton 24155

For 98 years, success escaped the men of Hampshire. Yet by the mid-1970s they were recognized as one of the most powerful county sides in England.

It all began with the County Championship triumph of 1961, contrived, against all the pundits' predictions, under the merry captaincy of Colin Ingleby-Mackenzie.

Hampshire waited 12 years for their next honour, but since lifting the Championship again in 1973 they have booked their place among the country's elite. Their mighty bid to retain the title was thwarted more by weather than by Worcestershire and in 1975 they led the pack again for much of the race before conceding to Ray Illingworth's Leicestershire.

In 1975 and again in 1978 Hampshire won the John Player League and at last supported the theory that their spectacular talent was well-suited to the limited-over game.

Recent triumphs owe much to the captaincy of Richard Gilliat, Hertfordshire-born and an ex-skipper of Oxford University. Gilliat led Hampshire from 1971–78 and was fortunate to have such international stars as Barry Richards (South Africa) and Gordon Greenidge and Andy Roberts (West Indies) under his wing. Richards and Greenidge formed an exciting opening partnership while Roberts became one of the deadliest strike bowlers in county cricket. During the 1978 season, however, Richards and Roberts were released from their contracts, apparently disenchanted with seven-days-a-week cricket.

The lone survivor from the 1961 title, Peter Sainsbury, a tireless exponent of the spin-bowling art and a more than useful middle-order batsman, became county coach in 1976.

During that first season of triumph, Sainsbury shared the bowling honours with Derek Shackleton, a master craftsman in the field of swing bowling, and pace bowler David 'Butch' White.

The main batting force was carried by West Indian Roy Marshall, one of the most exciting stroke-makers of his day. Marshall completed 1000 runs 18 times for Hampshire and was succeeded by Richards in recent years as the golden boy of the county's batting.

Richards was only denied the right to prove himself the finest batsman of the era by South Africa's rejection from the world's Test match circuit. His partner Greenidge, and fast bowlers Roberts and Malcolm Marshall established themselves in the West Indian Team in the mid 1970s.

Even before that momentous 1961 year, Hampshire possessed many splendid players, particularly batsmen. Yet they seldom achieved the correct blend to make a serious assault on the honours, despite the efforts of several outstanding captains, including Desmond Eagar who led the side from 1946 to 1957.

Hampshire also produced the outstanding batsman of his time in the left-handed Phil Mead. Only three batsmen have bettered his 55,061 runs in first-class cricket. Twice, in 1921 and 1928, he scored more than 3000 runs in a summer.

His name still dominates the Hampshire record books and his aggregate run total of 48,892 for the county will surely never be beaten. He holds the record for runs in a season of 2854, most hundreds in a season (12) and most hundreds in a career (138). Another name of the same period which still features in the Hampshire records is that of medium-paced bowler Alec Kennedy whose 190 wickets in the summer of 1922 remain a county record.

For many years Kennedy and Jack Newman, an off-spinner who also used the new ball effectively at medium pace, constituted the Hampshire attack, both finishing with more than 2000 wickets in their careers. Supporting Mead with the bat was Charles Fry, a brilliant all-round athlete who moved to the county from Sussex when taking a naval post in Hampshire, and George Brown. When these batsmen retired within a few seasons of each other Hampshire found them difficult to replace and in the late 1920s and throughout the 1930s they were one of the weaker counties. Nevertheless they continued to produce fine players, including Johnny Arnold, a quick-witted batsman whose England career was surprisingly limited to one match on the cricket field, but he also gained international honours for England at football.

Best in County Championship: Winners 1961, 1973. **Best in Gillette Cup:** Semi-finalists 1966, 1976. **Best in NatWest Trophy:** Quarter-final 1982. **Best in John Player League:** Winners 1975, 1978. **Best in Benson and Hedges Cup:** Semi-finalists 1975, 1977.

Kent

Formed: 1870

St Lawrence Ground, Old Dover Road,
Canterbury. Tel: Canterbury 56886

Kent hold the record for the earliest date by which the championship has been won when they secured the title by August 12 in 1910. They were also involved in one of the most dramatic title hunts in their centenary year of 1970 in which they fittingly carried off the championship again—after a lapse of 57 years.

Their main run of championship titles came in the early days of the competition. They won the title four times between 1906 and 1913 and twice came second in that period under the captaincy of C. H. B. Marsham and E. W. Dillon. Both were members of a brilliant batting side when the championship was first won in 1906, along with J. R. Mason, C. J. Burnup and the strong-hitting K. L. Hutchings. They had much to do with the county's triumph, but it was in the field that Kent really shone, inspired by wicket-keeper Fred Huish.

That season also saw the start of one of Kent's most noted and elegant batsmen, the left-handed Frank Woolley. A great stylist, a model for any watching youngster, Woolley scored more first-class runs than any other player apart from Hobbs, making 58,969. He reached 1000 runs in 28 consecutive seasons from 1907 to 1938, once obtaining 3000 runs in a season and scoring 2000 runs a season on 12 occasions.

During their early years in the championship Kent were fortunate to have the inspiration of Lord Harris to lift them, not only as a captain for 18 years but often doubling as honorary secretary and in one year, holding the office as President.

Kent had another such influential figure in the 1930s when Percy Chapman, a dashing left-handed bat and glorious fielder, especially at silly point, led the county and captained England. He skippered MCC to Australia in 1928–29 and returned with the Ashes, winning the series 4–1.

Two other great influences on Kent cricket between the two world wars were wicket-keeper/batsman Les Ames and leg-break and googly bowler 'Tich' Freeman, who often bowled all day.

Ames was an outstanding wicket-keeper to spin bowling, and during his career made 415 stumpings, which still stands as a record. He was also a brilliant batsman against spin, scored 1000 runs in a season on 17 occasions, more than 37,000 runs in his career and hit 102 centuries.

Only the best of batsmen could play the leg-breaks of Freeman with any confidence. In 1928 he took 304 wickets during the summer—more than any player has achieved—and on seven other occasions took more than 200 wickets in a season. Only the great Wilfred Rhodes took more wickets in a career than Freeman's 3776 at an average of 18·42.

His role in the Kent side was taken over in the mid 1930s by another fine leg-break bowler, Doug Wright, who bowled at a faster pace than Freeman. In his career, interrupted by the war years, Wright took more than 2000 wickets and achieved the hat-trick on no fewer than seven occasions.

In more recent years the class batting in Kent has been provided by Colin Cowdrey, a player who has not always played to his full potential, yet has scored more runs in Test cricket—over 7000—than any other England player except Boycott. He could play all types of bowling, being a superb timer of the ball and a master of placing. He led Kent for 15 seasons.

Derek Underwood has proved a master as a left-arm bowler at near medium pace and is virtually unplayable on rain-affected wickets. In his first season, at the age of 18, he took 100 wickets.

Kent's other tradition has been in producing outstanding wicket-keepers from Huish, through Hubble, G. E. C. Wood, Ames and 'Hopper' Levett, down to Godfrey Evans who played 91 times for England, claiming 219 victims, and Alan Knott who shared the dismissal of 269 batsmen in 95 Tests.

Scottish-born batsman Mike Denness took on the captaincy in 1972 and helped Kent the following season to win the John Player League and the Benson and Hedges Cup. Denness also led the side to another Gillette Cup triumph in 1974 and captained England 19 times. Subsequently Asif Iqbal and Alan Ealham guided Kent to further honours, Ealham in his first season as leader taking them to a Championship and Benson and Hedges 'double' in 1978.

Best in County Championship: Winners 1906, 1909, 1910, 1913, 1970, 1978. Shared in 1977. **Best in Gillette Cup:** Winners 1967, 1974. **Best in NatWest Trophy:** Second round 1981, 1982. **Best in John Player League:** Winners 1972, 1973, 1976. **Best in Benson and Hedges Cup:** Winners 1973, 1976, 1978.

Lancashire

Formed: 1864

Old Trafford, Manchester 16.
Tel: Manchester 8720261

Four victories in the Gillette Cup Final and two triumphs in the John Player League are proof of how successfully Lancashire adapted to the demands of limited-over cricket. Without a doubt one-day cricket has been the saving of the Red Rose county. The crowds who almost deserted the famous ground after years of disappointing results in the championship flocked back to Old Trafford in the 1970's.

As far as championship cricket is concerned Lancashire have enjoyed two wonderful periods in their history. They were the outstanding side from 1875 to 1905 during which time they won the championship outright on three occasions, shared the title in four other seasons, and finished in second place eight times.

Their second period of joy was after the First World War when they won the championship five times between 1926 and 1934. They won it four years out of five between 1926 and 1930, finishing in second place in 1929. Not until 1950 were they to win the championship again (with Surrey).

Their fine run around the turn of the century was inspired largely by the batting feats of A. N. Hornby who led the side at various times between 1880 and 1898 and played with tremendous vigour both from the crease and in the field, plus R. G. Barlow, a patient man who broke the heart of many a bowler by his great powers of concentration.

In support Lancashire had Albert Ward and Archie MacLaren who was the opposite to Barlow in almost every way. He believed the ball was there to be hit and proceeded to do so, even on the most difficult of wickets.

Bowling strength at the time was supplied by A. Mold, a fast bowler who was later accused of throwing, and Johnny Briggs, a slow medium left-arm bowler who took more than 2000 wickets in his career, all 10 in a match against Worcestershire and 100 in a season on 11 occasions.

The other force in the batting was provided by John Tyldesley and the graceful R. H. Spooner. Soon after the start of the century John Tyldesley was joined in the side by his younger brother Ernest and their records are remarkable for their similarity. In his 27 years of first-class cricket Ernest scored

30

38,874 runs in 961 innings. John played 30 innings more and scored just 1000 runs less.

Unlike their neighbours Yorkshire, Lancashire have never insisted on their players being born inside their own county borders although the policy has caused numerous disputes over the years among supporters. They were always willing to import players and justified the policy by their achievements during the 1920s. This time their strength lay in the quality of their bowling attack and they won the title in 1926 largely on the performance of fast bowlers C. H. Parkin from Durham and the mighty Australian E. A. McDonald. By this time McDonald had already established a world-wide reputation as a fast bowler by his deeds for Australia.

In Lancashire's hat-trick of championship victories in 1926, 1927 and 1928 McDonald took 484 wickets in championship games, magnificently supported by the well-flighted leg-spin of Richard Tyldesley who took 303 championship wickets in the same period.

Those years also saw the emergence of that outstanding wicket-keeper George Duckworth, who was to play 24 times for his country, and later the aggressive left-handed batting of Eddie Paynter. Towards the end of the 1930s another batting figure was starting to dominate Lancashire's innings in the form of Cyril Washbrook.

He was to serve England well in the tough period after the Second World War as regular opening partner to Hutton, as was fast bowler Brian Statham, a model of length and direction, whose haul of 252 wickets for England has been bettered only by Trueman and Underwood.

Statham was captain for a time when Lancashire rebuilt their side, handing over a team of promise to Jack Bond whose enthusiastic leadership channelled the ability into winning the Gillette Cup in 1970, 1971 and 1972 and the John Player League in 1969 and 1970. A fourth Gillette success, in 1975, was guided by new captain David Lloyd. His namesake, Clive Lloyd, the West Indies batsman, was appointed county skipper in 1981.

Best in County Championship: Winners 1881, 1897, 1904, 1926, 1927, 1928, 1930, 1934. Shared title in 1879, 1882, 1889, 1950. **Best in Gillette Cup:** Winners 1970, 1971, 1972, 1975. **Best in NatWest Trophy:** Semi final 1981. **Best in John Player League:** Winners 1969, 1970. **Best in Benson and Hedges Cup:** Semi-finalists 1973, 1974, 1982.

Leicestershire

The County Ground, Grace Road,
Leicester. Tel: Leicester 832128

Leicestershire, formed in 1879, had to wait until 1975 for their first success in the County Championship. It was a triumph that capped the finest period in the club's history, having won the Benson and Hedges Cup in 1972 and 1975 and the John Player League in 1974 and 1977.

For all their efforts down the years, Leicestershire have become a major force only during the last decade. Much of the credit for the transformation must go to tireless secretary Mike Turner and to Ray Illingworth who led the county for ten years.

With only a small population from which to draw their players, Leicestershire have come to rely on proven players from elsewhere. They certainly secured a bargain in 1969 when they persuaded Yorkshire and England off-spinner Illingworth to join them and take over the captaincy.

Recent successes are in stark contrast to their early years in the championship when the club finished in the top half of the table on only six occasions in their first 65 years of playing first-class cricket.

Some of their most profitable years took place before they were admitted to the county championship in 1895. Once accepted they struggled to maintain the required standard, despite the rather fast but successful off-breaks of A. D. Pougher, the first Leicestershire player to score 1000 runs in a season. His most notable performance was for MCC against the Australians at Lord's in 1896 when he took five wickets without conceding a run.

Leicestershire also possessed considerable batting strength in those formative years, including C. E. de Trafford who led them for the first 12 years in the championship, V. F. S. Crawford who later became a tea-planter and one of Ceylon's most successful batsmen, and C. J. B. Wood, a solid rather than stylish batsman. On no fewer than 17 occasions he batted right through a Leicestershire innings.

Two others to add character and style to the batting were A. E. Knight and the left-handed J. H. King who both played for England against Australia early this century.

Just before the outbreak of the First World War three of the greatest characters in Leicestershire cricket began to emerge, all-rounders W. E. Astill and George Geary and fast bowler Alec Skelding who later became the most popular of umpires.

Astill and Geary both played for England, Astill scoring 22,720 runs and taking more than 2000 wickets in his career. Geary more than 13,000 runs and 2000 wickets, but even their combined talents could not take Leicestershire higher than sixth place in the table. That position was reached in 1935 when Astill was captain, the first professional to be appointed regular captain of any county side in this country.

Two other bowlers were to feature strongly in Leicestershire cricket after the Second World War when the county was captained by another professional, Les Berry, the only Leicestershire player to score 30,000 runs in a career. Both were from Australia—off-spin bowler Vic Jackson and left-arm spinner Jack Walsh. Maurice Tompkin, a most attractive batsman, was also a major force when he died in 1956.

Charles Palmer had already moved from Worcestershire to take over as captain and secretary and he led the county to their highest position of third in 1952, a position not reached again until 1967 when they brought back former Surrey and England left-arm spinner Tony Lock to take over the captaincy. Among their most prolific run-getters in recent times was Maurice Hallam who three times in his career scored centuries in each innings of a match, twice scoring double centuries and a century.

Leicestershire first began to rebuild the club under the influence of Palmer, and full use of their Grace Road headquarters in the 1960s, together with fund-raising schemes have enabled the county to attract a higher standard of player, including that fine Australian fast bowler Graham McKenzie who retired after the title triumph of 1975.

The emergence of a young left-handed batsman, David Gower, who made his England debut in 1978, confirmed the growing talent being developed by Leicestershire.

Best in County Championship: Winners 1975. **Best in Gillete Cup:** Semi-finalists 1977. **Best in NatWest Trophy:** Third round 1981. **Best in John Player League:** Winners 1974, 1977. **Best in Benson and Hedges Cup:** Winners 1972, 1975.

Middlesex

Formed: 1863

Lord's Cricket Ground, St John's Wood
Road, London N.W.8. Tel: 01–289 1300

Two names glow with special pride in the memory of older
county cricket supporters whenever the story of Middlesex is
recounted. Those of Denis Compton and Bill Edrich, who became
known as 'The Terrible Twins' for the havoc they created among
opposition bowlers with their thrilling stroke play immediately
after the Second World War.

When these two were in harness no bowler in the country
could keep them quiet. Not surprisingly, therefore, Middlesex
enjoyed their most successful period for a number of years while
this ebullient pair were chastening attacks.

Compton was blessed with a fine eye, lightning reflexes and
superb temperament. He would use his feet magnificently
against the spin bowler, and delighted spectators by his daring
and unorthodox excursions down the wicket. Edrich, of smaller
stature, possessed tremendous courage and was at his best
when the odds were stacked against him. They also did their
share of bowling—Compton with his brand of left-arm slow
deliveries and Edrich as a fast bowler, when Middlesex won the
championship in 1947. This was the first time for 26 seasons
that they had taken the title which they shared with Yorkshire
two years later.

Those few years after the Second World War were the golden
age of Middlesex cricket. In the summer of 1947 Compton
scored 3816 runs which included 18 centuries. Both are still
records. Edrich scored 3539 runs, the second highest aggregate
for a summer, and both hit more than 30,000 runs in their careers.

They were not alone in being Middlesex batting heroes during
that 1947 summer. Jack Robertson and Sid Brown, who scored
11 and three centuries respectively that season, were a good
opening partnership. In 1949 Robertson scored 331 not out *in a
day* against Worcestershire.

Between the wars the Middlesex team's performances were
enlivened by another remarkable personality, the Irishman Patsy
Hendren whose career aggregate of 57,611 runs including 170
centuries has been exceeded only by Jack Hobbs and Frank
Woolley. Along with J. W. Hearne (37,252 runs), he carried the
Middlesex batting between 1909 and 1935.

Throughout the first 70 years of their championship life

Middlesex relied for much of their main strength on a high number of talented amateurs. With these players not available for much of the season, Middlesex were constantly forced to change their side and this produced a lack of consistency.

They emerged as a recognized force in the Championship when they were undefeated in 1878. In 1885 A. E. Stoddart arrived to supply their main batting strength. They were undisputed champions for the first time in 1903 and by then possessed a sound bowling attack led by J. T. Hearne and Australian Test player Albert Trott, supported by B. J. T. Bosanquet who introduced the googly to English cricket.

Throughout their history Middlesex have been served by a number of outstanding captains including 'Plum' Warner, a sound opening batsman, who brought the championship back to Middlesex again in 1920, the year of his retirement. They won it again the following season under F. T. Mann.

Warner, F. T. Mann and F. G. Mann all led their country on tours overseas as did G. O. 'Gubby' Allen, an outstanding fast bowler between the wars who captained England in Australia and the West Indies.

After Compton and Edrich, Middlesex struggled to provide a consistent challenge in the championship until the seventies, yet it was rare to find the county without one representative in the England side. The most regular was off-spinner Fred Titmus whose 158 championship wickets in 1955 broke the county record held by Trott for 55 years. Titmus also completed the double on eight occasions, the last player to perform this feat in England. Left-handed batsman Peter Parfitt scored more than 25,000 runs before leaving the county in 1972.

Under the shrewd captaincy of Mike Brearley, who also led England successfully, Middlesex won the County Championship in 1976, 1980 and 1982, and shared it with Kent in 1977. They also provided four players—Brearley, Clive Radley, Phil Edmonds and John Emburey—for the final Test against New Zealand at Lord's, 1978.

Best in County Championship: Winners 1878 (Disputed), 1903, 1920, 1921, 1947, 1976, 1980, 1982. Shared title 1949 and 1977. **Best in Gillette Cup:** Winners 1977. **Best in NatWest Trophy:** Semi-final 1982. **Best in John Player League:** Second 1982. **Best in Benson and Hedges Cup:** Finalists 1975.

Northamptonshire

Formed: 1878

The County Ground, Wantage Road,
Northampton. Tel: Northampton 32917

Handicapped, like Essex, Leicestershire and Somerset, by having a small population from which to draw players, Northamptonshire have the worst record in the county championship of any side. During one particularly melancholy period they went from May 1935 to May 1939 without gaining a single victory.

Throughout their first-class life, which began in 1905, they seldom provided a worthwhile challenge until 1957 when they finished runners-up, a position they have occupied twice more, in 1965 and 1976. But between the two world wars their highest position was 11th in 1925. In those 25 seasons, they finished bottom eight times and last but one five times.

They have been unfortunate in losing many of their best or most promising players for a variety of reasons long before the county had seen the best of them.

The performances of one man were largely responsible for Northamptonshire's good position in the county championship of Edwardian times. He was George Thompson, a fast medium bowler who was selected to play for an England Eleven against the Australians in 1902 while playing in Minor Counties cricket; he later became the first Northants player to win a Test place.

The bowling of Thompson, who was also a solid batsman when the need arose, supported by the medium pace of William East, proved the strength of the Northants team in 1912 when they won 10 of their 18 matches and finished as runners-up to Yorkshire.

During their lean years after the First World War there seemed a hope of better things to come when A. H. Bakewell came into the side in 1928 and impressed everybody with his confidence and the power of his stroke play. Within three years he was playing for England, and Northants appeared to have a fine opening partnership in the making when he was joined in the county side by A. W. Snowden. Then tragedy struck when Bakewell was badly injured in a car accident. He was compelled to give up playing cricket when only 27, and Snowden found his playing opportunities limited because of business pressures.

There was some compensation when Dennis Brookes joined the side to start a career that was to bring him more than 30,000 runs but the rest of the side still lacked strength and their dismal record continued.

Rebuilding after the Second World War, Northamptonshire looked around the rest of the country to cover their weaknesses. To support Brookes they brought in Yorkshireman Fred Jakeman and Desmond Barrick, secured Test batsman Norman Oldfield from Lancashire and, perhaps their best capture, Freddie Brown from Surrey to captain the side. Brown was then nearing the end of his career but his influence on Northants was immediate, and within months of leading his county for the first time he was named captain of England and took them to Australia for the 1950–51 tour. Only once in his four years as captain did Northants finish in the top half of the table but it was the start of a better period. Two Australians, Jack Manning and George Tribe, strengthened the side with their spin bowling and Northants produced Frank Tyson, the fastest England bowler since the war, whose heroic deeds in Australia helped Len Hutton retain the Ashes in 1954–55.

In 1957 Northants rose to second place in the championship but the side began to break up within the next two seasons, Tyson deciding to move to Australia although he was still at the top of his playing career in England.

Perhaps the greatest blow to hit Northants in recent years was the loss of their 18 stone batsman, Colin Milburn, after a car accident which robbed him of the sight of his left eye. David Steele, grey-haired and bespectacled, burst on to the England Test scene in 1975 after many seasons in obscurity and his tenacious batting did much to earn a drawn series against the Australians. The following year the county won their first major honour after almost a century of trying, unexpectedly defeating Lancashire in the Gillette Cup final.

In 1980 they won the Benson and Hedges Cup, beating Essex by six runs. Allan Lamb, South African-born, Geoff Cook, Wayne Larkins and Peter Willey, all played for England during the early 1980's.

Best in County Championship: Second 1912, 1957, 1965, 1976. **Best in Gillette Cup:** Winners 1976. **Best in NatWest Trophy:** Finalists 1981. **Best in John Player League:** Fourth 1974. **Best in Benson and Hedges Cup:** Winners 1980.

Nottinghamshire

Formed: 1866

Trent Bridge, Nottingham.
Tel: Nottingham 861381

When county-championship sides were given the go-ahead in 1967 to sign an overseas player on an immediate registration without a residential qualification Nottinghamshire saw the change of rule as a golden opportunity to try and recapture some of their former glory.

They went straight to the top to sign the West Indies captain Gary Sobers, the greatest all-rounder of his day and probably the greatest cricket has produced. In Sobers Nottinghamshire saw the player and the personality they needed to bring back the success of the early years, when they won the championship outright for four seasons and shared it six times in the space of 17 years.

Not even the all-round talents of Sobers could provide the transformation needed and after the 1974 season he retired, taking with him a knighthood.

Long before the county championship was formed and Trent Bridge became one of England's most famous Test centres, cricket in Nottinghamshire was flourishing under the influence of a William Clarke, one of the leading under-arm bowlers of his day, who launched the All England team and turned a meadow into a cricket ground. That is Trent Bridge.

A most notable batsman in his side was George Parr who perfected the sweep stroke and used it so effectively in hitting the ball over a line of trees on the edge of the ground that one famous old elm still standing is known as 'Parr's tree'. Two fine bowlers were Alfred Shaw and Jimmy Shaw; Arthur Shrewsbury and William Gunn, who hold the record for the highest opening stand for Notts—398 v. Sussex in 1890, were others whose contributions helped set a standard that was to bring one triumph after another.

By the time the championship was taken again in 1907 Nottinghamshire had developed into one of the strongest batting sides in the country, largely through the exploits of William Gunn's nephews. George, the younger of the two brothers, was the more exciting player scoring 35,190 runs in his career—the highest made by a Nottinghamshire batsman. His brother John was a more solid left-hander and more than useful bowler. Both played for England, as did their uncle William Gunn in the 1880s.

George Gunn's son also played for the county and in 1931 both he and his father scored a century in a match against Warwickshire, the only instance in cricket of a father and son scoring hundreds in the same innings. A contemporary of George Gunn was Joe Hardstaff whose son also played for the county between the wars and up to 1955.

The next most successful period for Nottinghamshire came between the two world wars when Joe Hardstaff junior was at the top of his career, although he did not play for the first eleven when they won the championship in 1929. He made his debut the following season. Nottinghamshire were rarely outside the top five in the championship, much of the credit going to their captain, A. W. Carr. He had a strong team at his command. Carr was a sound batsman himself and could call upon George and John Gunn, Hardstaff (senior)—and later Hardstaff (junior)—and William Whysall whose 2620 runs for the county in that 1929 championship-winning season is still a Nottinghamshire record. Their bowling attack was probably the best of the day.

At one end Carr could call upon Harold Larwood, said by many to be the fastest England bowler of all time and the central figure of the famous 'bodyline' tour of Australia. Sharing the new ball attack was the powerful figure of Bill Voce, a left-arm swing bowler. Between them Larwood and Voce played 48 Tests for England. Voce was still playing after the war along with Hardstaff junior, but the lean years were starting.

In 1953 Bruce Dooland, a leg spinner from Australia strengthened the attack. Nottinghamshire still produced their share of personalities, including Reg Simpson, a fine player of fast bowling; the left-handed Cyril Poole and Derek Randall who scored 174 for England in the 1977 Melbourne Centenary Test. In 1981 under the captaincy of a South African, Clive Rice, they won the championship for the first time for 52 years. New Zealand Test fast bowler, Richard Hadlee, also played a notable part in this success.

Best in County Championship: Winners 1883, 1884, 1885, 1886, 1907, 1929, 1981. Shared title in 1873, 1875, 1879, 1880, 1882, 1889, 1981. **Best in Gillette Cup:** Semi-finalists 1969. **Best in NatWest Trophy:** Third round 1981. **Best in John Player League:** Fifth 1975. **Best in Benson and Hedges Cup:** Finalists 1982.

Somerset

Formed: 1885

The County Ground, St James's Street,
Taunton. Tel: Taunton 72946

Although success in the form of a county-championship title has
eluded Somerset, their contribution to cricket has been rich in
the colourful characters they have provided. The championship
would have been a poorer competition without them and their
habit of securing surprise victories over the strongest teams.
They have given the game such names as Arthur Wellard, one of
the mightiest six hitters of all time, Harold Gimblett, Bill Andrews,
Maurice Tremlett and Ian Botham and such overseas personalities as the Australians Colin McCool and Bill Alley, and West
Indians Peter Wight, Viv Richards and Joel Garner.

From their first moments in the championship when admitted
in 1891, Somerset had a real character in the shape of Sammy
Woods who captained the side for 12 seasons from 1894. He
was an outstanding fast bowler, clean striker of the ball, and a
wit. His influence on the side was immense, as was that of
another all-rounder of the same period, L. C. Braund who played
in 23 Test matches against Australia and South Africa and took
part in three tours of Australia.

This tradition for producing all-round players was maintained
after the First World War by John White, a slow left-arm bowler
who took 100 wickets in a season 14 times and in two of those
seasons went on to complete the double by scoring more than
1000 runs. His strength was in his exceptional accuracy and
flight, and was rewarded with 15 England matches.

He was still a leading bowler for Somerset when Wellard
joined the county from Kent and became an immediate hit with
his new employers in more ways than one. The cricket was rarely
short of excitement when Wellard had the ball in his hand or
stood at the crease. Spectators around the boundary in the area
between mid-wicket and mid-on were never safe when Wellard
was batting. He is credited with as many as 500 six hits, 72 of
them coming in one season. Twice in his big-hitting sprees he
took five sixes off an over, the first against T. F. Armstrong of
Derbyshire in 1936 and again off Frank Woolley when playing
against Kent two years later.

Another of Somerset's powerful stroke-makers in the 1930s
was Harold Gimblett who made an amazing debut in 1935 when
batting against Essex at Frome. He was called into the side as a

late replacement, sent in to bat well down the order and exploded with 123 runs—including three sixes and seven fours.

His century took only 63 minutes, the fastest of the season. Gimblett was to make the opening position his normal role in the county side—along with the steady Frank Lee—and his 310 not out against Sussex in 1948 remains the highest individual score by a Somerset batsman. His 21,108 runs and 49 centuries also stand as county records.

A series of poor returns in the championship in the late 1940s and early 1950s led Somerset—as Nottinghamshire had done—to seek players from overseas, and they engaged Australian Colin McCool, who had been a member of the 1948 Australian party under Donald Bradman, Wight from the West Indies and another Australian off-spinner, Jim McMahon, who had been playing for Surrey.

There was an immediate improvement in results but a greater success story belongs to another Australian, Bill Alley, who had been playing in Lancashire League cricket from soon after the Second World War.

He was 38 when Somerset gave him his chance of first-class cricket in this country in 1957 and the following season Somerset finished third in the table, equalling their performance back in 1892, their second season of championship cricket. Alley was to play for Somerset for 12 seasons until the age of 49, his most remarkable summer coming in 1961. In that season he scored 3019 runs—the last player to score 3000 runs in an English summer—setting a county record by scoring 2761 for Somerset, including 10 centuries, another county record.

By the late seventies Botham had made a sensational impact as an all-rounder and shattered various Test records. He became the third player in Test history to complete the double of 2000 runs and 200 wickets in 1981–82 and in fewest matches (42).

Best in County Championship: Third 1892, 1958, 1963, 1966, 1981. **Best in Gillette Cup:** Winners 1979. **Best in NatWest Trophy:** Quarter-final 1982. **Best in John Player League:** Winners 1979. **Best in Benson and Hedges Cup:** Winners 1981, 1982.

Surrey

Formed: 1845

The Oval, Kennington, London S.E.11.
Tel: 01–582 6660

Whatever the achievements of Surrey in the future, it is unlikely that they will surpass their remarkable feat during the 1950s when, under the leadership of Stuart Surridge for the first five years and with Peter May at the helm for the final two, they won the county championship for a record seven successive summers.

It proved to be the second time in their history that Surrey had ruled supreme in English cricket. In the nine years between 1887 and 1895 they won the title eight times, shared it in 1889, but missed out completely in 1893. To complete this wonderful run they also won the championship in 1899.

Between these periods Surrey rarely finished in the bottom half of the table but only on two other occasions were they able to finish on top, outright winners in 1914 and sharing the title once more in 1950. Yet in this period they produced some of the greatest names in sport.

Among them were Sir Jack Hobbs, Andy Sandham and Tom Hayward who each scored 100 centuries in a career, Hobbs reaching the staggering total of 197.

During his time he scored 61,167 runs, more than any other player has achieved, scoring 1000 runs a season 26 times. In 16 of those summers his aggregate exceeded 2000.

Before these three were able to join forces Surrey had already left their mark on the game by their record towards the end of the last century. Much of their success was due to the influence of their captain, John Shuter.

Under Shuter they were more than a match for any other county. He, in turn, was served by a series of fine players. Little Bobby Abel was the pick of the batsmen until Hayward joined the side towards the end of that run. Abel scored more than 30,000 runs. Bill Brockwell was a fine all-rounder and Shuter could not have had a better spearhead than fast bowlers George Lohmann, Tom Richardson and Bill Lockwood—among the finest of their type.

Another famous name was the wicket-keeper, Herbert Strudwick. In 25 seasons—less the break for the First World War—he claimed 1493 victims, 1235 of them caught, both world records until 1975.

Making sure that all this talent was expressed in the right

way, Surrey continued to have some fine leaders, including H. D. G. Leveson-Gower before the First World War, Percy Fender from 1920 to 1931, succeeded by Douglas Jardine who made his name in cricketing history by the 'bodyline' tactics he employed, as England's captain during the 1932–33 tour of Australia. Fender set a fine example in everything he did, as a fielder, a leg-spin bowler and a dashing batsman whose century against Northants in 35 minutes in 1920 still stands as the fastest scored. Six times he achieved the double.

Bill Hitch and Maurice Allom were outstanding fast bowlers of this time, and later came Alf Gover who, in 1936 and 1937, took 200 wickets in a season. He was at his peak when another remarkable bowler joined Surrey, Alec Bedser along with his identical twin brother Eric.

Both were to serve in the memorable period during the 1950s. The wicket, too, had changed at the Oval, giving some help to the pace bowlers early on and then the spinners. Surrey had the players capable of taking advantage with Alec Bedser, fast bowler Peter Loader, and the spin 'twins', Jim Laker with his off-breaks and Tony Lock with left-arm spinners. The fielding was of a high class, set by the captain, Stuart Surridge. The batting while not quite as strong, still contained stroke-makers of high quality, led by the elegant Peter May and the patience of Bernard Constable and, later, Ken Barrington.

Since those days Surrey continued to produce Test players of note, including Barrington (31,000 career runs) and Edrich of the famous Norfolk cricketing family (nearly 40,000 career runs). Under Micky Stewart—another England batsman—they took the championship again in 1971.

Edrich was appointed captain in 1973 and led Surrey to victory in the Benson and Hedges Cup the following year. Then in 1975 Edrich, Geoff Arnold and Graham Roope all played for England against Australia.

Best in County Championship: Winners 1887, 1888, 1890, 1891, 1892, 1894, 1895, 1899, 1914, 1952, 1953, 1954, 1955, 1956, 1957, 1958, 1971. Shared 1889, 1950. **Best in Gillette Cup:** Finalists 1965, 1980. **Best in NatWest Trophy:** Winners 1982. **Best in John Player League:** Fifth 1969, 1980. **Best in Benson and Hedges Cup:** Winners 1974.

Sussex

Formed: 1857

The County Ground, Eaton Road, Hove.
Tel: Brighton 732161

Sussex cricket today follows very much the pattern played throughout the history of the club. The side has always contained notable performers but has never quite possessed sufficient all-round strength to make them a championship-winning combination. In the third year of recognized championship cricket in 1875 they did finish at the top of the table but shared the honour with two other counties.

Since then they have been runners-up on seven occasions, perhaps slightly unlucky not to win the title in the early thirties when they had their strongest side and finished in second place for three successive seasons, 1932, 1933 and 1934. In 1981 they finished two points behind Notts.

The most remarkable feature of their history is the large number of families who have served Sussex splendidly, starting with one of the most fascinating figures to play for them, Ranjitsinhji, who took over the captaincy from that outstanding Australian player, W. L. Murdoch, who led his countrymen to England in 1880.

Ranji was the most elegant of batsmen both in his stroke play on the field and in his dress off it. In 1899 and 1900 he scored more than 3000 runs each season. The family link with Ranji was provided by his nephew Duleepsinhji who captained the county in the early thirties. Duleep, another attractive batsman and agile fielder, arrived in Sussex when they were struggling for class batsmen in the middle order.

In the Sussex side at the same time as Ranji were the brothers Albert and Robert Relf. Albert was the more successful, a fine all-rounder but better known for his well-flighted spin bowling with which he took 100 wickets a season on 11 occasions. George Cox started his career in Ranji's time and became a considerable force for almost 30 years with his left-arm bowling.

Later his son George Cox became a leading batsman, making his presence felt just before the Second World War and blossoming when cricket started again afterwards.

Another player in the side at the turn of the century was off-spinner Fred Tate whose son Maurice was to become the greatest bowler in Sussex's history and a more than useful batsman. He started to follow in the footsteps of his father as an off-spinner but found his form and fame as a fast medium bowler, taking 2784 wickets in his career, 155 of them for England in 38 Test matches. He had one tremendous period between 1923 and 1925 when he scored 1000 runs and took 200 wickets in three successive seasons.

The era of Tate saw several other family connections springing up. Brothers John and James Langridge were emerging as two of the highest scoring batsmen in Sussex history, John scoring 34,380 runs in a 28-year career interrupted by the Second World War, and James 31,716.

In the side with the Langridge brothers were the Parks, batsman Harry and all-rounder Jim who had a most memorable season in 1937 when he scored more than 3000 runs and took 100 wickets, the only player to have performed this feat. His son, also named Jim, kept the family name going, scoring more than 30,000 runs and playing in 46 Test matches while at Sussex.

Among the long line of outstanding Sussex players have been E. H. Bowley, a tower of strength in the early part of this century, Arthur Gilligan who shone as a leader, fast bowler and fielder during the 1920s. Rev. David Sheppard, a fine opening batsman whose appearances were limited by his calling, Ted Dexter, a most aggressive all-rounder, Ian Thomson who, after the Second World War, proved to be a bowler in Tate's mould, taking 100 wickets a season 12 times, and more recently John Snow, the outstanding fast bowler in the world at the start of the 1970s.

The limited-over competitions in England gave Sussex a new setting to show their worth. Under Dexter's leadership they won the Gillette Cup at Lord's in the first two years of the competition and again in 1978, led by Arnold Long.

In 1973 Sussex appointed the South African Tony Greig as captain. He also led England until he was replaced in 1977 for his involvement with World Series Cricket. Under John Barclay's enthusiastic leadership they won the John Player League in 1982. Imran Khan from Pakistan and Garth le Roux from South Africa, proved valuable all-rounders.

Best in County Championships: Shared title 1875. **Best in Gillette Cup:** Winners 1963, 1964, 1978. **Best in NatWest Trophy:** Third round 1981. **Best in John Player League:** Winners 1982. **Best in Benson and Hedges Cup:** Semi-finalists 1982.

Warwickshire

Formed: 1884

The County Ground, Edgbaston,
Birmingham. Tel: 021–440 3521

The summer of 1972 saw Warwickshire end 20 lean years and capture their third County Championship title. It was a just reward for the unstinting work by their committee over the preceding years.

The success was also richly merited on account of the quality and enterprise of their batting. Warwickshire had finished level on points with champions Surrey the previous season but took second place because Surrey had won two games more. Nobody could deny Warwickshire the right to the title in 1972.

Yet there were some who begrudged Warwickshire their success, complaining that they had 'bought' the title by importing some of the leading players from overseas to fill the weaknesses in their own side.

Certainly it was sad at one stage of the summer to see an England Test player, Dennis Amiss, left out of the side early on in favour of a largely unknown quantity, the West Indian Kallicharran. Amiss fought his way back into the team—as an opening batsman—and set up the championship success with a string of thrilling centuries in the second half of the summer.

In addition to Kallicharran, Warwickshire regularly included three other West Indian Test players in Kanhai, off-spinner Gibbs and Murray who put captain Alan Smith out of his wicket-keeping role. Warwickshire's answer to those who objected to their policy was that they took fair advantage of the rules in existence which other county sides had helped to frame.

Not until the championship had been in progress for nine years were Warwickshire really established as a county organization in 1882. Another 13 years were to go by before they could persuade the other first-class counties that they were worthy opponents.

They had a comparatively short—and not very impressive—period to wait before they won the title for the first time in 1911. The achievement surprised most people, for only the season before Warwickshire had gone through their worst summer and finished 14th in the table. The 1911 success coincided with the appointment of Frank Foster to the captaincy, his fourth year with the county, and he played a leading role in claiming the title.

He was a fine left-arm medium bowler who combined

devastatingly with Sydney Barnes in Australia on the 1911–12 tour, and a successful, fierce-hitting batsman, restricted in technique but strong in courage. A motor-cycle accident cut short his career. Quality batting on his side was provided by Willie Quaife, probably the finest batsman Warwickshire produced in the first 50 years of the club. He scored more than 36,000 runs in his career. His brother Walter also played for Warwickshire. Sept Kinnear was another powerful influence on the batting order during that period and 'Tiger' Smith was a great strength behind the wicket.

The county produced a number of other fine captains during the next 40 years without having a balanced side for them to lead; these included the Hon. Frederick Calthorpe, Bob Wyatt (1000 runs a season 18 times) who also led England and later Worcestershire, and Peter Cranmer. The right blend was not to be found until 1951 when, with Tom Dollery in charge, Warwickshire took the championship a second time.

His main striking force on the bowling front was provided by a New Zealander, Tom Pritchard, and the cunning leg-spin of Eric Hollies. Dollery and Hollies had started to make their mark with Warwickshire about the same time in the middle thirties and played side by side for 20 years, Hollies taking more than 2000 wickets. Another fine bowling combination began to develop in the late 1950s between Tom Cartwright and Jack Bannister, two expert seam bowlers. Mike Smith brought his immense batting talent from Leicestershire and later took over the captaincy—as well as leading England—as Warwickshire began to build again.

The change in registration laws relating to overseas players enabled Warwickshire to field a balanced side, and add to the skill of Jameson, Amiss, Brown and Bob Willis, a fine fast bowler who captained England in the eighties.

Best in County Championship: Winners 1911, 1951, 1972. **Best in Gillette Cup:** Winners 1966, 1968. **Best in NatWest Trophy:** Finalists 1982. **Best in John Player League:** Winners 1980. **Best in Benson and Hedges Cup:** Semi-finalists 1972, 1975, 1976, 1978.

Worcestershire

Formed: 1865

The County Ground, New Road,
Worcester. Tel: Worcester 422694

There can be no better way to celebrate the centenary of a
county cricket club than by topping the championship table at
the end of the season. This is exactly what Worcestershire did
in 1964 under Don Kenyon. The success was given added
significance because it was the first time in their history that
they had won a major honour.

Worcestershire repeated their victory the following season
after an astonishing late run. The basis of these triumphs lay in
the balance of the side which was equipped for all conditions. In
Kenyon they possessed an experienced craftsman to open the
innings with Ron Headley, the exciting stroke-making son of
George Headley, the 'Black Bradman' of the West Indies. Dick
Richardson and Tom Graveney, who had transferred his affec-
tions from Gloucestershire, gave them batsmen of 'England
stature' in the middle order.

Roy Booth was a wicket-keeper of high quality, Gifford and
Slade provided their own specialized left-arm spin and the
opening attack of Coldwell and Flavell was a test for any
batsman, particularly on the fast Worcester wicket. The following
season, in 1965, the side was further strengthened by the
inclusion of Basil D'Oliveira, the Cape Coloured cricketer from
South Africa who was denied the opportunity of playing first-
class cricket in his own country and came to England to find
success in a fairytale story.

D'Oliveira was still a vital member of the team when they won
the Championship again in 1974, edging out Hampshire in a
thrilling climax. Gifford had taken over as skipper but his success
turned sour the following year, 1975, when the players staged a
protest against wages and conditions.

Just as Gloucestershire owe their early success to the
influence of the Grace family, so Worcestershire are heavily
indebted to the Fosters. Seven Foster brothers played for the
county at various stages and three Fosters led the county.
Undoubtedly the most famous was Reg Foster who took over
the captaincy from his brother in 1901 for one season. Unfortunately for Worcestershire, he was not always available and was
even forced to turn down the captaincy of England in Australia
in 1907, although he did lead England in South Africa and toured

Australia in 1903–04, scoring 287 in seven hours in his Test debut in Sydney. The total stood for a number of years as the highest individual Test score.

Against Hampshire in 1899 he scored 134 and 101 not out, his brother W. L. Foster making 140 and 172 not out, the only instance of brothers scoring a century in each innings in the same county match.

Another player to score a century in his first Test against the Australians was the Nawab of Pataudi in Sydney on the 1932–33 tour. He had joined Worcestershire in 1932, one of the few players to play Tests for two countries, leading India when they toured England in 1946. The season before the Nawab joined, Worcestershire lost a great bowling stalwart in Fred Root whose controlled inswing bowling brought him 204 championship wickets in 1925—still a county record—and gained him three Test appearances against Australia the following season. He retired in 1931 after taking 9 for 23 against Lancashire, another county record.

At the time of Root's retirement Worcestershire's bowling strength was growing, although they always lacked the right blend to make them potential champions. In 1930 Reg Perks began his long career with the county as a fast bowler, a career that was to gain him more than 2000 wickets, taking 100 wickets a season 16 times even in his final season.

They continued to supply England with players after the Second World War, including Kenyon, who made more than 30,000 runs in his career, the Richardson brothers—Peter and Dick—Coldwell, Flavell and Gifford, although it was not until the 1960s that Worcestershire discovered the team to bring home the championship.

More recently Worcestershire found another Test player in the New Zealander Glenn Turner who, in 1970, set a new county record of 10 championship centuries in the summer. In 1971 Worcestershire were among the honours again when they won the John Player League. They had already displayed the talent as limited-over cricketers by reaching the final of the Gillette Cup in 1963 and 1966, and they were again beaten finalists in 1973 and 1976 when losing to Kent in the Benson and Hedges Cup.

Best in County Championship: Winners 1964, 1965, 1974. **Best in Gillette Cup:** Finalists 1963, 1966. **Best in NatWest Trophy:** Second round 1981, 1982. **Best in John Player League:** Winners 1971. **Best in Benson and Hedges Cup:** Finalists 1973, 1976.

Yorkshire

Formed: 1891

Headingley Cricket Ground,
St Michael's Lane, Leeds 6. Tel: 0532–787394

The Yorkshire record of triumph is such, the list of personalities and famous players so long, that it is impossible to recount them all, but three captains stand out in their history.

The one great influence on the life and ways of Yorkshire cricket—and cricket in England—was Lord Hawke who was actually born in Lincolnshire. He led the county for 28 years, taking over in troubled times, patching up the quarrels, to assume command in 1883.

Throughout most of his first 10 years of captaincy Yorkshire were frequently in a challenging position for the title. In his last 18 they won the championship eight times and finished runners-up four times. Their first success under Lord Hawke was in 1893. Even when he retired his influence was still felt, for he was President for a further 25 years. From 1933 until 1947 Yorkshire came under another outstanding leader, Brian Sellers. He was not quite in the top flight as a player, but for his fearless fielding, competitive spirit and tactical flair alone he was worth a place. He took over a side that had won the championship in the two previous years and in his nine summers as leader brought the title back to Yorkshire on six further occasions.

He was chairman of the club in the 1960s during the controversial captaincy reign of Brian Close, at 18 the youngest player to appear for England. Close ruled for eight seasons—during which he also captained England without losing a Test match—and won the championship four times, taking the Gillette Cup in two seasons when the championship was not to be Yorkshire's.

The captain who never captained his county by appointment was Len Hutton, the first professional player to lead England; he successfully retained the Ashes in Australia in 1954–55. During his playing career Yorkshire still persisted in the policy of an amateur leading the county.

Lord Hawke, Sellers and Close were all helped by having some of the greatest players of their day. During Lord Hawke's time Yorkshire possessed two of the finest all-rounders cricket has seen, Wilfred Rhodes and George Hirst in harness, supported by Stanley Jackson, later Sir Stanley, another who captained England but not his county.

Even more devastating with the bat than Rhodes and Hirst was David Denton who in 22 summers scored 36,000 runs. As these three were beginning to reach the end of their respective careers the next great Yorkshire side was already beginning to take shape. In 1913 Percy Holmes made his debut and six years later Herbert Sutcliffe came into the side. These two formed the finest opening partnership Yorkshire have possessed and their association finally ended in 1933, the year after they had established a world-record opening partnership of 555 against Essex at Leyton. The year after Sutcliffe started, Yorkshire introduced another youngster, the left-handed batsman Maurice Leyland. All three scored more than 30,000 runs in their careers, Sutcliffe making more than 50,000.

When Rhodes was on the decline as a bowler Yorkshire had a ready-made replacement in Hedley Verity who bowled his left-arm spin just below medium pace. In only his second season of championship cricket he returned the remarkable figures of 10 for 10 against Nottinghamshire at Leeds in 1932.

Under Sellers, Hutton started his great career that was to bring him 40,000 runs and 129 centuries, the finest England opening batsman of modern times. After the war Close and Trueman emerged together, Trueman an aggressive fast bowler with a record of 307 Test wickets, 2304 in his career. Shortly afterwards came Illingworth who served Yorkshire for 17 years before finding even greater personal success with Leicestershire and, more recently, Geoff Boycott, one of the world's most reliable opening batsmen. In 1971 he became the first Englishman to finish a summer with an average over 100. Then in 1975 he led a young side to runners-up position in the Championship and two years later scored his 100th century in Leeds Test against Australia. At the end of 1978 Illingworth rejoined Yorkshire as manager and in 1982, aged 50, he was made captain.

Best in County Championship: Winners 1867, 1870, 1893, 1896, 1898, 1900, 1901, 1902, 1905, 1908, 1912, 1919, 1922, 1923, 1924, 1925, 1931, 1932, 1933, 1935, 1937, 1938, 1939, 1946, 1959, 1960, 1962, 1963, 1966, 1967, 1968. Shared 1869, 1949. **Best in Gillette Cup:** Winners 1965, 1969. **Best in NatWest Trophy:** Semi-final 1982. **Best in John Player League:** Second 1973. **Best in Benson and Hedges Cup:** Finalists 1972.

Oxford University

The presence of Pakistani Test all-rounder Imran Khan from 1973 to 1975 gave a significant boost to Oxford University cricket. Without him, they might have struggled to match the strength of Cambridge, but in fact only five results had been achieved in 23 University matches up to 1982: two victories to Oxford, three to Cambridge.

They did break a run of six drawn University matches by beating Cambridge by an innings and nine runs in 1966 when Richard Gilliat led the side. They also won in 1976, skippered by Victor Marks.

Captaining Oxford in 1956 was Mike Smith, later captain of Warwickshire and England, who set a record by scoring his third century in successive University matches. His 201 not out in 1954 was the third highest score in a University match.

There can be no more pleasant setting in the country for a young freshman to receive his introduction to first-class cricket than Oxford University's ground, spread over 10 acres in the Parks, with its tree-lined background. This has been their headquarters since 1881. Previously Oxford were 'hosts' in five University matches played on Cowley Marsh, which was their first home until it was sold.

The list of players who have gone on to star in county sides or represent their country is not as long as that at Cambridge, but still impressive and contains a number of notable players from overseas. The famous Foster brothers from Worcestershire— R. E., H. K. and G. N.—all played for Oxford, as did Charles Fry and Bernard Bosanquet.

In the 1920s came Errol Holmes and Douglas Jardine and the Nawab of Pataudi who later played for England and captained India. Ian Peebles and Alan Melville (South Africa) played in the thirties. After the Second World War came Abdul Kardar from Pakistan and that gifted left-hander Martin Donnelly from New Zealand, Fellows-Smith and Clive van Ryneveld from South Africa and the Nawab of Pataudi, following the path his father trod 30 years before.

They all played in a period when Oxford cricket flourished. Donald Carr played from 1949 to 1951 and Colin Cowdrey graced the Parks and Lord's for the following three years.

Cambridge University

Time was when the majority of the Cambridge side packed their bags immediately after the University match and rushed off to play a vital role for a county championship side.

Those days are gone: the universities no longer provide the classic breeding-ground for England's talent. But Cambridge still hold a reputation for promoting potential first-class players, as they demonstrated in 1975 when captain Chris Aworth joined Surrey. Alastair Hignell (Gloucestershire) and Paul Parker (Sussex) are other recent examples.

County batsmen make the most of the practice these matches provide and the one difficulty of a University side is finding bowlers in their early twenties experienced and cunning enough to cope with batsmen who have been in the game for years.

In some lean years it has been suggested that the matches should not be labelled 'first class', but with the constant change-over in personnel the strength of a University side can be low one year and high the next. In 1971 and 1972 Cambridge fielded Majid Khan (captain), Dudley Owen-Thomas, John Spencer and Phil Edmonds, all capable of holding down a regular place in a county side.

In the University matches which date back to 1827 when the first one was played at Lord's—largely as a result of an old rivalry between Herbert Jenner (Cambridge) and Charles Wordsworth (Oxford) who had played against each other during their Eton and Harrow days—Cambridge hold the edge, winning 53 of the 138 games, Oxford's score standing at 45.

Before the turn of the century Lord Hawke, Stanley Jackson, Ranjitsinhji and Gilbert Jessop made their name with Cambridge. The 1920s produced such players as Percy Chapman, Gubby Allen, Duleepsinhji, Maurice Allom and Maurice Turnbull, followed by F. G. Mann, Norman Yardley, Freddie Brown and Kenneth Farnes.

Since the Second World War Cambridge's greatest period was in the late 1940s and early 1950s when they produced a string of fine batsmen including Dewes, Doggart, Bailey, Insole, Dexter, Sheppard, May and Subba Row—all England players. More recently Barber, Lewis, Brearley, Edmonds, Paul Parker, and Pringle are among those to win England caps.

The Minor Counties

Only Durham, Lincolnshire and Hertfordshire defeated county teams in the Gillette Cup. That in itself speaks volumes about the gulf that exists between the part-timers and the first-class professionals.

Some of the Minor County clubs can afford professional playing help, paid for on a match basis, but money is scarce. The best players are not always able to seek time off from their occupations to play in all the matches, particularly when travelling is involved.

Promising youngsters are often snapped up by the first-class counties. Colin Milburn, for example, was beginning to emerge as a force in Durham when he left to sign for Northamptonshire, later to become an England player. Paul Allott began with Cheshire before becoming a Lancashire and England fast-medium bowler during the late 1970's and early 1980's.

The gulf in class has not always existed. Indeed there was probably little difference in the 1890s when the 'second-class' counties joined together at the suggestion of Worcestershire to start their own competition, which was launched by seven counties in 1895. No doubt many of them thought this would provide a stepping stone towards becoming accepted as 'first class'. In fact Worcestershire, Northamptonshire and Glamorgan succeeded in following that trail.

The second elevens of the first-class counties were also eligible to join the new competition in 1899 but today only two—Lancashire and Somerset—remain.

Finance has always been a problem. At one stage the Minor Counties competition was played on a regional basis for an experimental period but this was abandoned. To qualify for the competition each side has to play eight matches, four home and four away, and they usually play the eight sides geographically nearest to them. Most counties have a fixture list of 10 games, some 12, the winners being the side with the highest average points return. If the side in second place has not met the side on top of the table, they are entitled to challenge, the championship going to the winner.

The Minor Counties Cricket Association receive a share of Test-match profits and they field a representative team against the touring side. Their most famous victory was against the Australians in 1977 by six wickets.

Bedfordshire: Having taken a long time to make their presence felt, Bedfordshire made up for it by winning the championship in 1970 and 1972. Their second victory was achieved after defeating Yorkshire's second eleven in the challenge match when their opponents fielded a side containing nine players with first-team experience. They had given notice of their improved standard by finishing in second place in 1969. Their previous best period was soon after the Second World War, finishing in second place in 1948.

Berkshire: They have produced a number of notable players throughout the years, some of whom have gone on to play for England. The first was Percy Chapman, the strong left-handed batsman who later captained Kent and England, followed by Tom Dollery who led Warwickshire to their second championship success in 1951 and more recently Peter May, another who was to captain England as well as leading Surrey and Ken Barrington and Graham Roope, also of Surrey.

Buckinghamshire: Along with Staffordshire, Buckinghamshire have proved an outstanding side in the Minor Counties championship, winning the title eight times. Much of the credit for their success belongs to W. B. Franklin who played for them for 35 years, the last 27 as captain until handing over the position in 1946. During his time they won the title five times including winning all their 10 matches in 1932. After the Second World War they were helped for a period by former Australian wicket-keeper Ben Barnett who took over the captaincy in 1952 and guided them to win the championship again in his first year as leader.

Cambridgeshire: From time to time Cambridgeshire are able to call on undergraduates, but although they first competed in 1898 they had to wait until 1963 before winning the championship. Jack Hobbs played with them for one season in 1904 before he joined Surrey. Finding suitable batsmen has seldom presented a problem but they have often lacked bowling strength. This was partially solved in 1963 when they engaged former England and Yorkshire left-arm spinner Johnny Wardle whose 55 wickets that season played a prominent part in winning the title and in 1974 when South African Peter Swart bowled them into third place.

Cheshire: After struggling throughout most of their life in the Minor Counties, dating back to 1909, Cheshire finally broke through in 1967 to win the championship for the first time. Their success was a tribute to the splendid work of their long-service captain, Fred Millett, who had provided both the bowling and batting strength for a number of years previously. Until recent times Cheshire have had to be content, in the main, with a place in the lower half of the table though they were fourth in 1980.

Cornwall: First-class cricketers to emerge from Cornwall have been few. Among them have been the former Gloucestershire and England batsman Jack Crapp, Mike Harris of Nottinghamshire and Jack Richards of Surrey—and this possibly explains the lack of success of Cornwall in the Minor Counties competition. League cricket has such a hold in the area that they have difficulty in prising players away to appear for the county. They achieved their most successful seasons in 1974 and 1976 when taking second place.

Cumberland: Although founded in 1884, it was not until 1955 that they entered the Minor Counties Championship. Their baptism was tough, with only two victories recorded in their first eight years of the competition, this despite the influence of former Yorkshire opening batsman Harry Halliday who joined them in 1957. They were strengthened by Geoff Edrich when he finished playing for Lancashire but Cumberland have still to make their presence felt in the competition.

Devon: Entering the competition in the first year they formed, Devon won their first championship in 1978. They have been able to discover a number of players who have played first-class cricket, including George Emmett who went on to play for Gloucestershire and England. Rarely, however, have they achieved consistent all-round strength. They finished third in 1926, and were champions in 1978. Some of their more recent players have done better. Roger Tolchard, Leicestershire wicket-keeper, started with Devon. Doug Yeabsley has captained the Minor Counties South team and Len Coldwell played for Worcestershire.

Dorset: Dorset's record in the Minor Counties Championship is rather similar to that of neighbours Devon. The great majority of their summers since entry in 1902 have been spent around the middle of the table. The story of their early years in particular is of one struggle after another to climb out of the bottom half of the table, something they achieved in the 1920s when finishing third and fourth in successive seasons. They had to wait until 1959 before reaching such heights again. In the meantime they had been helped by two Somerset players, M. Walford and G. Woodhouse. They were third in 1982.

Durham: Durham set themselves a high standard by winning the championship three times in their first seven years in the competition. They have remained a considerable force, winning the title again in 1926, 1930, 1976, 1980 and 1981. They created history in 1973, their Gillette Cup victory over Yorkshire being the first success by a Minor County against first-class opposition. Since the war Harold Stephenson (Somerset), Reg Spooner (Warwickshire), Colin Milburn and Malcolm Scott (Northants) are among those who started with Durham.

Hertfordshire: Conclusive winners of the 1975 championship in their first season under the leadership of Minor Counties wicket-keeper Frank Collyer. One of the original seven counties who took part in the first competition in 1895, Hertfordshire first won the championship in 1936; it was largely gained for them that summer by the bowling feats of E. Roberts who set a club record with 97 wickets. In their early years Hertfordshire found comfort in the batting of C. H. Titchmarsh, one of the heaviest-scoring batsmen, season after season in Minor County cricket until he died in 1930. They were runners-up in 1980.

Lincolnshire: Another county who have found the recent years the most rewarding in their history. They won the championship for the first time in 1966 when they proved to be one of the outstanding fielding sides in the competition. The leading figure in their championship success was Norman McVicker. He formed a penetrative opening attack in that year with J. Evans, both finishing the season with 71 wickets. They came near to winning the title again in 1970, when they lost the challenge match to Bedfordshire and finished second.

Norfolk: Largely through the exploits in the first-class game of former Middlesex and England batsman Bill Edrich, Surrey and

England's John Edrich and former Lancashire batsman Geoff Edrich, Norfolk have become one of the most familiar names for Minor County cricket. The cricketing Edrich family come from within the county border and Bill Edrich led the side for several seasons. In 1981, captained by Phil Sharpe, formerly of Yorkshire and England, they finished runners-up. Their first success came in the first year of the competition when they shared the title with Durham and Worcestershire, winning it again in 1905, 1910, 1913 and 1933.

Northumberland: Northumberland have enjoyed two brief periods of near success in their history but have yet to win the championship. The first period was in the middle 1920s when they were forced to settle for second place in successive seasons after losing challenge matches against Berkshire and then Buckinghamshire to decide the outright winner. In the 1950s they twice again finished runners-up.

Oxfordshire: By far the oldest of the Minor Counties—they are able to trace a side playing in 1779—Oxfordshire have won only three championships, in 1929 and more recently in 1974 and 1982. Three times Oxfordshire have been denied the Minor Counties Championship by the more professional second elevens of first-class sides. In 1949 they lost the challenge match against Lancashire and finished as runners-up. They met the same fate in 1958 when losing to Yorkshire and in 1961 had to be content with second place again, this time losing to Somerset.

Shropshire: Although one of the oldest county associations dating back to before 1850, Shropshire are the youngest of the Minor County clubs. They did not enter the competition until 1957. Upon entry they found the standard a little above them, for half their matches were played against the second elevens of first-class sides. When the majority of the second elevens dropped out of the championship, forcing Shropshire to seek more fixtures against genuine Minor County sides, their playing record improved, culminating in a championship triumph in 1973.

Staffordshire: They have finished first seven times. Even so their last win was back in 1927. The run of success in the early part of the century was due to England fast bowler Sydney Barnes, the only player regularly to appear for his country while

58

playing Minor County cricket. In his 22 seasons he took 1432 wickets and was still playing for them at the age of 61. John Ikim, Lancashire and England left-handed batsman, captained Staffs for 10 years.

Suffolk: Even with the help for two seasons of Phil Mead, the former Hampshire and England batsman and the fourth highest aggregate scorer in cricket history, Suffolk have only won the Minor County Championship three times, in 1946, 1977 and 1979. Mead ended his association with them in 1939 when he was 52. His two summers with the county brought him more than 800 runs. Suffolk first played in the competition in 1904 but insufficient support resulted in their not taking part when the competition resumed after the First World War and it was not until 1934 that they rejoined.

Wiltshire: Fortunate in being able to call upon masters at Marlborough School with a sound cricket background, Wiltshire have generally been able to give a good account of themselves in the championship. On several occasions they have come close to repeating their achievement in 1902 and 1909 when they won the title. The best remembered of the Marlborough masters was B. W. Hone, the Oxford blue from Australia who played for them in the late 1930s and for the Minor Counties in their match against the touring side in 1939. Another was J. R. Thompson, a Cambridge blue. They finished runners-up in 1982.

Second Elevens: Since the majority of the first-class counties decided to form their own second-eleven competition in 1959 only two are left to compete in the Minor Counties competition, Lancashire and Somerset. As the first-class game became more professional after the Second World War the second-eleven teams began to dominate the competition. Between 1947 and 1962 the title was won only twice by genuine Minor County sides. Lancashire have been the most successful, winning the title on seven occasions.

The MCC

During the last few years the Marylebone Cricket Club has gradually started to revert to the role intended when it was founded in 1787, that of a private cricket club. With the game still expanding and the management of first-class cricket becoming an increasingly complicated task, the process is likely to continue.

The year of 1969 marked the beginning of the change. As with all other sports, cricket became eligible for grants from public funds to encourage the growth of the game at the lowest level and it was felt wrong that such grants should be made available for a private club to administer instead of a national body. To solve the problem the Cricket Council came into being, with the National Cricket Association looking after the game beyond the first-class level.

The Cricket Council was formed to take charge of the government of the game as a whole and the Test and County Cricket Board were given responsibility for the first-class game in this country and for MCC tours abroad. The MCC, however, still retain considerable influence on the game for they are well represented on the Cricket Council. The MCC secretariat also act for the Cricket Council; they remain responsible for the laws of the game and they own the ground at Lord's.

Until 1969 the MCC was undoubtedly the most important organization in the world of cricket, although it was a responsibility heaped on them rather than one they sought. They were formed in 1787 and quickly became the leading private club in the country, moving their headquarters to the present site in 1814. Such was the respect in which their members were held that other organizations looked to the MCC to settle disputes, particularly with regard to the laws.

It was only natural that as the game gained in popularity, and began to take a hold overseas, the MCC should be asked to organize and control the development. This led to a body being formed to look after the interests of the county championship. Then they took on the task of organizing Test matches at home and the selection of the England teams which had been chosen previously by the ground authority staging the Test match.

The Gillette Cup and NatWest Trophy

Faced with yet another depressing set of figures showing that championship cricket attendances had fallen away still further while costs continued to rise, the first-class county administration in England took a decision in 1962 that opened up a whole new way of life.

Sponsorship was re-introduced to cricket on a large scale and the Gillette Cup was launched the following year. Limited-over cricket had arrived to stay. The game was given a welcome injection of cash and a new pattern for the future that began to be felt in international cricket at the start of the 1970s. The first year demonstrated that cricket was on a winner. The Gillette Cup provided an answer to those who wished to see a start and finish in one day, unless rain interfered. Batsmen were forced to play shots before their side ran out of their permitted number of overs, whatever the strength of the bowling. The knock-out element brought in a new public which had found three-day cricket lacking in appeal and sometimes difficult to comprehend.

In some aspects the competition has not lived up to its aggressive image. After the first season the captain of the fielding side found the safer course was to restrict the run-scoring efforts of the batsmen by setting defensive fields. Spin bowlers were often dispensed with as uneconomic, although this view is slowly changing.

Lancashire, who set a record in 1972 by winning the final at Lord's for the third successive year won it again in 1975.

The outstanding success of the competition can be gauged by the fact that all tickets for the final are always sold out weeks before the finalists are known. Perhaps the most surprising revelation for the organizers has been the size of the crowds in mid-week when championship cricket failed to attract more than a handful of spectators.

The first year the competition was played on a 65 overs basis, but this was reduced to 60 overs the second year to ensure a finish in a day.

In 1981 NatWest Bank took over the competition from Gillette and Derbyshire won the inaugural final. In a thrilling match at Lord's, the scores were tied but Derbyshire lost fewer wickets than Northamptonshire.

The John Player League

After the success of the Gillette Cup it was only a matter of time before first-class cricket attempted to profit from the appeal of limited-over cricket, and the right formula was found in 1969 to launch a new league sponsored by the John Player tobacco company.

Matches are played every Sunday, limited to an early-afternoon start to avoid the accusation that sport might disrupt the religious inclinations of the general public. In order to ensure a finish by the normal closing time of 6.40 p.m., the match is played over 40 overs each side, bowlers are limited to a 15-yard run-up and no bowler may bowl more than eight overs.

As the game is over within a five-hour period county clubs have been able to take the matches to more outlying grounds which are unfit for first-class games. These centres are ideal for the family man who can take his wife and children along without danger of their becoming bored.

Four points are awarded for a victory, two points if rain rules out play. If rain does interfere, matches can be played over a minimum of 10 overs per side in an effort to achieve a result. Where rain interferes after the match has been started, an over is deducted for every three minutes lost. As an extra attraction to the players each batsman hitting a six takes a share of prize money which is awarded each season, the share being calculated according to the number of sixes hit during the season, each bowler who takes four wickets in a match earning prize money on a similar basis.

In one aspect the John Player League has certainly helped to improve the game—the art of fielding. This was proved beyond question in the first two years of the competition when the title was won by Lancashire. Essex, winners in 1981, have always been a force in this competition, finishing level on points with Worcestershire in 1971 but relegated to runners-up because Worcestershire's run rate per over during the season was faster.

In 1972 the result was again in doubt until the final Sunday when Kent beat the 1971 champions, Worcestershire, and pipped Leicestershire by one point to win £2000 first prize. Kent repeated their success in 1973 and 1976. Leicestershire won in 1974 and 1977; Hampshire in 1975 and 1978. Somerset (1979), Warwickshire (1980) and Sussex (1982) have been other winners.

The Benson and Hedges Cup

The attraction which limited-over cricket has gained on the summer sport was fully demonstrated in 1972 when room was found for a third competition, the Benson and Hedges sponsored cup. To make way for this competition, the championship three-day programme was reduced.

The games are played over 55 overs each side and a gold medal is awarded to the outstanding performer in each game. This competition provides added interest in its early stages by its local rivalry.

The country is split into four groups of five teams, which are now altered each year to provide a balanced and varied competition. The Minor Counties supply a team, and Oxford and Cambridge enter a Combined Universities team.

In these groups each side plays the other once, two points being awarded for victory. For the first year of the competition, 1972, an extra point was awarded for dismissing the opposition but this was swiftly abolished.

The top two teams in each league make up eight quarter-finalists who go into a draw. The rest of the competition is played on a knock-out basis. Over the first four years of its existence, the competition was dominated to some extent by Leicestershire. Before the birth of the Benson and Hedges Cup, Leicestershire were without a major honour in 90 years of playing first-class cricket. They killed that unwanted record by beating Yorkshire in the first final and have since reached the final twice more, losing to Surrey in 1974 but defeating Middlesex in 1975. Their achievements owed much to the shrewd tactical brain of skipper Ray Illingworth.

In 1973, 1976 and 1978 Kent won the solid gold trophy and in 1981 and 1982 Somerset triumphed in one-sided finals after crowd-pleasing matches in earlier rounds.

League Cricket

Weekend cricket in Great Britain was for many years split clearly into two categories: the hard, play-for-points attitude dominated much of the nation but in the south, the traditional friendly club fixtures continued.

Now, however, a wind of change has blown. Almost every county in the south has formed its own league; new competitions spring up annually and the vast majority of leading club sides are involved in at least one competitive championship.

There is still a major difference, though. Whereas leagues in the north of England and in Scotland monopolize club cricket and include the employment of star professionals, the south remains purely amateur and combines league competition with the privately arranged 'friendlies'.

The development of league cricket on a highly competitive and commercialized basis, with the use of professionals to attract a large paying public, took place in Yorkshire—mainly through the Bradford League—and the two main leagues over the border, the Lancashire and Central Lancashire Leagues. Originally, the engagement of professionals was designed to improve the technique, understanding and playing ability of the amateur club members.

Former county cricketers or those not quite good enough to hold down a regular place in a county side made ideal professional coaches.

The First World War brought a change of attitude. When the County Championship programme was suspended, numerous players were forced to look elsewhere for a game. They found the more adventurous and wealthy league clubs in the north only too willing to accommodate them. Such players as Jack Hobbs, Frank Woolley and Sydney Barnes made their way into the Bradford League.

Their presence quickly proved an attraction and drew large crowds. The lesson was not lost in Lancashire where demands were soon being made by the public for greater personalities in their weekend cricket. The hunt began, and spread all over the world, when the County Championship returned after the war and the clubs lost their star players to the first-class game. At this stage the West Indian-born player was beginning to demonstrate his individual skill and enthusiasm. The Caribbean became a favourite source of players for the Lancashire and Central Lancashire Leagues, with such cricketers as that wonderfully gifted all-rounder Learie Constantine and George Headley, the man they dubbed 'The Black Bradman', fascinating the Lancashire public. Ted McDonald, one of the greatest of Australian fast bowlers, also joined the league. Indeed, one or two leading England players, including Sydney Barnes, preferred to be paid for weekend cricket rather than involving themselves in full-time employment in the first-class game.

Almost all the members of the great West Indies side of the late 1950s and early 1960s under Frank Worrell had played in league cricket at some stage. Vinoo Mankad, that fine Indian all-rounder, Ray Lindwall of Australia and John Reid of New Zealand were others attracted by the financial rewards of playing cricket all the year round. Leading sides in the North Staffordshire and South Cheshire Leagues also decided to seek famous professional help.

Today the Lancashire and Staffordshire clubs still go for the most attractive drawing card they can find, but the field has been limited by the easing of the qualifications rule for players in first-class cricket. Overseas players attracted by the thought of playing full-time cricket naturally turned to the county championship game in England for employment and greater reward. Nevertheless, league sides still attract some of the world's finest cricketers. Indeed, not only the major clubs sign them but smaller ones such as Rishton, a village club, which in the early 1980's secured the services of West Indies fast bowler Michael Holding. During the same period Nelson recruited Kapil Dev, the brilliant Indian all-rounder.

Not everybody in Lancashire cricket circles has agreed with the influx of paid professionals of Test class. Some believed it affected the flow of home talent into the leagues.

They maintained that youngsters turned their back on it because they felt their opportunities were limited. Moreover some promising boys saw no hope of improving their batting when their innings were liable to be cut short by express deliveries from such fast bowlers as Lindwall, Charlie Griffith, Roy Gilchrist, Wes Hall and Gary Sobers on wickets not up to first-class standard.

Their view was given weight in 1959 when the Oldham captain caused a sensation by conceding a Central Lancashire League match against Middleston because he did not want his younger batsmen to face what he considered 'unfair and dangerous' bowling by the West Indian Test player Gilchrist.

The players who survived the onslaughts from these fast bowlers obviously possessed potential as well as courage and Lancashire County Cricket Club have been grateful over the years for having such a fine breeding ground on their own doorstep. Brian Statham, Peter Marner, Malcolm Hilton, Geoff Pullar and Jack Bond all grew up in the Lancashire leagues. Yorkshire, too, have benefited greatly from the league system inside their own county borders where the demand for high-class professionals has never been as great as in Lancashire. The vast majority of the Yorkshire players gained their early experience of tense, competitive cricket in league cricket and, consequently, when given the opportunity, found the step up into first-class cricket easier to accomplish.

Similarly Warwickshire and Worcestershire have profited from the Midland leagues, Glamorgan from the Welsh leagues, while other counties—notably Derbyshire and Northants—have found Staffordshire, Durham and Northumberland profitable recruiting areas.

By far the most famous of the leagues is the Lancashire League. It came into being in 1980, serving the main population areas in the eastern side of the county and made up of 14 clubs, Accrington, Bacup, Burnley, Church, Colne, East Lancashire, Enfield, Haslingden, Lowerhouse, Nelson, Ramsbottom, Rawtenstall, Rishton and Todmorden.

In the League Competition Nelson have proved the most successful. They set the trend for the 'star' system when they persuaded Learie Constantine to play for them in 1929, the year after he made such an impact on the West Indies tour of England. He was an immediate hit, spectators flocked to see him and the other league sides were forced to follow Nelson's lead. Nelson obviously found the policy rewarding in the way of championships, and in the 1930s won the title four years in succession. They won it again three years out of five in the late 1960s, the first time helped by Pakistan all-rounder Saeed Ahmed, the second and third occasion by Australian opening bowler Neil Hawke.

Burnley also found that the 'star' system paid off when they signed West Indian fast bowler Charlie Griffith whose 144 wickets in taking them to the title in 1964 at an average of 5·20, set a club and league record.

Griffith's great West Indian opening bowling partner Wes Hall helped Accrington to the title and another West Indian, Everton Weekes, holds the record for the highest aggregate in a season, with 1518 for Bacup in 1951. Australian opening batsman Bobby Simpson scored 1444 runs for Accrington in 1959, including a remarkable run of 11 successive half centuries. A feature of league cricket has been the collection among the crowd for players scoring half centuries or taking five wickets in an innings.

Two years after the formation of the Lancashire League came the birth of the Central Lancashire League in 1892. Nine clubs took part in the first year and today the league consists of 14 clubs, a total reached in 1937. Rochdale claim the greatest number of titles and Indian all-rounder Dhatu Phadkar—who toured England in 1952—holds the record for the highest number of wickets in a season when taking 154 on Rochdale's behalf in 1955. Frank Worrell set the batting score standard with 1694 runs in the 1951 season for Radcliffe. The same club tempted Sobers into league cricket and only a knee injury late in the season in 1962 prevented him performing the double of 1000 runs and 100 wickets for the third successive year.

In Yorkshire there is little emphasis placed today on the signing of Test-class professional help. That has not always been the case. The Bradford League, perhaps the best known of all the various Yorkshire leagues, started the star system when offering regular cricket to England-class players during the First World War. The Bradford League was started in 1903, and later came a second division, leading to a promotion and relegation system which added spice to their weekend cricket.

Many of Yorkshire's finest cricketers started in the Bradford League, among them Len Hutton, Brian Close and Ray Illingworth, three who went on to captain England. By the very fact that Herbert Sutcliffe, Hutton and Illingworth were born in Pudsey, the Pudsey St Lawrence Club is more widely known than any other in the league, including that of Bradford whose Park Avenue ground is used by the county for first-class matches. To the embarrassment of Yorkshiremen, the player who made the most impact on the record section of the league has been Eddie Paynter, the Lancashire and England batsman who scored 14 centuries for Keighley when he turned to league cricket for an eight-year spell towards the end of his first-class days. Sydney Barnes also left his mark when playing for Saltaire, who later employed England and Gloucestershire off-spinner Tom Goddard.

The Bradford League has not been alone in proving to be a splendid nursery for Yorkshire. Several players have emerged from the Huddersfield and District League, formed in 1891, including Willie Watson, George Hirst and Wilfred Rhodes. Still more have come from the Yorkshire League which was launched in 1936 and caters for the larger towns close to Leeds. Smaller clubs compete in the Leeds and District League.

Leading the way in the formation of leagues were the Birmingham League, started in 1888, and the North Staffordshire League, founded a year later. These two were the main leagues in the midland area for almost 80 years until a disagreement resulted in many of the leading North Staffs league clubs breaking away in 1962 to form the North Staffs and Southern Cheshire League.

The Staffordshire clubs had little hesitation in following the example of the Lancashire sides, and hired such overseas help as Frank Worrell who played for Norton, Trevor Goddard from South Africa (Great Chell) and Sonny Ramadhin (Ashcombe Park). They have also produced a number of fine players for England, there being no better example than Jack Ikin who started with Bignall and returned to them when his Lancashire and England days were over. More recently Ken Higgs (Lancashire, Leicestershire and England) and Bob Taylor (Derbyshire and England) started their careers with Staffordshire clubs.

The main clubs in the North Staffordshire League switched to the new league at the beginning of the 1960s and persuaded such players as Cec Pepper and Gary Sobers away from the Lancashire area. Both played for Norton. Wes Hall was signed by Great Chell.

League cricket has proved a popular way of cricketing in the north-east of England since the start of this century, with North Yorkshire and South Durham, Durham Senior and the Northumberland the best known leagues. Similarly, league cricket has been properly organized in Wales for the last 40 years and the south-west of England is well served by the leagues in Cornwall and Devon.

Cricket in Scotland

Scottish cricket has a history dating back more than 200 years and for more than 100 of these years there has been regular competition between club sides. Yet the game has never become the popular pastime it might have done, considering its proximity to England.

Few Scottish cricketers have shown either the willingness to take up the game as a profession or the ability to become a recognized force in English county cricket, although Scotland has produced several Test players.

Certainly the most notable of these is Mike Denness, who captained England 19 times between 1973 and 1975, leading MCC on overseas tours to West Indies and Australia. Denness began his serious cricket at Ayr Academy and first played for England in 1969 after gaining experience of representative cricket in Scotland's team while still a schoolboy. He captained Kent from 1972 to 1976.

Leg-spinner Ian Peebles was born in Scotland and went to Glasgow Academy. He played 13 times for England, touring South Africa in 1927 and 1930, and captained Middlesex in the 1939 season.

Scottish representative cricket is on a small scale, rather similar to that played in Ireland. Indeed, one of the highlights of their season is the annual fixture between these two countries, and also the individual matches which they fulfil against MCC.

Scotland are normally visited by the side touring England for Test matches and in 1882, the year the Australians beat England at the Oval to start the story of the Ashes, the Scots gained a famous victory over the Australians in an exhibition match lasting one day. A match against Warwickshire, whom they beat for the first time in 1959, is almost a regular feature of their fixture calendar, as, too, are matches against other county sides when they can be arranged. The Scottish Cricket Union is hoping these may become more frequent with the reduction of county championship matches which will leave more time for county sides to cross the border.

The game was introduced into Scotland, as it was to the rest of the world, by the English army and became accepted by several of the leading schools at the start of the last century. Cricket coaching still forms part of the sports education at the fee-paying schools, but it is not generally practised among the rest of the schools.

The climate is one reason why the game failed to gain the popularity which it did 200 miles further south in England. The Scottish sporting scene is largely dominated by association football and rugby football, and both golf and bowls are other popular pastimes.

Despite these factors Scotland has been fortunate to be served by a number of outstanding cricketers. Several undoubtedly would have found places in first-class cricket in England if they had wished, notably J. Kerr who played for Scotland regularly in the 20 years after the First World War. He made more than 20,000 runs for his club side, Greenock, and one of his five international centuries was scored against the 1921 Australian touring side of Warwick Armstrong.

Even more prolific in Scotland's cause was the Rev. J. Aitchison. His calling gave him little time for practice, but he possessed sufficient natural ability, coupled with a keen eye and sound footwork, to become the first batsman to score 3000 runs for Scotland. He scored hundreds against the Australians, the South Africans and against both the 'Roses' counties. In W. Nichol, Scotland possessed a sound all-rounder who batted left-handed and bowled slow left arm, so effectively that he scored 1000 runs for Scotland and took 50 wickets. Leg-spinner/bowler K. Laidlaw failed by only three to take 100 wickets while bowling for Scotland just before and for some years after the Second World War. R. H. E Chisholm was a reliable batsman who made 80 appearances for Scotland.

Another who gave sterling service was J. Brown, a wicket-keeper batsman who played 85 times between 1953 and 1973.

Left-arm spinner J. M. Allan made such an impression during his three years playing for Oxford University at the start of the 1950s that he was invited by the MCC to join their 'A' side on the 1955–56 tour of Pakistan, an invitation he was forced to turn down because of examinations. He played county cricket for Kent and later Warwickshire when they were short of spinners in the middle 1960s. About the same period T. B. Racionzer, from Queen's Park Secondary School, Glasgow, joined Sussex, but could never establish a regular batting place in the county side and returned to Scotland.

Scotland's most successful current cricketer is Brian Hardie, an opening batsman with Essex. Born in Stenhousemuir, he played in the East of Scotland League and made his debut for Scotland in 1970, at the age of 20. His father and elder brother have both played for the country.

Several leagues operate—notably the Scottish Counties, Border, Western Union, and East and Strathmore Union. In 1980 Brian Close, former England, Yorkshire and Somerset captain, was appointed manager of Scotland's team which was included in the Benson and Hedges Cup.

To improve their cricket, Scottish clubs have followed the example of the Lancashire and Staffordshire Leagues in engaging professional cricketers from overseas, although on a small scale. Aberdeenshire, in the Scottish Counties League, employed West Indian batsman Rohan Kanhi and he rewarded them with 10 centuries in 1959. Pakistan Test captain Intikhab played for West of Scotland for several seasons in the Western Union before going to Surrey. His post was taken by another Pakistan Test player, Salahuddin. Sadiq Mohammad played for the Glasgow club, Poloc and Australian opening bowler Bob Massie assisted Kilmarnock.

Cricket in Ireland

The day of July 2nd, 1969 will always be proudly recalled in any history of cricket in Ireland. For that was the occasion when the all-Ireland team created front-page news at home and overseas by beating the West Indian touring side by nine wickets in a one-day match at Sion Mills.

Only the previous day the West Indies had emerged from a five-day Test battle against England at Lord's with a creditable draw, and six of those players, plus the manager and former West Indies batting star Clyde Walcott were in the team to play Ireland. Sobers was missing but players of the ability of Joey Carew, Maurice Foster, Basil Butcher and Clive Lloyd were playing. Yet they were dismissed for 25 runs on a green wicket.

Ireland's bowling heroes were the captain, D. Goodwin (five for six), and A. O'Riordan (four for 18), both bowling medium pace. Ireland scored the 26 runs needed to win for the loss of one wicket. Over the next two days the West Indies played another match against Ireland, this time in Belfast, and had the better of a drawn game.

The start and growth of cricket in Ireland follows a pattern similar to that in other parts of the world. The game was introduced mainly by the army when the whole country was under British rule. Most of the early matches involved the army and the local civil authorities who were, in the main, from England. Nevertheless, it took almost 100 years before the Irish started expressing more than a passing interest in the pastime of the English and it was not until the middle of the last century that clubs, started by Irishmen, began to spring up.

Today there are three main competitions. In the south there is the Leinster Senior League, administered from Dublin, while the Northern Senior League, run from Belfast, serves the north. The third competition is for district sides—six of them competing—for the Guinness Cup which is the Irish version of the county championship in England.

The Leinster Senior League caters for 10 clubs. Not all the sides play the same number of matches and the final league placings are worked out on a percentage basis. The Northern Senior League caters for 12 clubs.

The amount of true representative cricket played by the full Ireland side varies from season to season, although they do have regular fixtures against Scotland and MCC, the matches being played at home one season and away the next. All the main Test-playing countries have visited Ireland at some stage when they have been on a tour of England, although it is not automatic that the touring side visits Ireland.

Ireland also play matches against other countries in Europe. They have visited Holland, and they played a match in Denmark for the first time in 1971. Denmark have visited Ireland, and Holland did so for the first time in 1971. In that same year the match against Wales was revived after a lapse of 45 years. Other matches Ireland seek are against the Combined Services when they are in England to play MCC. The Pakistan International Airways cricket team, composed almost entirely of Test players, has toured Ireland and several national sides have played there when they have been visiting England on an 'A' tour.

Among the celebrated Ireland players in the past was R. H. Lambert who helped bring about the formation of the Irish Cricket Union—linking the north and the south—in 1923. Lambert scored almost 2000 runs for Ireland in representative matches and took more than 130 wickets. His performances so impressed W. G. Grace that he invited Lambert back to play in the London County side which he organized when he left Gloucestershire after a dispute. Lambert's brother S. D. and his son N. H. also played representative cricket for Ireland.

Just when R. H. Lambert was bowing out of Irish cricket—in a playing capacity—one of their most successful bowlers was stepping in. He was J. C. Boucher who took 307 wickets in a 25-year career for Ireland with his fastish off-spin. He was partnered in the same period by leg-spinner E. Ingram who, in one memorable spell against the 1938 Australians, captured five for 29.

More recently Ireland's bowling hero, with his left-arm medium fast deliveries, has been A. O'Riordan, the youngest player to captain Ireland in a representative match—of which he has played more than 50. He was supported in 1971 by the left-arm slow bowling of J. D. Monteith when Ireland went through the season unbeaten, winning three and drawing the others in their six-match programme.

Monteith was the leading wicket-taker, breaking the record of 44 wickets in a season, set up by Boucher in 1937. Monteith took 11 for 66 when Ireland beat Wales by 260 runs, and 13 for 126 in the 138-run victory over Holland in Dublin. Against the Combined Services at Portsmouth he took another 13 wickets, this time for the cost of 78 runs and then 12 for 110 in the 96-run victory over the MCC at Lord's. He also proved one of his country's most successful captains before signing for Middlesex in 1981.

In 1966 O. D. Colhoun, in sharing a dismissal for the 54th time, established a new wicket-keeping record for Ireland, and in 1971 increased his total to three figures.

O'Riordan is the only player who has completed the double of 2000 runs and 200 wickets for Ireland. In 1980 I. J. Anderson became the first to score 3000 runs for Ireland. S. F. Bergin passed 2000 runs and Monteith and J. C. Boucher have each also taken more than 200 wickets.

The Irish cricket authorities have done much to encourage young cricketers and, in 1979, their Under 19 team won a seven-team 'Round Robin' tournament in Toronto.

Cricket in Australia

County cricket organizations were already being formed and cricket had been played regularly for almost 100 years in the mother country before the game started to take a hold in Australia. Yet Australians proved such keen students that within 40 years of the first inter-club matches taking place they had learned the techniques required to match the power and strength of the early touring sides from England.

Australian cricket has one great natural advantage—the climate which encourages people to pursue outdoor recreational activities for most of the year. Nevertheless, when the game was first introduced, they discovered one *disadvantage*—the type of soil in many parts of the country was unsuitable for making cricket wickets. This has been largely overcome by scientific means, so that today the wickets in Australia are truer and produce an evenness in bounce not generally found in England. Clearly, such conditions are a great boon to batsmen and explain why they tend to reach international standard at a younger age than their English counterparts.

Compared with England, there is little first-class cricket in Australia. Only five sides take part in their major championship, the Sheffield Shield. They are New South Wales, Queensland, South Australia, Victoria and Western Australia. They play each other twice and this is the limit of the first-class game, apart from Test matches and state games against the touring side.

This small programme allows the leading players to appear for their club sides in grade cricket at weekends. The standard is therefore high at the top level of grade cricket and could almost be compared with that of championship cricket in England, although the games are played over shorter hours, demanding a more positive approach. The cricket, as the title suggests, is graded throughout the whole network in each state. Players have every opportunity to find their own level and those with extra talent can quickly make progress up the scale, whatever their age.

The Australians had the advantage of organizing their cricket system virtually straight away because they adopted the rules and regulations fashioned out of years of trial and error in England. This largely accounts for the speed with which Australian players were able to grasp the essential skills so soon after the game started taking a hold in the main population centres of Sydney and Melbourne in the early 1800s.

Deep rivalry has always existed between the states of New South Wales and Victoria, and is as intense as that between Yorkshire and Lancashire. This stems from the early days of the game in Australia when Sydney and Melbourne vied for the leadership and development of the game in their country.

There is no doubt that cricket was exported from England to Australia mainly by the Royal Navy and introduced to the local inhabitants by games played between sailors or between sailors and the authorities looking after the prison colonies. Early in the 1800s cricket clubs were being formed, mainly in Sydney, Melbourne and Tasmania whose much smaller population from which to draw players inevitably meant it could not keep pace with the development of the game on the mainland.

By the middle 1800s the club sides were starting to search for wider horizons for fixtures, even crossing into other states. The rise of the game was spread even more quickly by touring sides from England, the first in 1861 under H. H. Stephenson and the second two years later. On each tour at least one player stayed in Australia to coach either in Sydney or Melbourne.

Within 15 years of Stephenson's tour the Australians felt they had progressed sufficiently to challenge the best of England. The first recognized Test match was staged in Melbourne in March 1877, Australia winning by 45 runs. Charles Bannerman from Melbourne, who opened the Australian innings, scored an undefeated 165 which was the first century in Test cricket. A return match was played a fortnight later and this time England succeeded by four wickets to level the series.

Meanwhile the Melbourne Cricket Club had forged ahead of the Australian, Maitland and Albert cricket clubs of Sydney, becoming the most influential in Australia, and raised the money for the early all-England sides to tour. In fact, it was not until the 1890s that cricket authorities in Sydney took on the responsibility of inviting the England touring side and the rivalry between the two centres flared again. Overall responsibility was finally settled in 1905 when the Australian Board of Control was formed, with Victoria and New South Wales as founder members. They were soon joined by Queensland and South Australia. Tasmania became a member in 1908 and Western Australia some 10 years later. The first Australian side to be selected by this body was in 1909 for the tour of England, but even then their troubles were not over.

The Australian players on tour had always selected their own manager. The Board agreed to continue their policy, provided they approved the choice. Then, for the 1912 tour of England, the Board insisted on their own nominee for manager, whereupon six of the Australian players refused to go, including such towering players as Victor Trumper, Clem Hill and Warwick Armstrong. The Board stood by their decision, however, and the tour went on with six replacements.

Twenty years before this incident Australia's major cricketing competition had been launched in 1892. Inter-state challenge matches had been played but not on any properly organized footing, and the new competition began after Lord Sheffield, who had taken a touring side to Australia, gave the Australian authorities a sum of money to help promote the game. The money was used to buy the Sheffield Shield and the competition started during the 1892–93 season.

At the start New South Wales, Victoria and South Australia competed for the trophy. Queensland were admitted in 1926, and staged a Test match for the first time two years later. Poor travel facilities kept Western Australia out of the competition until new air routes were opened after the Second World War, and they joined in 1947, although it was not until the MCC tour of 1970–71 that they really achieved equal status with the other states by staging a Test match for the first time at Perth.

In the 1970–71 season, an inter-state knockout competition was introduced. Initially sponsored by V & G, then by Coca-Cola, it ultimately became the Australasian Gillette Cup in 1973–74. Apart from the five Sheffield Shield states, New Zealand annually enter their national team.

A limited overs competition for the McDonald's Cup was introduced in 1979–80 and Victoria, its first winners, collected £35,000 in bonuses, sponsorship and other rewards from their triumphs in the Shield and in the various limited overs tournaments.

The Sheffield Shield

Just as Yorkshire have dominated the county championship over the years, so New South Wales have been the outstanding side in the Sheffield Shield, the major cricketing competition in Australia, winning the title 36 times since it was first launched in 1892–93.

For the most part, the story of the Sheffield Shield has been a battle for supremacy between New South Wales and Victoria, with occasional interruptions by South Australia and, more recently, Western Australia who emerged as the strongest state side in the late 1960s, largely under the leadership of former Surrey and England left-arm spinner Tony Lock. Queensland have not won the Shield.

Twice in the first three years of the competition the title went to Victoria who were able to call upon such players as G. H. S. Trott, H. Trumble and C. E. McLeod. South Australia took it in the second year, helped by the all-round ability of G. Giffen, and New South Wales gained the title for the first time in 1895–96 when Victor Trumper was beginning to demonstrate his power as a batsman.

Between the two wars the balance of power was divided equally between Victoria and New South Wales, each winning the title nine times, South Australia coming into the picture in the middle of the 1930s when Don Bradman moved to Adelaide from Sydney for health reasons.

When cricket resumed after the Second World War New South Wales became supreme once more. They won the championship a record nine times in succession between 1953 and 1962.

Western Australia, Victoria and South Australia have emerged as the strongest sides in recent years. South Australia have received outside help from the redoubtable Gary Sobers who helped them win in 1963–64 and South African Barry Richards in 1970–71. Richards became an Australian hero, topping the averages with 109·86. Western Australia entered the competition after the Second World War on a limited basis, winning the title in 1947–48. They gained equal status in 1956–57 and won the title again in 1967–68 under the leadership of Lock and the help of Colin Milburn. They then finished champions five times in seven seasons including 1976–77 when they also won the Gillette Cup.

Queensland

Although admitted to the Sheffield Shield competition in 1926–27 season, Queensland have lived in the shadows of their more successful state opponents, New South Wales, Victoria and South Australia, and at the end of the 1981–82 season they were still searching for their first Shield title.

They were slow to gain Shield recognition in Australia largely because travelling difficulties made it impossible for them to obtain matches against Victoria and South Australia. Visiting Western Australia was out of the question until air travel became as familiar to Australians as hopping on a bus.

Becoming organized was a long, slow process. Representative games were few and there was little to encourage the younger, more promising player. Nevertheless Queensland had Test players in their cricket, including A. Coningham, C. B. Jennings, J. W. McLaren and R. J. Hartigan who all appeared for Australia against England or South Africa earlier this century. Not all of them, however, were Queensland-born.

The problem of whether to stay and help Queensland gain first-class recognition or lend his talents to another state, faced left-arm spinner H. Ironmonger in the 1920s. He eventually decided on helping Victoria and later played in 14 Test matches. Half way through his Test career Queensland were finally accepted into the Sheffield Shield competition. This was for the start of the 1926–27 season and almost immediately the state produced a Test player in R. Oxenham who bowled medium pace and made his Test debut against England in the 1928–29 series. Another Queensland player, P. Hornibrook, also appeared for Australia against England during the 1928–29 season. In the middle of the 1930s Queensland cricket received a great boost when Test batsman Bill Brown decided to switch from New South Wales and throw the weight of his considerable talent behind Queensland's cause. Brown was one of Australia's leading batsmen of the day, making 22 Test appearances, including three tours of England. Almost half those Test appearances came during his Queensland days.

He took his place in their state side just as Don Tallon was starting to attract the attention of the selectors with his smooth and efficient wicket-keeping style, although he was not to be rewarded with a Test place until England toured Australia in 1946.

Tallon's entry into Test cricket along with that of Colin McCool—who switched to the state after starting with New South Wales and later came to England to play for Somerset—was the start of a trail travelled by several Queensland players in the last 20 years, the most celebrated being the burly, aggressive Peter Burge and the jovial wicket-keeper Wally Grout.

Burge liked nothing better than fighting against the odds and then going on to slaughter the bowling with the power and fury of his driving. He was a tower of strength in the Australian middle-order batting as well as Queensland's star for 10 years from 1955 when he was chosen for his first tour to the West Indies. His highest score in Tests was 181 at the Oval in 1961.

Keeping Burge company in the Australian team was wicket-keeper Grout who made 51 Test appearances, and his haul of 187 Test victims is fifth only to the record of 302 by Rodney Marsh after 83 Tests. In all Grout dismissed 479 batsmen, some of them taken by spectacular diving catches way down the leg side which was always a remarkable feature of his keeping. Queensland provided two other regular Test players in the 1950s, one being Ken Mackay, an obstinate middle-order batsman and medium-paced bowler. He was Australia's answer to England's Trevor Bailey in almost every way, possessing unlimited patience and great powers of concentration.

Another was opening bowler Ron Archer. He joined Ray Lindwall in the Australian Test team and soon the two were operating as Queensland's spearhead.

Australian Test batsman Greg Chappell accepted the state captaincy in 1973–74 after spending several years with his home state, South Australia. He inspired Queensland to second place in his first season, and with the arrival of Test opening bowler Jeff Thomson from New South Wales the following season, they have made a significant challenge in recent seasons. In 1979–80 Chappell's average was 104.

When Lindwall retired they employed West Indian fast bowler Wes Hall whose 43 wickets in 1961–62 set a state record. At the end of the 1978–79 season John Maclean, the state's captain and wicket-keeper, retired with a record 313 dismissals.

New South Wales

The omission of Doug Walters from the final Test against England at the Oval in August 1972 meant that the Australians took the field without a New South Wales member in the side. The event was such a rarity that it caused widespread comment among the game's historians. Certainly from the time cricket became organized in Australia, New South Wales has produced an almost ceaseless flow of brilliant batsmen, bowlers and wicket-keepers.

In the domestic Sheffield Shield competition New South Wales have won the title more times than any other state. Their record is a tribute to the skills of the team and the direction provided by a long line of outstanding leaders.

Long before the Sheffield Shield competition was conceived New South Wales were playing inter-state matches against their greatest rivals, Victoria. Their star batsman of those days was Murdoch who later moved to England and captained Sussex in the championship. He was actually born in Victoria but gave his batting genius to New South Wales. Murdoch was the first player to score a double century in Tests when making 211 against England at the Oval in 1884.

Murdoch was soon replaced in the New South Wales side by one of Australia's greatest batsmen and most popular of figures, Victor Trumper whose career was cut short by a fatal illness in 1915 when he was only 37. Trumper made a quiet start to his career but then sprang into prominence with an innings of 292 not out against Tasmania and became the inspiration behind New South Wales' run of title wins before the First World War.

Murdoch and Trumper provided a high example for later New South Wales batsmen to follow. The fast bowling standard had been set in Murdoch's time by Frank Spofforth who gained the nickname 'The Demon' because of his speed, accuracy and the amount he could move the ball back off the wicket. In 18 Tests against England he took 94 wickets.

Joining Trumper in the slaughter of the bowlers for New South Wales during that period was Noble, a gifted all-rounder who often opened the bowling for Australia and batted at number four. He performed the Test match double of 1000 runs and 100 wickets and was supported in the New South Wales side by another of their famous characters, Charlie Macartney, who is remembered mainly for his correct and punishing right-hand batting. Macartney was also a polished left-arm spinner whose 45 Test wickets included a best performance of seven for 58 against England at Leeds in 1909.

The second of the New South Wales outstanding fast bowlers emerged after the First World War when Jack Gregory, a fearsome fast bowler, shared an outstanding opening bowling partnership for Australia with Ted McDonald. Gregory was also a forceful left-handed batsman—whose century in 70 minutes against South Africa in 1921 is still a record—and a brilliant slip fielder. He was a member of a famous New South Wales cricketing family and he played for the state for nine seasons. Gregory was fortunate in having one of the finest wicket-keepers of all time in Bert Oldfield who took his bowling in both state and Test matches.

Oldfield was adept at handling fast and spin bowling alike. He had plenty of experience, for in addition to Gregory, he kept to the spin bowling of Arthur Mailey and the cunning leg-breaks and googlies of Bill O'Reilly who, in only 27 Test matches, captured 144 wickets. New South Wales had batting qualities to parade alongside their bowling in the early 1930s with the courage of Stan McCabe who stood unflinchingly against the bodyline tactics employed by England on the 1932–33 tour, the class of Bill Brown and the master of them all, Don Bradman, who made his debut in 1927 and stayed until moving to South Australia in 1934.

After the Second World War, New South Wales could justifiably claim both the finest opening batting partnership in Sidney Barnes and Arthur Morris and the best new ball attack in Ray Lindwall and Keith Miller—who had started his career with Victoria. When these great names started to disappear from the scoreboards still more were ready to take over during the record run of nine Sheffield Shield titles in the late 1950s and early 1960s, among them Brian Booth and Norman O'Neill in the middle-order batting and Alan Davidson, one of the finest left-arm fast bowlers cricket has seen. The brilliantly aggressive left-handed batsman Neil Harvey was to switch from Victoria to New South Wales halfway through this run, and he became the second highest scorer in Australian Test cricket, with 6149 runs. His arrival coincided with the appointment as captain of Benaud, who developed as Australia's leading wicket-taker in Tests, and the emergence of Simpson as an opening batsman.

South Australia

South Australia were seldom able to match the all-round strength of New South Wales and Victoria during the first 65 years of the Sheffield Shield competition. Some of their most rewarding times have occurred during the last 20 years, notably their title win in 1976 under Ian Chappell who, despite brushes with authority, was a prolific scorer into the Eighties.

Their sparkle in the early 1960s was largely explained by the presence of Gary Sobers. He played for them for three seasons from 1961–62, culminating in South Australia winning the title in 1963–64. This was the first time they had achieved the feat for 11 seasons.

Sobers took a while to settle during his first season but he gave an indication of what was to come in his final innings when scoring 251 against New South Wales. More was to come when Sobers returned in 1962–63. This time he scored 1006 runs and took 51 wickets, the first time that particular double had been achieved in a season of Australian first-class cricket. The following season he repeated the feat while taking South Australia to the title.

Barry Richards, the South African opening batsman, was tempted to try his hand and proved the inspiration behind their Sheffield Shield triumph in 1970–71, the second time in three seasons they had won the title. Richards' batting was brilliant. He topped the Australian averages with 109·86, scoring 1538 runs in 16 first-class innings.

Add, that season, the battling strength of Ian Chappell, who had taken over the captaincy from the long serving Les Favell, and his younger brother Greg and the reason for South Australia's title victory was clearly seen. The performances of Sobers and later of Richards were reminiscent of two other great periods in South Australia's history when Clem Hill and Joe Darling were in full flow at the start of this century and when Don Bradman joined them from New South Wales to take over the captaincy in 1935.

Hill was a master left-handed batsman, the best Australia has produced. He still holds the individual Sheffield Shield record for South Australia of 365 not out made against New South Wales in 1900–1.

Almost matching Hill for power but contributing even more in the way of captaincy was another brilliant left-handed batsman

83

Joe Darling. They were both in the side when South Australia won the Sheffield Shield in 1893–94, the second season of the competition. Darling was an astute captain who led Australia on three tours of England, his finest season in Tests being in the home series in 1897–98 when he made three centuries against England. He had not then taken over the captaincy and they were his only centuries in Test cricket. Another famous pair, G. Giffen and J. J. Lyons, helped provide the strength to match New South Wales and Victoria before Shield cricket was organized. They were on the scene within 10 years of the South Australia Cricket Association being formed in 1871. The more notable of the two was Giffen, the best all-rounder of his day, whose 31 Test appearances brought him 1438 runs and 103 wickets with his slow medium-flighted deliveries.

His contemporary was J. J. Lyons who made three tours of England in the last century, and his total of 14 Test appearances were all against England. The second outstanding period for South Australia this century was between the wars when Vic Richardson, grandfather of the Chappell brothers, was in the side at the start of the 1930s and Bradman the main batsman at the end of the decade. Serving with them both was another outstanding import Clarrie Grimmett who was born in New Zealand, started with Wellington and arrived in South Australia via six seasons with Victoria.

He was one of the finest spinners of his type, turning his leg-spinner appreciably, his top-spinner a deadly delivery. In all he took 1424 wickets, 216 of them coming in only 37 Test appearances, a figure bettered only by Lillee, Benaud, Lindwall and McKenzie in Australian Test cricket.

He was 33 when first chosen for Australia and on his Test debut took 11 for 82 against England at Melbourne in 1925. Bradman's influence was immediate with a triple century, double century and century in his first three innings for South Australia, taking them to the title in 1935–36 and again in 1938–39.

Their success in the 1968–69 season was achieved without any 'outside' help and after Neil Hawke, their leading opening bowler in recent years who took 91 wickets in 27 Tests, had decided to settle in England. It was a tribute to the captaincy of Les Favell who retired a year later after being with them 20 years, during which he became one of the most consistent batsmen Shield cricket has seen. David Hookes led them to the title in 1981–82.

Victoria

The second most successful state side in the Sheffield Shield, Victoria, has never managed to dominate the competition in the same way New South Wales has done, their nearest approach being in the 16 seasons between 1921–22 and 1936–37 when they won the title nine times.

This was the era of Bill Ponsford and Bill Woodfull, the finest state opening partnership the country has produced and one Australia was grateful to call upon through a number of Test campaigns.

They came into the Victoria side within 12 months of each other at the start of the 1920s and both announced their retirement after Australia had visited England in 1934, Woodfull as captain of the tour party.

Opposition bowlers in Australia treated Ponsford with the respect with which they held Bradman, so difficult was he to remove, especially once he had survived the opening attack. For an opening batsman of such a reputation he was suspect against the really fast delivery which explains his modest record against England when Harold Larwood was bowling against him. His first season in Shield cricket was not particularly successful but an innings of 429 against Tasmania in the 1922–23 season launched him on the road to fame. Five seasons later he scored 437 against Queensland, the only player to have played two innings exceeding 400.

His most successful series against England was his last in 1934 when he returned an average of 94 including 266 at the Oval when he and Bradman added 451 for the second wicket. In all he scored 13,819 runs, 2122 in Tests. Woodfull's record was remarkably similar with 13,392 career runs, 2300 in Tests. As Australia's captain he twice won series against England and was captain when England's Jardine unleashed the 'bodyline' tactics in 1932–33. When Woodfull retired after the 1934 series it ended a run of 35 successive Test appearances covering seven series.

Woodfull's entry into Victoria cricket followed the retirement of another Victoria and Australia captain, the powerful figure of Warwick Armstrong who weighed around 20 stone throughout most of his cricketing life. He was a giant of a man in every way, as a powerful batsman, clever spin bowler and a hard captain.

Armstrong appeared in the Victoria side soon after the state had lost the first Australian wicket-keeper John Blackham. He was chosen for what is regarded as the first Test match in 1877 and made such an impression he stayed to take part in the first seven recognized tours of England.

The loss of Ponsford and Woodfull at the same time in 1934 was a blow to Victoria but they were not long in finding suitable replacements. Lindsay Hassett had already played a few games for the state in the 1933–34 season and three seasons later Keith Miller appeared on the scene to stay until the war years and then moving on to New South Wales.

Hassett was perhaps a little unfortunate to start his Test career in the shadow of Bradman. Standing 5 ft 6 in., he was small for a batsman, yet his batting lacked nothing and he made more than 3000 runs in Test cricket from 69 innings, often carrying the batting when Australia's strength was not up to usual standards in the early 1950s. The same applies to Colin McDonald, a sound opening batsman and courageous player of fast bowling who served Victoria for 16 years.

Victoria were also blessed by having two fine bowlers during the time of Hassett, Bill Johnston, a left-arm medium paced swing bowler, and off-spinner Ian Johnson. Johnston was used as the foil for Lindwall and Miller but was so successful he finished the leading Australian wicket-taker against England in 1948. Johnson was never fast enough through the air to become a successful bowler in English conditions—he took only 13 Test wickets in two tours to England—but proved extremely effective in Australia and in the West Indies. He captained Australia in five series.

Victoria also produced the only Australian batsman to approach the Test figures of Sir Donald Bradman. He was Neil Harvey who spent the most rewarding years of his cricketing life with the state before moving over to New South Wales. An aggressive left-hander who refused to allow bowlers to dictate to him, Harvey played in more Test matches than any other Australian, a total of 79.

His role as Victoria's main batsman was taken over by the dour Bill Lawry, the third highest run scorer in Australian Test cricket. Lawry, another left-hander was almost the opposite in attitudes at the crease to Harvey. He was a specialist in blunting attacks. Lawry was replaced by the aggressive Keith Stackpole, a successful number one for Australia until his retirement and Graham Yallop led Victoria to Shield wins in 1979 and 1980.

Western Australia

Anxious to make up for lost time—not having been given a full home-and-away Sheffield Shield programme until the 1956–57 season—Western Australia have considerably improved the state's image and playing reputation during the last 20 years.

One of their most successful moves was to employ Surrey and England left-arm spinner Tony Lock when he was left out of the 1962–63 MCC tour party to Australia. Lock enjoyed the experience so much that he emigrated to Perth and took over as the state's player coach. The next step was the captaincy and under his aggressive leadership and with the help of his superb bowling Lock steered the side to the Shield title in 1967–68. It was their first title since becoming full playing members in the Shield competition.

By the time he retired from first-class cricket in 1971 Lock had made sure that Western Australia cricket was in good shape and they won the Shield again in the 1971–72 season under the leadership of John Inverarity, repeating the triumph in 1972–73, 1974–75, 1976–77, 1977–78 and 1980–81.

Over these victorious seasons they possessed the best-balanced side in the country. Inverarity and Ross Edwards provided the backbone of the batting along with Test wicket-keeper Rodney Marsh, while the bowling attack contained Australia's past pace king Graham McKenzie alongside his successor Dennis Lillee.

In addition to Lock, Western Australia tried several other players from overseas. Rohan Kanhai was among the first in 1961–62 but he was not the success they had hoped. Alan Jones of Glamorgan also played for a season and Bill Playle, the New Zealand opening batsman, spent several seasons with them. Their next most successful 'foreigner' was another England Test player Colin Milburn who delighted the Australian crowds with his big-hitting, fast-scoring performances.

He did not score as many centuries as Sobers but made his runs so quickly that the later batsmen often found the opposition attack a spent force by the time they arrived at the crease. The contributions of Lock, Milburn and company all played a part in the growth of Western Australia cricket and the establishment of their headquarters at Perth as a Test-player centre in the 1970–71 series against England.

Cricket had taken hold in Western Australia in the middle of the last century, about the same time as it was gaining in popularity in the other states. The Western Australia Cricket Association was formed in 1885 and within two years they had engaged professional coaches. Yet their cricket was to remain a purely local affair for a number of years.

Their first breakthrough came immediately after the Second World War when they were admitted to the Sheffield Shield but were not given a full programme of matches because of the travelling difficulties. They were on trial but proved their worth by winning the competition in their first season 1947–48 under the leadership of their captain and coach Keith Carmody, the former Royal Australian Air Force, Services and New South Wales batsman.

Even today travelling poses a problem. In order to fulfil their away engagements against the Eastern States, the Western Australia team have to undertake a mini-tour of their own. This causes problems for the players who have to take their holidays to go on the tour or rely on the generosity of their employers.

During the first half of this century Western Australia's lack of competition meant they had few players good enough to attract the attention of the national selectors but this position changed once they were playing regularly. One of the first to catch the eye was Bobby Simpson who was born in New South Wales, transferred to Perth for his employment and broke into state cricket—and Tests—via Western Australia.

Jack Rutherford was also picked for Australia but their leading Test player has been fast bowler Graham McKenzie with his jogging, economical run-up and deceptive speed and bounce. He was undoubtedly helped by Perth having the fastest wicket in Australia but proved his ability in Test cricket everywhere—including the slow wickets of India. By the finish of the 1970–71 MCC tour to Australia, McKenzie stood only two wickets behind Benaud's then record Australian Test haul of 248.

Des Hoare and Laurie Mayne are two other fast bowlers who have benefited from Perth's wicket and gone on to play in Tests just as Lillee and Bob Massie have done. On the batting front the beefy figure of Barry Shepherd took Western Australia's colours into the Test side in the 1960s before switching to New South Wales, a trend continued by John Inverarity and Ross Edwards.

Tasmania

Tasmania, youngest of the Sheffield Shield competitors, entered in 1977. They were captained and coached by Jack Simmons, the Lancashire all-rounder, and in 1978–79 caused a major surprise by defeating Western Australia by four wickets–their first Shield victory, and then beat the same opponents in the final of the Gillette Cup. Jackie Hampshire, then with Yorkshire, and Brian Davison of Leicestershire, succeeded Simmons but Tasmania have never quite managed to emulate those heady triumphs.

Cricket in South Africa

Any analysis of South African cricket must start with events which occurred more than 150 years after the game was introduced to the country. In 1968 the South African Government found the inclusion of Basil D'Oliveira, a Cape Coloured cricketer, 'unacceptable' in the MCC party to tour South Africa for a five-Test match series.

Despite an innings of 158 in the final Test against the Australians at the Oval that summer, D'Oliveira, who left Cape Town in 1961 to start a cricketing career in England, had been left out of the original tour party. When he was brought in to maintain the balance of the side after the Warwickshire (later Somerset) bowler Tom Cartwright withdrew because of injury, the South African Government refused to accept him as a member of the team and the MCC cancelled the tour.

In doing so they announced that no future MCC tour of South Africa would be considered until they were satisfied that proper steps were being taken inside South Africa towards complete non-racial cricket. In 1968 cricket played by white cricketers in South Africa came under the control of the South African Cricket Association who selected the Test team and touring parties. Cricket played by coloured players was largely administered by the South African Cricket Board of Control. They have their own grounds—poorly equipped by white standards—and white and coloured cricketers do not take part in matches against each other.

Since that decision in 1968 South African cricket has been isolated by the rest of the world. As a result of the government's policy towards coloured people South Africa have never played Test series against West Indies, India or Pakistan.

The Australians made a short tour in 1969–70 but scheduled South African tours of England in 1970 and Australia in 1971–72 were both cancelled, as several have been in more recent years, primarily because it was felt the South African cricketers and the games they were due to play could not be guaranteed freedom from interference by demonstrators who had threatened to disrupt the tours at every possible moment. It was a tragedy for cricket in general and South Africa in particular because they had developed their strongest side since the British Army introduced the game to the country about the start of the last century.

By the middle of the last century cricket clubs had been formed in Cape Town, Port Elizabeth and Pietermaritzburg, and the influence of the game spread rapidly. Challenge matches were issued between army personnel posted to South Africa and people born in the sub-continent. Soon the main townships were challenging each other and in 1874 a competition was started between centres for a trophy known as 'The Champion Bat'. Ten years previously the Western Province Cricket Club had been formed.

The year of 1888 marked a great advancement in the game when negotiations were started for a side from England to tour during the season of 1888–89. This team was led by Aubrey Smith who later settled in South Africa before becoming a film star. To celebrate the visit, the famous cricket grounds of Newlands in Cape Town and Wanderers in Johannesburg were prepared. The England side, though not a full representative side, proved far too strong for the local opposition, but the tour led to the start of the Currie Cup competition, South Africa's main domestic first-class programme.

The competition was launched when Transvaal challenged Kimberley, and in 1890 the South African Cricket Association was formed to organize the game on a proper footing. Meanwhile local associations were established in the provinces where the game was being played at an advanced level. Nowadays there are nine district sides competing in two divisions. Several teams from England toured South Africa after Aubrey Smith's visit, including two led by Lord Hawke, and all of them found the opposition lacking in strength, but the picture changed drastically when 'Plum' Warner took the first side representing the MCC in 1905–6. The South African side then contained such figures as Dave Nourse, George Faulkner and Albert Vogler, the first of the great googly bowlers. They won the series 4–1, and made their first fully representative visit to England in 1907. South Africa was now launched as a Test-playing country along with England and Australia.

The next change in their cricket occurred in the 1930s. All the earlier matches had taken place on matting wickets. The South African authorities had been urged by several touring sides to try to make turf wickets. Some provinces had already experimented with turf wickets and for the 1930–31 MCC party under Percy Chapman, the two Tests at Durban and one at Cape Town were played on turf. All three were drawn, though South Africa won the five-match series with the one victory of the series at Johannesburg.

One step behind in the development of cricket came Rhodesia but the game quickly grew in popularity and within 10 years of the first recorded match in Rhodesia they were admitted to the Currie Cup, in 1902. Few South African Test players emerged from Rhodesia, now Zimbabwe, which left the South African Cricket Union in 1980.

Side by side with the growth of the game by white players came the development of the coloured groups, particularly the Cape Coloureds and the South African Indians, although they did not enjoy the same freedom and facilities as the white players. Griqualand West was the first centre to have an organization looking after the interests of the coloured players and administered their main competition, the Barnato Memorial Trophy.

Other provinces then formed their own organizations and these were all linked to the South African Coloured Cricket Board, formed in 1904. The running of this organization was disrupted in the 1930s when the different racial groups went their own way. This led to three different associations controlling cricket for the Coloureds, Indians and the Bantu. These internal squabbles had the effect of halting the progress of cricket for coloureds as a whole and it was not until 1950 that they got together again when the South African Cricket Board of Control was formed.

Occasionally, in recent years, representatives of the Board of Control and Cricket Association have met to try and resolve their differences. In 1971 leading white South African players— including all their Test stars—walked off the field during the staging of a Transvaal v. Rest of South Africa game, to announce their support for a move towards non-racial cricket and selection of touring sides on a non-racial basis.

On September 18, 1977, a single body was formed, the South African Cricket Union, incorporating the three previous national organizations. Political factors, however, continue to prevent South Africa's return to Test cricket.

The Currie Cup

Since 1977 when all players, of whatever colour, were involved with one cricketing authority, the S.A. Cricket Union, the Currie Cup and Castle Bowl competitions have had no racial barriers.

Yet the small number of first class matches played in the Republic has meant its best cricketers spending much of their careers in Australia and England. Those to make their marks beyond South Africa include Eddie Barrow, Peter Kirsten, Allan Lamb (now qualified for England Test selection), Ken McEwan, Mike Procter, Clive Rice, Barry Richards, Garth Le Roux and Kepler Wessels (now qualified for Australia Test selection).

Natal and Transvaal have dominated the Currie Cup, apart from occasional triumphs by Western Province.

The competition started in the 1888–89 season during a visit by an England touring party. They arrived in South Africa on a ship owned by Sir Donald Currie, and he presented a trophy to the team who put up the best performance against the England side.

During the first season it was won by Kimberley, later to be swallowed in the district of Griqualand West. They were challenged by Transvaal, successfully, the following season and the Currie Cup competition was launched.

Western Province joined in the competition in the 1892–93 season, quickly followed by Natal, Eastern Province and Border before the turn of the century. Orange Free State and Rhodesia were both taking part in 1904–5 and North East Transvaal had grown sufficiently in population to form their own side just before the Second World War.

Natal

Although Natal's record in the Currie Cup competition since the Second World War surpasses anything they achieved in the first 40 years of the competition, the province has provided South Africa with some of its greatest players.

Dave Nourse, known as the first of South Africa's 'great' batsmen, started his career with Natal. He was a solid and courageous left-hander whose 304 not out against Transvaal in the 1919–20 season stood for a number of years as the record individual score in South Africa. After 29 years with Natal he moved to Transvaal and was still playing first-class cricket when he was past 50, this time for Western Province, when his son Dudley Nourse was playing in Tests. Dudley, a right-handed batsman, spent all his career with Natal, scoring 12,472 runs in all and playing in 34 Test matches.

He arrived on the South African cricket scene just as they were regretting the departure of Herbie Taylor, another magnificent right-handed batsman who was a master on South Africa's matting wickets. He made his name for the way he stood up to the fast medium bowling of Sydney Barnes—probably the best bowler of his kind on *all* wickets England has produced—the only South African batsman to do so when England won four of the five Tests on the 1913–14 tour.

Yet Natal had won the Currie Cup only four times outright by the start of the Second World War. Their greatest period was to come in the 1960s, most of it under the leadership of opening batsman Jackie McGlew.

For the first 10 years after the war they were helped by off-spinner bowler Hugh Tayfield whose 170 Test wickets are the highest aggregate in South African Test cricket. He later moved to Rhodesia and then Transvaal. Supporting Tayfield was all-rounder Trevor Goddard, with 123 Test wickets and more than 2500 Test runs. Roy McLean was another batting stalwart.

Goddard stayed with Natal during the 1960s helping McGlew, when Natal produced such exciting talent as in Barry Richards, Mike Procter, Lee Irvine, Dennis Gamsy and Hylton Ackerman. Richards became captain for the 1973–74 season and led them from bottom place to the championship—their first title in six years. They won again in 1975–76, in 1976–77 when Procter took a record 59 wickets and 1980–81 when Van der Bijl dismissed 54 batsmen.

Transvaal

Transvaal, who twice won the Currie Cup four years in succession before the Second World War, enjoyed a more recent period of dominance in the early 1970s when they broke Natal's grip on the title with three consecutive triumphs.

Their early years of success were based on the best provincial bowling attack in the country, together with the batting strength of all-rounders Jimmy Sinclair and Aubrey Faulkner. Sinclair shared the opening attack, but then Faulkner, Albert Vogler and G. C. White took over with their googly bowling, helped by R. Schwartz and S. Pegler.

The reputation of Transvaal for finding top-quality bowlers continued over the years. In their success days in the 1920s they were helped by off-spinner E. Nupen who, despite only one eye, played in 17 Test matches. He was succeeded by another fine off-spinner, Athol Rowan, and they also had left-arm bowler C. L. Vincent who took 84 wickets in 25 Tests. In the 1950s Transvaal produced two of the country's finest fast bowlers, Peter Heine and Neil Adcock.

Transvaal's batting was particularly strong in the 10 years just before the Second World War when the central figure was opening batsman Bruce Mitchell, a solid reliable player who has scored more runs in Tests for South Africa than any other batsman.

Herbie Cameron, one of South Africa's finest wicket-keepers, was also in the Transvaal side of this period, as was Alan Melville, another South African captain. They found another Test wicket-keeper after the war in John Waite, who also doubled as opening batsman, and a splendid middle-order batsman in Russell Endean.

Natal dominated the Currie Cup throughout most of the 1960s. the run being ended in 1968–69 by Transvaal, champions again under the shrewd leadership of Ali Bacher and the strength of his middle-order batting.

Transvaal shared the title with Western Province the following season but were outright champions again in 1970–71, 1971–72 and 1972–73 before their run was broken by a Natal side under Barry Richards. They won again in 1978–79 when Graeme Pollock scored 961 runs (av. 96.10) and 1979–80, a season in which Clive Rice's brilliant all-round talents were often in evidence.

Border

Border have a special place in the record section of world cricket but not one of which they are proud. In the 1959–60 season they were dismissed for 16 in the first innings and 18 in the second innings of a Currie Cup match against Natal at East London. The combined two innings total of 34 is a record low for first-class match score anywhere.

Only occasionally have Border, situated in the Cape Province with East London as its centre, had sufficient strength in their playing staff to come near to matching the 'big three' of South African cricket.

Their Test players have been few. All-rounder G. Hartigan opened for South Africa in the triangular tournament which also involved England and Australia in England in 1912. Another all-rounder O. Dawson played nine Tests in the 1940s, including all five on the 1947 tour of England, followed by W. Farrer who played six Tests in the early 1960s. Tony Greig, who went on to captain England, began his first-class career with Border.

Zimbabwe—Rhodesia

Two century-making batsmen put the name Rhodesia among the record pages of Currie Cup cricket.   The first was R. Gripper playing against Orange Free State in the 'B' section during the 1967–68 season. He scored 279 not out at Bloemfontein. It was the highest individual score in Currie Cup cricket, beating, by two runs, Eric Rowan's total for Transvaal against Griqualand West 17 seasons earlier.

The next super effort was by South Africa, Gloucestershire and Natal all-rounder Mike Procter who, in the 1970–71 season, scored six successive centuries to equal the feat of Charles Fry in 1901 and Don Bradman in 1938–39.

Rhodesia, like Border, followed the yo-yo route between the two sections since the Currie Cup was divided in two. Before Gripper and Procter, their outstanding player was Bulawayo-born Colin Bland, a talented batsman and one of the greatest fielders cricket has seen, with a deadly accurate throw from any distance. In 21 Tests he scored 1669 runs.

In May, 1980, Zimbabwe quit the South African Cricket Union.

Eastern Province

Two of the finest players to represent South Africa in recent years have been produced by Eastern Province—the Pollock brothers, fast bowler Peter and left-handed batsman Graeme. Both of them starred on the 1963–64 drawn series in Australia when Graeme scored two Test centuries, five on the tour.

At the peak of his career Peter Pollock was probably the

second fastest bowler in the world, just behind Wes Hall of the West Indies.

Despite the presence of these two, Eastern Province have never won the Currie Cup and in recent years have switched between the 'A' and 'B' sections. For a time, in their early years, they were helped by South Africa's great googly bowler Albert Vogler, who once took 16 wickets in a day when playing for them against Griqualand West in 1906–7. They cost him 38 runs. This still stands as the best individual bowling performance in the Currie Cup.

Western Province

Western Province, the only province side with the strength over the years to challenge the supremacy of Natal and Transvaal, have taken the Currie Cup outright on twelve occasions and finished joint champions twice.

A number of fine Test players have come from the area. They include two of the best bowlers in the country in the early part of this century, fast bowler J. Kotze, a man of exceptional physique, and J. Commaille. S. Snooke was then their principal batsman and he played 26 times for South Africa. H. Owen-Smith, a rugby international, also played for Western Province and in 1929 shared a tenth partnership of 103 against England with another Western Province player, A. J. Bell, a bowler who found the turf wickets to his liking.

The most notable player since the Second World War has been Jack Cheetham, an outstanding captain who led his country in England, Australia and New Zealand as well as at home. More recently South Africa opening batsman Eddie Barlow led the province to the Championship in 1974–75 and they won again in 1977–78 and 1981–82. A. J. Lamb, P. N. Kirsten and G. S le Roux are other notable performers.

Orange Free State

The closest Orange Free State have come to winning the Currie Cup was in 1926–27 when they finished runners-up to Transvaal, but in other seasons they have been one of the weaker sides in the competition.

Twice in their history they have been defeated inside a day by Transvaal and Eastern Province. Nevertheless several of South Africa's Test players have appeared for Orange Free State at some stage during their careers, including K. G. Viljoen, J. Commaille and S. Coen, the last two sharing in a second-wicket partnership of 305 against Natal in 1926–27, which is still a South African record. Fast bowler Peter Heine also played for OFS.

Northern Transvaal

A state side which was born in 1971, succeeding the defunct North Eastern Transvaal, Northern Transvaal won the 'B' section in their first season of existence. They have since continued a spirited challenge and, in 1977–78, were first winners of the Castle Bowl domestic competition. Outstanding players produced by N.E. Transvaal include medium-fast bowler Jackie Botten and wicket-keeper Denis Lindsay, both of whom toured England with South Africa. Botten's record of 55 wickets in 1958–59 was beaten by Mike Procter (Natal) in 1977.

Griqualand West

Known as Kimberley, they became the first holders of the Currie Cup for their performance against the 1888–89 touring side from England. Griqualand West also won it two years later when it had become the major trophy in South Africa for the district sides.

Since then, however, they have gradually lost their power with the growth of such centres as Johannesburg, Durban and Cape Town, although in 1929–30 they twice topped 600 in an innings playing against Western Province and Rhodesia.

These days they generally struggle to hold their own with the sides in the SAB Bowl.

Cricket in New Zealand

A significant development in New Zealand's cricket growth was made in 1975 with the announcement that Shell Oil had offered sponsorship for the following five years—a move that prompted wholesale revision of the first-class programme.

The Plunket Shield, which consisted of five three-day fixtures for each of six districts, was replaced by the Shell Trophy. The new competition was to be run under similar lines to its predecessor but would be followed each year by an additional tournament culminating in a four-day final. As a result, New Zealand's season was increased from 45 to 67 playing days, giving the additional competition that has long been advocated in the country as New Zealand strives to gain improved standing as a major force.

The crowd potential in New Zealand is not high enough for them to be hosts to a touring party on their own. Furthermore, visits abroad are difficult to arrange for they do not possess enough star players to attract crowds and guarantee a large profit for any country they visit. For tours to their islands, New Zealand often have to rely on countries stopping over for an extra three weeks or a month at the end of a tour to Australia. This is not always popular with visiting players, some of whom regard this section of the tour as an anti-climax to the long and demanding Australian itinerary. For visits overseas, particularly to India and Pakistan, New Zealand have gone at the end of their visit to England. Again this is asking much of their players. Facing the English first-class counties and also competing in a Test series, is a stamina-sapping experience for basically weekend players, without having to find the extra energy for another tour on the way home. To add to these problems business commitments often prevent some of their leading players taking part on overseas tours.

Visiting players, understandably winding down physically after the Australian part of the tour, tend to be surprised that New Zealand do not manage to achieve more Test victories than they have to their credit. Yet it must not be overlooked that New Zealand's first-class programme is confined to a period of about five weeks in December and January and by the time the touring side has arrived, the New Zealanders have been without first-class practice for several weeks.

Between visits by other major touring sides to New Zealand,

the Australians have often helped by sending sides. But it was not until the 1973–74 season that a full-strength Australia party made the short trip to the islands—and during that tour New Zealand achieved the greatest success of her cricket history.

It happened at Christchurch on March 13, 1974, when their first-ever win over Australia was completed, entirely on merit and chiefly due to the brilliance of opening batsman Glenn Turner, who became the first New Zealander to score a century in both innings of a Test match.

In recent years there has been far more contact between New Zealand and her neighbours Australia, highlighted by the participation of a New Zealand team in the Australian Gillette Cup competition.

Despite the afore-mentioned drawbacks, the country has still managed to produce a number of players who could hold their own with any others in the world. With more experience other players might have reached this peak.

C. S. Dempster, T. C. Lowry, and K. C. James, a wicket-keeper of considerable ability who, like Dempster, played for Northants, Martin Donnelly, Bert Sutcliffe, John Reid, V. Scott, W. Wallace, Jack Alabaster, Walter Hadlee, T. B. Burtt, Dick Motz, Jack Cowie and Barry Sinclair are players good enough to hold their own in any company. Today Glenn Turner is among the top four opening batsmen in world cricket and Richard Hadlee one of the finest fast bowlers.

The cricket seed was planted in New Zealand about the same time as it started to flourish in Australia, around the middle of the last century. Before 1900 had been reached, touring sides from England had set the trend by going on to visit New Zealand—playing sides 22 in strength—and the Australians had sent over a side. With this growth came the calling for professional experience to help improve the technical ability of the New Zealanders. Three of the earliest coaches were Albert Trott and Charles Macartney from Australia and Albert Relf from England, all of them Test players.

By the end of 1894 cricket had advanced sufficiently for the need for a national body to exercise some control, and the New Zealand Cricket Council was formed in December of that year. Four years later New Zealand undertook her first tour when sending a team to Australia. Challenge matches between the leading provinces date back to about 1860 but it was not until

1907 that the Plunket Shield started, playing a challenge system until moving to a championship basis in 1921.

During the next 10 years New Zealand cricket made considerable progress and was mature enough to fulfil what has been regarded as the first Test series against Arthur Gilligan's MCC touring side in 1929–30. It was not a full-strength team as some leading English players were required on another MCC tour to the West Indies. The first full tour of England, including Test matches, took place in 1931, New Zealand captained by Cambridge blue and Somerset player Tom Lowry, perhaps the shrewdest captain they have possessed. From that moment tours to England have been regular.

Yet it was not until the 1950s that New Zealand began making tours to other countries to play Test matches, and new ground was broken during 1971–72 when they visited West Indies for a tour involving Tests. In fact it was against the West Indies in New Zealand that they secured their first victory in Test matches in 1955–56. In a four-match tour West Indies were easy winners in the first three games but in the final game at Auckland the West Indies, set 268 to win in four hours, lost their first six wickets for 22 and were all out for 77. New Zealand's hero was medium-paced bowler H. B. Cave who took eight wickets in the match in New Zealand's 190-run victory.

New Zealand had to wait until 1969–70 for their first series win. They played three matches against India and Pakistan. The India section was shared but New Zealand won the second Test match against Pakistan by five wickets in Lahore to take the series.

As this victory followed a tour of the West Indies when they held their hosts to a draw in all five Tests, New Zealand looked to the future with confidence—a feeling that was justified by the win over Australia. Then in 1978 they beat England for the first time in the 50th meeting between the countries and, in 1979–80, they won a Test rubber at home for the first time, defeating West Indies in a three-match series.

The Plunket Shield

After more than half a century as New Zealand's major domestic championship, the Plunket Shield was replaced in 1975–76 by an extended first-class programme known as the Shell series.

Only in one period since the Plunket Shield was made into a championship in 1921–22 has a team dominated the competition. This was immediately before the Second World War when Auckland took the title for four successive seasons, under the batting influence of V. Scott, the first player to score 3000 runs in Shield cricket, and the bowling of J. Cowie.

The tournament first came into use for the 1906–7 season after Lord Plunket, who was then Governor-General, had presented the shield. The first season the New Zealand Cricket Council awarded it to Canterbury for their performance during the season. Until the 1921–22 season it was left to the other districts to challenge the holders to a match, the winners taking the shield.

Auckland, Canterbury, Wellington and Otago—covering the area around the southern township of Dunedin—were the four original centres operating under the challenge system. Hawke's Bay was also declared first class in 1914–15 and twice made a challenge for the shield—both unsuccessful—before being relegated to second-class cricket.

First-class cricket was not lost to the area completely, however, for in 1950–51 Hawke's Bay, along with several other surrounding areas, were amalgamated for first-class cricket purposes to form Central Districts. Six years later Northern Districts entered the Shield on a similar basis.

The two finest batsmen New Zealand have produced, Bert Sutcliffe, who played for Auckland, Otago and Northern Districts in turn, and John Reid, who played for Wellington and for a short time, Otago, dominate the record section of the Plunket Shield. Sutcliffe's 385 for Otago against Canterbury in the 1952–53 season remains the highest score in first-class cricket anywhere by a left-handed batsman. He also hit 355 against Auckland in season 1949–50. Bob Blair of Wellington and Central Districts was easily the most successful Plunket Shield bowler, with 352 wickets.

Having a large population from which to draw their players, Auckland and Wellington have won the title on most occasions since the league system was introduced in 1921–22.

Auckland

Auckland, the most consistently successful side in New Zealand until the Second World War, have found success much harder to achieve in the last 20 years.

They won the first inter-provincial match in New Zealand by beating Wellington in 1859–60 and they continued to have the better of the exchanges for the next 90 years.

Their outstanding period, however, was in the 1930s when they had the help of two of New Zealand's finest batsmen, W. Wallace and V. Scott. They were at the start of their respective careers and both played regularly in Test cricket after the Second World War. Auckland's attacking strength was then in the hands of fast bowler J. Cowie who took 359 wickets either in New Zealand or playing for them overseas.

During and immediately after the Second World War Bert Sutcliffe played for Auckland, but his best years came after he had left for Otago. Hedley Howarth, a top-quality left-arm spinner, M. G. Burgess who led N.Z. and J. F. Reid have been more recent successes.

Canterbury

The first winners of the Plunket Shield in 1906–7, Canterbury have produced a number of New Zealand's finest captains in their comparatively short time as a Test-playing country.

Canterbury's line of Test captains started with the 1931–32 visit by South Africa when M. Page led New Zealand; he also captained the 1937 team to England. Walter Hadlee, another Canterbury player, was leader of the 1949 tour to England.

More recently Graham Dowling has led both Canterbury and his country, captaining New Zealand when they won their first Test series during their visit to Pakistan in 1969–70. He is the fifth highest scorer in New Zealand Test history, with more than 2000 runs to his credit. He came into the Canterbury side when it still contained A. MacGibbon, who played in 26 Test matches after the Second World War.

Dick Motz, the first bowler to take 100 wickets in Test matches for New Zealand, B. E. Congdon, S. L. Boock, B. F. Hastings and the Hadlee brothers, have all distinguished themselves for Canterbury.

Central Districts

Admitted to the Plunket Shield in 1950–51 season, Central Districts, comprised of seven of the minor provinces, had won the championship four times by the end of the 1971–72 season. For two of those championships they were indebted to Lancashire-born Vic Pollard who took them to the top in successive seasons 1966–67 and 1967–68.

They won the title for the first time in 1953–54, four years after being admitted to the competition and again in 1970–71 when middle-order batsman Bev Congdon was in charge. Congdon, who served Central Districts throughout the 1960s with a top score for them of 202 not out against Otago in 1968–69, is the highest run-getter in New Zealand Test cricket.

In the early 1960s Central Districts benefited from the help of the two experienced Wellington and New Zealand Test bowlers Blair and Cave and the batting of M. Chapple, another Test player, who has switched from Canterbury. In 1980–81, Central Districts were unbeaten and G. N. Edwards, a powerful stroke-maker, won a Test recall.

Northern Districts

Not all the cricketing authorities in New Zealand were in favour when Northern Districts was formed and admitted to the Plunket Shield in 1956–57, but they justified their existence seven seasons later when they won the trophy. In 1976–77 they took the Shell Cup.

They had considerable outside help that season, including the experience of Bert Sutcliffe, then in his 40th year, who had just joined them from Otago. He was past his best but still good enough to gain a place in the New Zealand tour party for England in 1965. Another Otago player helping Northern Districts that season was Grenville Alabaster, brother of Test player Jack, whose bowling was to play a leading part in clinching the title. Captaining the side was the West Indian Bruce Pairaudeau who played in 13 Tests for his country.

Northern Districts also had a Test player of their own in wicket-keeper Eric Petrie who had toured England under John Reid in 1958, playing in all five Tests. Glenn Turner, who averaged 81.75, captained Northern Districts to their Shell Cup triumph in

1976–77 and G. P. Howarth led them to their Shell Trophy win in 1979–80.

Otago

Otago, the southernmost province of New Zealand, has enjoyed the rich and prolific run-making of three of the country's greatest batsmen, Roger Blunt, Bert Sutcliffe and Glenn Turner. Yet only in the late 1960s and early 1970s, when they achieved three titles in six years, did they rise to powerful prominence in the Plunket Shield.

In the 1974–75 triumph, captain Turner set a Shield record by scoring 703 runs, beating Sutcliffe's 683 22 years earlier. He also twice scored two centuries in a match.

Blunt was the first of the country's high-scoring batsmen, but his feats during the 1930s were all overshadowed by the brilliance of left-hander Sutcliffe. An Otago player from 1949 until 1962, he twice raised the Plunket record for individual scores and still holds the career aggregate record with 6894. One of New Zealand's other great batsmen, John Reid, played with Sutcliffe for Otago between 1956 and 1958.

Wellington

No other player for Wellington has matched the outstanding achievements of John Reid, a forceful right-handed batsman and aggressive captain.

He also doubled as a medium-paced bowler and has kept wicket in Test matches, but it is as a batsman that Reid made his name second only to Sutcliffe in his Plunket Shield exploits, and New Zealand's second top scorer to B. E. Congdon in Tests with 3431. He also took 85 Test wickets. His highest innings was 296 against Northern Districts in 1962–63 when he set a world record by clearing the boundary 15 times for sixes.

The bowling strength in the Reid period was supplied in the early years by H. Cave and later by Bob Blair whose 46 wickets in the 1956–57 season stands as a Plunket Shield record. Other bowlers who contributed much to Wellington's performances were E. J. Chatfield and R. O. Collinge.

Cricket in the West Indies

There has been no richer breeding ground in international cricket than the island of Barbados, measuring a meagre 166 square miles in area. Add Trinidad, Guyana on the mainland of South America, and Jamaica, and it is easy to see why West Indies quickly became a leading cricketing power, although they pipped New Zealand to Test status by only 18 months in 1928.

Several reasons account for their rise. The climate has played a leading part with hard and fast wickets speeding the technical development of the players; their natural athleticism plus the social climate in which there was little work and cricketing ability allowed the players a station in life they might otherwise never have known.

Inter-island jealousy has always been strong and this, in the early days of a national team, spread into the dressingroom. The very way they play the game has sometimes told against them. They are, in the main, gay, aggressive, attacking cricketers who tend to lose patience and even interest in the slowing down, tactical ploys used against them on the Test fields.

In its early days cricket, once again introduced by the British Army and the early traders, was very much a game for the richer families on the islands. Slavery had not long been abolished when the game began to spread in the middle 1800s and the islanders were used as bowlers and fielders.

It did not take them long to show they were as good, if not better, than their masters, although the early touring sides from West Indies contained a high percentage from the upper social classes on the islands. The first inter-island match took place in 1865 when Barbados entertained a team from Demerara, later British Guiana, now known as Guyana. In the next 30 years teams left the West Indies to play in Canada, but the game really began to take shape when the early sides came over from England. In 1900 a West Indies side toured England and included L. S. Constantine who scored a century at Lord's against MCC. He was the father of Learie Constantine who was to score more than 1000 runs and take 100 wickets on the first official West Indies tour to England in 1928 when they played three Tests, losing them all. It was the start of what has been an impressive Test history.

During the first 100 years of cricket in the West Indies Jamaica was always a step behind the other main islands because of the island's position. It took several days to reach it by boat and because of this it could not join in the triangular tournament organized for Barbados, Trinidad and Guyana. Air travel solved this problem and in 1965–66 a new national championship was organized for the Shell Shield, sponsored by the Shell Oil Company, but administered by the West Indies Board of Control. The two island groups, the Leeward Islands and the Windward Islands took part as a Combined Islands' team until 1982 when the West Indies Board decided they should compete as separate entities. In their final season as a joint side they won the Shell Shield for the first time, captained by the brilliant Vivian Richards.

West Indies have dominated world cricket in the past two decades. Their seemingly never-ending supply of top-class fast bowlers and brilliant batsmen has made them a major crowd attraction wherever they play.

Such has been the range of their talents that they have triumphed both in Tests and one-day internationals. They carried off the inaugural Prudential World Cup in 1975 and retained it fours years later, each time led by Clive Lloyd.

Barbados

Barbados will always be associated with the all-round genius of Sir Garfield Sobers and, before him the magnificent batting feats of the 'three Ws', Frank Worrell, Clyde Walcott and Everton Weekes.

Cricket was played there–in one form or another—before 1800. It took a giant step forward when Barbados beat Demerara—now Guyana—in 1865, to start representative cricket between the islands. The first triangular tournament involving Trinidad and Guyana took place in Bridgetown, Barbados in 1891.

The great days were still to come, however, with the emergence of Weekes, Worrell and Walcott who were all born within 18 months and two miles of each other in the mid 1920s. They grew up under the influence of John Goddard, the Barbados captain who led West Indies on two tours of England as well as Australia, New Zealand and India.

Worrell's achievements as Test captain lifted him just above the other two, the first man to blend the various individual talents into a team effort. He made his debut for Barbados in 1942 at the age of 18, and soon showed his batting power when sharing in an unbroken 502-run partnership with Goddard against Trinidad in 1943–44 and, two seasons later, a 574 partnership with Walcott, Trinidad suffering again.

Walcott was only 16 when he made his first-class debut. His highest score was 314 not out, made during that 574 partnership with Worrell. He was at his best in the mid-50s.

Weekes was the only one to stay with Barbados, serving them 20 years as batsman and, later, captain. Between 1947 and 1949 in series against England and India he set a record by scoring five centuries in successive Test innings.

The scoring feats of these three were beaten by Sobers, the greatest run-scorer in Test history. Sobers was in such demand all over the world that he was not always available to lead Barbados, but he took them to the Shell Shield Championship in the first two years of the competition, helped by such other great talent as Conrad Hunte, Seymour Nurse and the menacing fast bowlers Wes Hall and Charlie Griffith. More fine pace bowlers–the quartet of Sylvester Clarke, Wayne Daniel, Joel Garner and Malcolm Marshall—helped Barbados retain the Shield in 1980 for the fifth successive year. They won it again in 1982.

Guyana

Known as British Guiana until it became independent, Guyana, situated on the mainland of South America, has produced as many famous cricketers as Barbados in the last 30 years, headed by Rohan Kanhai who stands second to Sobers as the highest run-getter in Test cricket for the West Indies and the left-handed Clive Lloyd.

Much of the credit for this rise in talent belongs to Clyde Walcott, the former great West Indian batsman from Barbados who moved to Guyana in 1954 to take a coaching appointment and later led Guyana in tournament matches against the West Indies islands. His arrival was the start of the greatest period in Guyana cricket history, although the Georgetown Cricket Club has been in existence for more than 100 years. The club did much to foster the game, not only in Guyana but elsewhere in the West Indies.

Nevertheless after these early performances Guyana was seldom a match again for the other islands until the 1930s, when Bob Christiani began to flower as a middle-order batsman and Berkeley Gaskin rose to Test standard as a fast bowler. Christiani played regularly for the West Indies for the first eight years after the Second World War. When he retired from Test cricket in 1953 Guyana was not long in supplying his replacement in the West Indies middle-order batting. In fact they supplied two, Basil Butcher and Joe Solomon, making their Test debuts on the 1958–59 tour of India and Pakistan.

They came into international cricket at an awkward period as Test replacements for Weekes and Walcott in the middle order. Solomon had to fight hard to keep his place for his 27 appearances, but Butcher became a regular in the side.

Along with Kanhai, Butcher and Solomons, the other great personality in the Guyana side of this time was off-spinner Lance Gibbs who took over as the spin-king from Ramadhin.

In the 1960s Guyana produced three other Test batsmen for the West Indies, opening batsman Roy Fredericks and Steve Camacho and the thrilling middle-order hitting Clive Lloyd, a cousin of Gibbs and later to become West Indies most successful captain. More recently still has come Alvin Kallicharran.

Under the captaincy of Kanhai, Guyana came from behind to win their first Shell Shield title in the 1972–73 season.

Jamaica

Lacking the playing reputation of the other three countries making up the main West Indies group, Jamaica has still managed to provide some of the most famous names in Caribbean cricket, and became the first side to halt the dominance of Barbados in the Shell Shield when winning the title in the 1968–69 season.

Mainly as a result of being positioned so far from the other islands, Jamaica's cricket was slow to reach the standard of the others and it was not until after the First World War that they became a power to be reckoned with by the early touring sides. Then the picture changed with the coming of J. K. Holt senior and E. A. Rae, whose sons J. K. Holt junior and Alan Rae both played for the West Indies in the 1950s. But the most famous name of all from the 1920s period was that of George Headley who was such a master right-hand batsman that he earned the nickname 'The Black Bradman'.

Headley was actually born in Panama but returned to the island with his Jamaican mother for his education, where he switched from baseball to cricket. In his career he scored a staggering 9921 runs in only 164 innings, including a highest score of 344 not out, made for Jamaica against Lord Tennyson's team in 1931–32.

As the 1950s approached and under the guidance of Worrell more stars began to emerge, including J. K. Holt junior, Alan Rae and Alf Valentine whose left-arm spin coupled with Sonny Ramadhin's spin mixture was to give West Indies their first series win in England in 1950. Perhaps the one with greatest potential was Collie Smith who was demonstrating his ability with two centuries against England on the 1957 tour. Many observers thought him as good as Sobers but he was killed in a car accident in England.

One of the brightest Jamaican stars in recent years has been Lawrence Rowe, who, in the 1971–72 season, passed three figures four times in three matches and scored the first double-century by a Jamaican on home territory for 25 years. Two years later Rowe scored 302 and 102 in the Test series with England. During the last decade Michael Holding has become Jamaica's greatest fast bowler.

Trinidad

English cricket has good reason to be grateful to the island of Trinidad for it was the birthplace of Lord Harris and Sir Pelham Warner who both captained England and served cricket as a whole by their administrative efforts off the field. They both did considerable work to boost the strength of the West Indies by taking sides there on tour. Sir Pelham's brother Aucher captained Trinidad for a number of years and also brought the first West Indies side to England in 1900.

Included in that side was L. S. Constantine, whose son Learie—later Lord Constantine—was to become Trinidad's most famous player as well as a firm favourite in League cricket throughout the Midlands and north of England. Before Learie made his mark in the 1920s, the cricket on the island had been taken to a high standard by another former captain. A. E. Harragin; he did much to organize the playing and the administration of the game on the island through the Queen's Park Cricket Club.

It was soon after the First World War that Learie Constantine became the toast of Trinidad for his exhilarating batting, his fast bowling, and wonderful performances in the field. He was on the first Test-playing tour to England in 1928 and was soon joined in the West Indies side by another Trinidad player, M. Grell. In the 1930s came G. C. and R. S. Grant and, as the Second World War approached, the Stollmeyer brothers and Gerry Gomez.

They were still playing when Sonny Ramadhin, Trinidad's bowling sensation, burst on the game, to start his successful Test match spin-bowling partnership with Valentine against England in 1950. At that stage Trinidad had a matting wicket at the Queen's Park Oval and it was not until 1954 that turf was used. Today the wicket usually takes more spin than the others in the West Indies.

Under the captaincy of Test opener Joey Carew and assisted by middle-order batsman Bryan and Charlie Davis, plus—in the first year—the speed of Wes Hall who had moved from Barbados to take a coaching appointment on the island, Trinidad won the Shell Shield in both 1969–70 and 1970–71.

Deryck Murray also captained the island and claimed 189 Test victims.

Cricket in India

The year 1971 will go down as the time when Indian cricket reached full maturity. In the space of seven months Ajit Wadekar took his team to the West Indies and England, and triumphed in both Test series. Each was won by one match to nil. The India victory acheived in the second Test in Trinidad of the five-match series was their first over the West Indies. Their win in the final Test at the Oval of a three-match series was their first victory in England.

They were helped in both series by the slowness of the wickets which, while suiting the Indian batsmen, blunted the edge both the West Indies and England held in fast bowling. Yet in the conditions that did exist—both the wickets in Trinidad and at the Oval, though far from menacing, favoured the spin bowler—India proved the better all-round team. Their victories were well deserved and demonstrated that their batsmen had learned to cope with conditions outside their own country.

Apart from their initial excursions into Test cricket in the 10 years before the Second World War India have always been difficult to beat on their own pitches. In the main their batsmen have been blessed with unlimited patience, born out of the high totals often compiled in their domestic cricket.

Once matting had been discarded, wickets were easy paced; rolled mud strips offered little help to any bowler apart from the wrist-spinner and handicapped the genuine fast bowler. These conditions helped the India teams to hold the opposition. Such feats were often regarded as a 'victory', but told against them overseas when their batsmen were exposed to fast bowling. Because of their physique and the hot climate, they produced few fast bowlers.

For a long time the early cricket in India—then including what is known as Pakistan today—remained a game for Europeans, only played between the British Army and the Europeans running the various trading companies in the country. The Calcutta Cricket Club, formed in 1792, was for Europeans only. The Parsees were the first Indians to develop an interest in the game to the extent of sending their own side to England in 1886. Gradually the other religions in India began to take up the game and started forming their own cricket clubs.

Interest quickened when privately arranged cricket touring parties came out from England and by news of the deeds of one of India's greatest players, Ranjitsinhji, for England, Cambridge University and Sussex, although he never played first-class cricket in India. The major domestic competiton in India, the Ranji Trophy, is named after him. In the early years of this century leading England professional players were engaged to coach in India.

The gradual improvement of the standard in India, coupled with the performances in English cricket of Duleepsinhji and the Nawab of Pataudi, led to the first Test match between England and India at Lord's in 1932. England won by 158 runs but it was a closer match than the majority had expected. England played virtually a full-strength side and India were blessed with probably the finest opening attack it has possessed in Nissar, a genuine fast bowler, and the fast medium-swing bowler Amar Singh. Between them they took 10 of the 18 England wickets to fall. The visit was returned in 1933–34 when Douglas Jardine took an MCC party on tour, including three Test matches, although Jardine and Verity were the only two of the 1932–33 MCC party to Australia to go to India.

The second and third tours by India to England fared no better than the first and they had to wait until England went there in 1951–52 for their first Test victory over England—their first Test win over any country—when Vinoo Mankad took 12 wickets in the match with his slow left-arm bowling. A series victory over Pakistan followed in 1952–53 and they have also beaten New Zealand and Australia in Test matches, as well as the West Indies.

Spin bowling has always been their attacking strength and in Mankad they had a brilliant all-rounder. He took 162 Test wickets and scored 2109 runs in 44 Tests Gupte, one of the finest leg-spinners in the world, captured 149 wickets and their spin attack of off-spinners Prasanna and Venkataraghaven, leg-spinner Chandrasekhar and slow left-arm bowler Bedi became the best in cricket. The leg-breaks of Borde and the left-arm spin of Durrani swept India to their first series victory against England when they beat Ted Dexter's side two–nil on the 1961–62 tour.

India's list of high-class batsmen is long and impressively headed—in terms of Test match returns—by Sunil Gavaskar who in 1982 had completed 6000 Test runs including an innings of 221 against England at the Oval in 1979.

He is followed by Gundappa Viswanath. Polly Umrigar, Manjrekar and Borde have each scored more than 3000 runs in their Test careers and then the younger Nawab of Pataudi who scored more than 2000 runs despite losing the sight of his left eye in a car accident while at Oxford University. Hazare, another who has topped 2000 Test runs for India, holds the world-record partnership with Gul Mahomed. They put on 577 for the fourth wicket, playing for Baroda against Holkar in 1946–47.

With the retirement of both Wadekar and Sardesai—who scored 212, 112 and 150 against West Indies in 1970–71—the Indian batting has lost some of its strength. But it still includes Gavaskar, plus D. B. Vengsarkar, G. R. Viswanath, S. M. Patil and Yashpal Sharma.

Gavaskar was another star of the West Indies series in 1970–71. After missing the first Test, he scored 65 and 67 not out in the second, 116 in the third, 117 not out in the fourth and in the fifth became only the second player in the history of cricket to score a century and double-century in a Test. Since then he has scored centuries against all the major Test playing countries.

In recent years Kapil Dev has emerged as India's finest fast bowler, in addition to being an aggressive batsman. He achieved the 'double' of 1000 runs and 100 wickets in only 25 Tests.

The main domestic competition in India is for the Ranji Trophy. This was started in the 1934–35 season on a knockout basis but now run in five zones—East, West, North, South and Central—with the two leading clubs in each zone going into a knock-out competition. It has been dominated by Bombay who have won it 28 times. They are followed by Holkar—for whom Denis Compton played when on war service in India—and Baroda who have won it four times each.

Cricket in Pakistan

Granted full Test status in 1952, Pakistan made a better start in international cricket than any other country, apart from England and Australia. Within seven years they had beaten West Indies, Australia and New Zealand in a Test rubber and recorded victories over England and India.

Pakistan embarked on a Test career with one major advantage. Many of the players in their early teams were seasoned cricketers, having gained experience with All India before partition in 1947 which led to the birth of a new nation. When Pakistan had to find replacements for these cricketers, the new players understandably lacked comparable technical ability and their Test cricket record suffered. Today, however, Pakistan are a formidable team. They proved themselves in England on a three-match Test tour in 1971. The first two Test matches were drawn and though eventually they lost the final Test at Leeds, they began the final day as favourites to win the rubber.

Inevitably Pakistan's cricket history is closely linked with the growth of the game in India. The British Army, once again, was the influence while it was on duty in the Punjab region and guarding the North-West Frontier with Afghanistan and the Khyber Pass. Lahore, which became one of the main cities in Pakistan, was an influential army centre and also the home of the University. Many of the leading cricketers of All India, and now Pakistan, came from the area. Karachi, as a trading post on the coast, was another rich area for cricketers.

Within two years of coming into being, Pakistan were playing representative cricket. West Indies took a team to India in 1948–49 and played some games in Pakistan. Pakistan made a tour of Ceylon the following year and when MCC fulfilled a Test-match tour of India in 1951–52 they also visited Pakistan. Pakistan's first official Test series was in 1952–53 when they played five matches against India. They won one Test and lost two.

Their strength in these early days was provided by their captain, Abdul Kardar, who played for India on their 1946 tour of England, plus two other former India Test players, Amir Elahi and Gul Mahomed. They also had an outstanding fast medium bowler in Fazal Mahmood who bowled leg-cutters in the style of England's Alec Bedser and was a deadly bowler on the matting wickets used in Pakistan at the time.

He was to become the first hero of Pakistan cricket for his

tremendous performance when England entertained Pakistan for the first time in 1954. Leading one-nil in the series and having had the better of two drawn matches when the final Test match at the Oval started, England fielded an experimental team with a view to helping the selectors choose a party for the 1954–55 tour of Australia. Pakistan, in the person of Fazal, made the most of it. He took six for 46 in the England second innings, helped by wicket-keeper Imtiaz Ahmed who held seven catches. Pakistan won by 24 runs to square the series.

Fazal continued to be Pakistan's main bowler in the series victory over New Zealand in 1955–56, against Australia in 1956 and on the high-scoring tour of West Indies in 1957–58. In all, Fazal took 139 wickets—including 13 in one Test against Australia at Karachi in 1956–57—in 34 Test matches, the first Pakistan bowler to have reached three figures.

Launched into Test cricket on the 1952 Pakistan tour of India, was one of Pakistan's most remarkable batsmen, Hanif Mohammad, whose family moved from India to Karachi during partition. During the 1957–58 tour of West Indies, Pakistan were in trouble in the Barbados Test, following on 463 behind, when Hanif rescued them with an innings of 337 in 16 hours 39 minutes, the longest innings on record. His elder brother Wazir scored 189 in a Test on the tour, and Sobers made his world record 365 not out in the third Test of the series.

Hanif developed a liking for long innings. The following home season he made a world-record score of 499 for Karachi against Bahawalpur, run out in the last over of the day trying for 500. He scored a century in each innings against England in 1961–62, and in 55 Tests a total of 3915 runs.

In the home series against West Indies in 1958–59 Hanif's younger brother Mushtaq joined the family in Test cricket. He was 15, the youngest player in Test history. Pakistan also provide the next three youngest. Aftub Baluch against New Zealand 1969–70, Nasim-ul-Ghani against West Indies 1957–58 and Khalid Hassan against England 1954, were all 16 on their Test debuts.

With his leg-spin Mushtaq became one of Pakistan's leading all-rounders. He served side by side with middle order batsman and off-spinner Saeed Ahmed who took over the captaincy from Hanif. Spin bowling is one of the country's strengths. Saeed was succeeded by Intikhab Alam, a gifted leg-spin and googly bowler and forceful batsman who completed 1000 runs and 100 wickets in Test cricket. Left-arm spinner/batsman Nasim served them well in 28 Tests. Their side until the emergence of World Series Cricket contained three of the most exciting stroke-makers in world cricket: Asif Iqbal, who shared with Intikhab a Test record ninth-wicket partnership of 190 against England in 1967; Majid Khan who hit 13 sixes in an innings of 147 not out for Pakistan against Glamorgan in 1967 and Zaheer Abbas who scored 274 in his first Test against England at Edgbaston in 1971. Wicket-keeper Wasim Bari is one of the most talented in the world today and Sarfraz Nawaz an outstanding opening bowler.

Under the lively captaincy of Imran Khan Pakistan proved a force in the early 1980s and Khan's immense all-round talents inspired them to a famous victory over England at Lord's in 1982. Khan, like Alam, has passed 1000 runs and 100 wickets in Tests.

In domestic cricket there are two main competitions, the Quaid-E-Azam Trophy started in 1953–54 and the Patron Trophy, formerly the B.C.C.P. Trophy which started in 1960–61. They have been dominated by Karachi, although in recent years the star-studded Pakistan International Airways team and the Banks' teams have provided formidable challenges.

In the 1979–80 Quaid-E-Azam tournament Aamer Malik, 17, playing for Lahore 'A' against Railways, scored a hundred in each innings. It was his debut in first-class cricket.

Cricket in Sri Lanka

Sri Lanka are the newest members to the International Cricket Conference. Admission in 1981 gave them full Test status which they had thoroughly merited by their performances against various countries and by their achievement in winning the ICC Trophy for associate member countries in 1979. They also defeated India in the Prudential World Cup that summer and further history was made in February 1982, when Sri Lanka played their first Test match, against England at Colombo.

The game was first played in Sri Lanka, then known as Ceylon, in the early 1800s but the Ceylon Cricket Association did not come into being until 1922. The Ceylon Board of Control was formed in 1948 and the island has produced a number of talented players who have appeared in English first-class cricket. They include F. C. de Saram, Gamini Goonesena, Laddie Outschoorn, Stanley Jayasinghe, Clive Inman and Gehan Mendis.

In recent years one of their most successful players has been Anura Tennekoon, who captained the team in England in 1979. He led his countrymen to wins over India, Malaysia, MCC, Pakistan and West Indies, and scored a number of centuries, including two in consecutive unofficial Test matches against India in Sri Lanka in 1974.

A serious blow was dealt to Sri Lanka's aspirations as a Test playing country when a party of 14 players left for an unofficial tour of South Africa in October 1982. The Sri Lanka Cricket Board reacted swiftly and suspended the players from international cricket for 25 years.

Cricket Elsewhere

Cricket does not belong exclusively to the eight countries who have played Test series. Almost everywhere the British navy, army and businessmen travelled in the late 18th century and early 19th century, they exported the game.

Outside the first-class countries who have been granted Test status, some of the best cricket can be found in Zimbabwe, formerly Rhodesia, and in 1982 they won the ICC Trophy from associate member countries, and thus qualified for a place in the third Prudential World Cup in England the following year.

A feature of the cricket in the Caribbean area 80 years ago was visits from touring sides from Philadelphia. They were particularly strong between the period of 1880 and 1910, and were encouraged by early Australian touring sides to England who, while returning home, played a series of games across America. In that period the United States claimed the best fast bowler in the world, John Barton King, who toured England three times about the turn of the century, and on one tour, headed the bowling averages in England when he took seven for 13 against Sussex. Former England cricket captain, turned Hollywood actor, C. Aubrey Smith encouraged the game on the West Coast of North America where it is still played and West Indian immigrants keep the game alive in New York.

Canada, too, has a healthy cricket-playing population and it is still played in Argentina, Brazil and Chile where it was introduced by British businessmen. The standard is quite high in Bermuda where they use matting over concrete and the game is played extensively throughout the central African countries, Malaysia, Singapore and Hong Kong. Papua New Guinea, Fiji, Bangladesh and Israel are among other areas where cricket flourishes. The MCC encourage the game in all these countries by sending out 'A' sides as often as possible and they have been visited by a number of privately organized touring sides. In Europe, English sides play in Cyprus, Germany, Denmark and Holland. The Dutch gained a famous three-wicket victory in the last over against Bobby Simpson's Australian side in 1964.

Women's Cricket

Most people look upon the growth of women's cricket as a comparatively modern phenomena, almost an early forerunner of the women's liberation movement which has swept the world in recent years. In fact, women were playing cricket in England from the middle of the 18th century. Exchange visits between countries for 'Test' series have been taking place since England's women cricketers went on tour to Australia in 1934.

The women players obviously lack the strength and stamina of the men. The fastest women bowler is no more than approaching medium in the men's world but in most other aspects of the game the women are equal. Technically they can play their strokes with all the timing and grace of male cricketers and in spin bowling are capable of producing considerable guile—as many men at the crease have found to their cost.

There is a record of a match being played between two women's teams in 1745 near Guildford, Surrey, and the game was taken up by women throughout the south-east of England. In 1890 there was even the formation of two teams of professional women cricketers which travelled the country playing exhibition matches under assumed names. They lasted one season.

Several of the larger schools for girls began to introduce cricket instructions in their sports programmes and the need for a national organization to help spread the game grew in the 1920s as its popularity increased. In 1926, at a meeting in London, the Women's Cricket Association came into being. The country was divided into five areas for administrative reasons, to help coaching and provide inter-territorial representative games. County associations began to spring up in the 1930s, and the game has continued to prosper under the driving force of its various administrators, notably the W.C.A's long-serving secretary, Netta Rheinberg.

The first overseas tour by women took place in 1934 when a team from England went to Australia and New Zealand. They were unbeaten in 21 matches and the party contained some of the best-known names in women's cricket, including Molly Hide who captained England in Test matches later in the 1930s and after the Second World War. She was a sound batswoman, as was Myrtle Maclagan who became the first Test century-maker in women's cricket when scoring 119 against Australia in the match at Sydney on that tour.

The women paid their own passage and they still do so. The profits are retained by the host country to plough back into the association funds and meet the expenses of touring sides once they land. The first Australian side to tour England came in 1937, the three 'Test' matches being shared.

Tours gained popularity after the Second World War when England produced another star player in Mary Duggan, a reliable batswoman and slow left-arm bowler. Her equal in Australia was Betty Wilson, said to be the finest player of her day. England toured Australia in 1948–49 and 1957–58.

Australia returned the visits in 1951 and 1963. New Zealand came in 1954 and in 1966 and England went to South Africa in 1960–61. Their cricket was encouraged by the number of county cricket clubs who allowed them to use first-class grounds. During the England tour to Australia in 1957–58 the International Women's Cricket Council was formed and a schedule of tours was drawn up for the following 20 years.

Another England team went to Australia and New Zealand in 1968–69, and the tour produced a memorable all-round performance from Enid Bakewell of England who scored 1031 runs in 20 matches and took 118 wickets with her left-arm orthodox spin. She scored three 'Test' centuries. Outstanding England players in recent years include Rachael Heyhoe, now Rachael Flint, a high-scoring batswoman, who captained her country for more than a decade, Mary Pilling, Sue Goatman and Jan Southgate.

West Indies have toured England and England sent teams to the Caribbean.

In Australia the earliest known public cricket match between women was in 1886 and the Australian Women's Cricket Council was formed in 1931. The New Zealand W.C.C. came into being in 1934 and the South African ruling body in 1952. The Dutch Association has been established since the middle 1930s.

The first-ever woman's World Cup was staged in England in 1973. Seven teams took part, with England beating Australia in the final, thanks to a century from Enid Bakewell.

The Women's Cricket Association celebrated their jubilee in 1976 with a tour of England and Australia.

Test Cricket

There can be few more thrilling sights for the cricket spectator than a batsman opening his shoulders and lifting the ball over the boundary for six or piercing the field with a stroke of perfect timing and execution. The prospect of Bradman, Hobbs, Hutton, Hammond, Compton, Trumper, Sobers, Weekes, Reid, Nourse junior, Graeme Pollack, Botham and the many other great batsmen who have bestrode the Test arenas of the world, savaging a bowling attack, has resulted in packed grounds from Manchester to Melbourne, Bombay to Barbados.

These players have captured much of the glory and the glamour. Yet in the final analysis the fortunes in international cricket have gone the way of the side providing the better-balanced bowling attack, especially if headed by a pair of top-class fast bowlers operating as a partnership.

Test-match spoils have been dictated by the fast men: Spofforth supported by Boyle and Palmer; Gregory and McDonald, Lindwall, Miller and Johnston, Davidson and McKenzie, Lillee and Thomson for Australia; Foster and Barnes, Larwood and Voce, Tyson and Statham, Trueman and Statham for England; Heine and Adcock, Peter Pollock and Procter for South Africa; Hall and Griffith for West Indies; Fazal and Khan Mohammad for Pakistan. When such combinations have been sharing the bowling, victory has never seemed far away for their sides.

A host of other great bowlers have also won matches on their own: Grimmett, Trumble, Benaud, O'Reilly for Australia; Laker, Tate, Alec Bedser, Rhodes, Verity, Richardson for England; Tayfield and Goddard for South Africa; Gibbs of the West Indies; India's spinners Gupte and Mankad; and Imran Khan of Pakistan. Many were expert spinners who created considerable damage after the spearhead made the initial breakthrough or pitches had turned in their favour.

The havoc which speed can cause was perfectly demonstrated in only the third of the 246 England v. Australia Test matches that have been played between 1876 and the final Test at the Oval in 1981. Spofforth provided that illustration in Melbourne when he swept Australia to victory by 10 wickets in the only Test played during England's visit of 1878–79. England were all out in the first innings for 113. Spofforth took six for 48. In the second innings England made 160. This time Spofforth's return was seven for 62 and the tales of outstanding bowling deeds were launched.

Spofforth did even better in the only Test during the Australians' tour of England in 1882, the famous Test at the Oval which led to the coining of that historic phrase—'The Ashes'. His figures: seven for 46 in the first innings, seven for 44 in the second, and Australia were home by seven runs despite the influence of W. G. Grace, who opened the innings for England.

Australia had won in England for the first time and matches between the two countries have dominated Test cricket ever since.

Other countries, too, have played their parts in some magnificent series. Historians will always recall the occasion in December 1960 when Australia and the West Indies produced the only tie in Test cricket—at Brisbane in the first match of the series. That tour evoked unprecedented scenes of enthusiasm and when it finally ended Australians lined the streets of Melbourne to say farewell to the ebullient West Indian team. Nor are the chronicles of such stirring events likely to forget the last over of the second Test at Lord's between England and the West Indies in 1963 which started with any one of *four* results possible.

There were great series . . . outstanding personal achievements . . . many emotion-filled occasions . . . and, regrettably, moments of bitterness, none more sharply expressed than when Douglas Jardine in England's 1932–33 tour unfolded his body-line theory, with the help of Larwood and Voce, to contain the threat of the Australian batting power. Once the shine had left the new ball the England bowlers directed their attack on line with the batsman's body. A ring of fielders crouched close in on the leg side ready to snap up the chances as the batsmen attempted to fend off the rising ball. A number of Australian batsmen suffered nasty blows, crowds became incensed, extra police were called in case of riots, and the air between Australia and Lord's was thick with cables threatening the whole future of the cricket relationships between the two countries. Atmospheres were strained too in 1958–59 when the England players thought some of Australia's fast bowlers were contravening the law which relates to throwing, and again when England toured Australia in 1970–71 short-pitched deliveries from their fast bowler Snow upset sections of the crowd.

Fortunately, these have been rare instances of discord in a

continuing series which has lasted over a century and provided countless hours of enjoyment. By the beginning of 1982 Australia had won 93 Tests against England's 82. This shifting emphasis of fortune which is so much part of the game's character has seldom been better illustrated than in the 1902 series. In the first Test at Edgbaston Australia were dismissed for 36 by the bowling of Hirst who took three for 15, and Rhodes seven for 17, in reply to a total of 376, but rain robbed England of certain victory. Yet before the final match the Australians had clinched the rubber. England were left to score 263 for victory in the fifth Test at the Oval and lost half the side for 48 before Jessop joined Jackson in a whirlwind partnership of 109 in 65 minutes. Jessop completed a century in 75 minutes and England gained their sole success of the series by one wicket.

The fourth Test match at Manchester had produced an Australian victory by just three runs when England collapsed in their second innings against the medium-paced bowling of Trumble whose 141 wickets in the England–Australia series is easily a record. In the Oval Test Trumble demonstrated his wonderful stamina by bowling unchanged throughout England's two innings, delivering 64.5 of Australia's 127 overs.

By 1911–12 England had a bowler of equal talents in Sydney Barnes who was brought in for the second Test of that MCC tour to Australia and struck fear into the hearts of batsmen by taking his first four wickets for one run, the first five for six runs and 30 wickets in all during the series. He was even more devastating in South Africa in 1913–14 when four Tests brought him a total of 49 wickets which still stands as a record. England won the series four–nil.

Barnes also took five wickets in the first innings to help England to victory by 244 runs over Australia in 1912, the only match between the two countries to reach a conclusion during the triangular tournament—which England won—in which South Africa was the third team. That was to prove England's last victory in a series against Australia until the 1924–25 season.

The reason can be found in the bowling figures of Australia's attacking spearhead, Gregory, McDonald and Kelleway as they went through the 1920–21 series in Australia, the 1921 series in England and the 1924–25 series in Australia winning 12 of the matches and losing one. Incidentally, Test matches in Australia between 1902 and 1946 were played to a finish; only in England was there a time limit.

Gregory and McDonald were at their best in England in 1921. Of the 71 England wickets to fall to the bowlers in the summer, 46 were captured by Gregory and McDonald. Mailey, with his remarkably accurate leg-breaks and googlies, was a splendid foil to them. At that time England were rebuilding an eleven after the ravages of war. Not until 1926 were England to taste a series victory again over Australia. The first four Tests were drawn, largely because of the poor weather but at the Oval, under the leadership of their young captain, Percy Chapman, England won by 289 runs. That final game has since been described as the greatest Test between the two world wars. Certainly the quality of the cricket was exceptional before the match swung England's way late on the third day.

The wicket gave some encouragement to the bowlers from the start, although runs were there for batsmen bold enough to play their strokes. With Sutcliffe scoring 76 and Chapman 49, England reached 280, despite the bowling of Mailey who took six wickets. Australia lost their first five wickets for 90 but recovered to reach 302, largely because of the application of Collins and Gregory who took part in a seventh wicket stand of 107. The turning point came on the third morning after a thunderstorm during the night had made the conditions just right for Grimmett and Mailey to exploit their spinners when Hobbs and Sutcliffe resumed England's second innings at 49.

At least Mailey and Grimmett *should* have been in command on a wicket which was drying out, but an artful tactical move by Hobbs and Sutcliffe kept them out. They pretended to make the leg theory bowling of Richardson look more difficult than it was. Richardson was kept on, while Mailey and Grimmett remained on the sidelines, until Hobbs and Sutcliffe had built the bulk of the opening stand of 172 which was to win the game. Both scored centuries. England reached 436 and Australia collapsed in the second innings on a worn wicket.

Thus after many years of waiting, England had regained the Ashes, which they easily retained in Australia in 1928–29, with one of the strongest sides sent overseas: Hobbs and Sutcliffe to open, followed by a new name, Hammond, and Jardine, Hendren and Chapman. Duckworth was the wicket-keeper, Tate the stock bowler, Larwood supplied the pace and White and Geary the spin. England won the series 4–1. For Australia there was consolation in the emergence in that series of a player who became the greatest run-collector cricket has known—Don Bradman.

He played in the first Test—the first to be held in Brisbane—but was dropped for the second. He came back for the third with scores of 79 and 112. He made 40 and 58 in the fourth and 123 and 37 not out in the fifth when Australia won. But not even Bradman could overshadow England's hero of the 1928–29 tour, Hammond who created a record totalling 905 runs in the series with scores of 251 in the second Test, 200 in the third, 119 not out and 177 in the fourth. The record was to stand barely 18 months.

Hammond watched it broken while playing in all five Tests for England in 1930 as Bradman cut loose. He started quietly, with eight in the first innings of the opening Test, but then warmed up in the second innings with 131, although he could not prevent an England victory. At Lord's Bradman scored 254 and one. At Leeds it was 334. He hustled to his double century in 214 minutes—the fastest in Test cricket—and actually scored 309 of the runs on the first day—another record! He had to be satisfied with 14 on a rain-affected Old Trafford wicket, but hit back with 232 at the Oval. Bradman had scored 974 runs in seven innings with an average of 139·14, a figure he was to better 18 months later against South Africa when he finished with 201·50, having scored 806 runs in five innings. Only four times between his debut in 1928 and his retirement in 1948 were Australia able to beat England without Bradman making a century in the Test match. Such was his immense contribution to Australia on the international field.

He was to see England regain the Ashes with their 'body-line' tactics under Jardine in 1932–33, but it was not until 20 years later that Australia were to lose them again when England appointed a professional captain for the first time in 1953. Hutton was the person to take over control.

Hutton had given evidence of his Bradman-like hunger for runs in 1938 when Hammond captained England for the first time. In the first match of the series at Trent Bridge Hutton and Compton both made centuries in their debuts against Australia. Barnett scored 126 while helping Hutton put on 219 for the opening partnership and Paynter scored 216 in England's total of 658 for eight declared. This high scoring was an indication of what was to come throughout the summer. The first two Tests were drawn. Australia won the fourth but England gained revenge in the record-breaking Oval Test. Batting first, Hutton set off on his marathon 13-hour 20-minute innings for 364 runs—both establishing new records for Test cricket. With Leyland scoring 187 and Joe Hardstaff junior 169, England reached 903 for seven before Hammond declared, the highest total by a side in Test cricket. Faced with this total, Australia submitted and were beaten by an innings and 579 runs—the heaviest margin of victory in Test cricket. Of the Australian bowlers Fleetwood-Smith came in for the most punishment, his 87 overs in the England innings costing 298 runs with only the wicket of Hammond to show for it.

Test careers, both for batsmen and bowlers, have been made or marred by controversial incidents. One such incident was partly responsible—in the opinion of many English observers—for Australia taking charge of cricket again once it resumed after the Second World War.

Bradman, suffering from ill health, had almost decided to give up playing the first-class game. When he recovered he found the call of the game too strong, tried his hand once more and accepted the Australian captaincy when England toured in 1946–47, although not entirely convinced that he was physically fit for the job. Failure in the first Test could have resulted in his retirement and the loss of an inspirational figure to the other Australian players. That moment almost came when, in Australia's first innings, Ikin in the slips appealed for a catch when Bradman was on 28. The claim looked justified, for the ball had deviated considerably to reach Ikin, but Bradman was given the benefit of the doubt when he stayed at the crease—and he stayed to score 187 as well as to torment England throughout two more series.

With Bradman to provide the batting backbone in the middle order, Hassett, Barnes and Morris to open and an attacking spearhead of Lindwall and Miller plus Johnston, Australia had the better-balanced team. England were certainly not short of batting strength with such stroke-makers as Hutton and Washbrook, Compton and Edrich, but the tireless Alec Bedser found himself very much both the spearhead of the attack *and* stock bowler. It was too much for one man.

Australia took the series in 1946–47 and 1948 in England when they brought probably the finest side to visit these shores. But not all the glory belonged to Don Bradman's team.

Some of it was earned by Compton, both for his ability and his bravery.

His talents showed through in the first Test at Nottingham. England faced an impossible task when they started their second innings needing 344 runs to avoid an innings defeat, after Bradman and Hassett had scored centuries in Australia's 509. All hope looked gone when England lost two wickets for 39 runs and Compton joined Hutton. They took the score to 150 before Hutton was dismissed on a fourth day in terrible conditions. The light was poor, rain continually caused stoppages and Lindwall and Miller bowled well, but Compton stuck to his task and, curbing his natural aggressiveness, stayed to score 184 runs. His innings was interrupted 11 times in its 395 minutes by one reason or another. England made 441 but lost by eight wickets.

Compton's courage was on display in the drawn Test at Old Trafford when England, batting first, lost wickets steadily except that of Compton. He hooked a no ball from Lindwall into his face and needed stitches in a cut forehead, but he came back later in the innings, still dazed from the blow, to score 145 in England's 363, an innings that might have won the match but for the fourth day being washed out when England were in a powerful position. By the time the Oval Test arrived Australia had already won the series and the only interest left was in seeing Bradman's farewell innings in Test cricket. He was to receive only one chance because England were bowled out for 52 and beaten by an innings. Bradman went to the wicket needing only four runs to make sure of a career Test average of three figures.

The crowd joined with the England players in giving the great man three cheers, but for once the emotion of the occasion proved too much. He was bowled second ball for a duck by Hollies and so ended his career with an average of 99·94 for a total of 6996 Test runs.

Throughout the success of Australia in those early years after the Second World War Hutton had been forced to take the fast-bowling barrage of Miller, Lindwall and Johnston, knowing England did not posess any big guns to fire in reply. He just waited for his opportunity and it came in the 1950s with the rise of Statham and Tyson. Hutton regained the Ashes for England in 1953 against Lindsay Hassett's side and then set off to defend them in 1954–55.

Even when the wickets suited the spinners Hutton kept his

pace battery going. Statham was a model of accuracy whereas Tyson concentrated on breathing fire and fury upon the Australians at the other end. The tour started disastrously for England when the first Test was lost by an innings and 154 runs, but then Tyson found his rhythm. England won the next three, taking a series in Australia for the first time since the 'bodyline' tour 22 years earlier.

Since then the exchanges have been evenly balanced. With the help of Laker's amazing 19 wickets for 90 runs at Old Trafford which established two world records, England retained the series in 1956, but then Australia found an outstanding captain in Benaud, a master tactician as well as a brilliant all-rounder. He became the first player to take 200 wickets and score 2000 runs in Tests. He saw Australia come out on top in three series.

England produced their own master tactician and shrewd thinker in Illingworth who regained the Ashes in 1970–71—the first time they had been regained in Australia since Jardine's 1932–33 tour. In doing so, Illingworth followed the pattern set by another Pudsey-born Yorkshireman, Hutton, by maintaining a speed attack. Snow was the shock bowler, supported by Lever and Willis, against Australian batsmen who were clearly suspect against genuine pace.

After retaining the Ashes in a drawn series on their own soil in 1972, England gave them up once more during a comprehensive annihilation in Australia in 1974–75. Under the captaincy of Scotsman Mike Denness, England were beaten 4–1, and although they regained some pride in a 1–0 defeat in their home series the following summer, the Ashes remained 'down under'.

In the next six full and part series, between 1976 and 1981, England won 11 of the 22 Tests, to Australia's six. These included a 5–1 win, under J. M. Brearley's captaincy, in Australia in 1978–79. No other captain has ever won by such a margin 'Down under', though it needs to be said that Australia's playing resources were reduced by the counter demands of World Series Cricket. England's 3–1 triumph in the 1981 series was due, very largely, to the remarkable all-round skills of Botham. He literally plucked victory from impending defeat at Headingley with a century off 87 balls; took five wickets for one run in 28 deliveries in the following Test at Edgbaston and then produced one of the most dazzling displays of controlled hitting ever witnessed in international cricket at Old Trafford to help England retain the Ashes. This time his hundred came off only 86 balls.

England made two disastrous tours of South Africa in 1905–6 and 1909–10. For the 1905–6 tour the South African selectors took the unusual step of announcing a side for all five Tests before the series began. At that stage South Africa had not beaten England in eight attempts, yet they took the first three Tests and the final match to win the series 4–1—England's heaviest defeat by South Africa. The series was a low-scoring one, with only two centuries recorded. South Africa's strength lay in a fine line of leg-spin bowlers, including Schwartz, Faulkner and Vogler who perfected the recently developed googly ball, although fast bowler Snooke finished leading wicket-taker in the series with 24 wickets.

The googly bowlers were even more in evidence in the 1909–10 visit when Vogler took 36 wickets and Faulkner 26. They took all 20 England wickets between them in the first Test, which South Africa won by 19 runs. They succeeded in two out of the next three and only in the final Test, when Hobbs scored 187, did England show any sign of mastering them.

Over the next 20 years South Africa's batting was dominated by the power of Taylor who made all his seven Test centuries against England, yet South Africa had to wait until the 1930s for their next series win against England.

They won the first Test of the 1930–31 series largely as a result of the off-spin bowling of Nupen who took 11 wickets for 150. The other four matches were drawn and in 1935 an innings of 164 by Mitchell at Lord's gave South Africa the series, again only one Test producing an outright result.

The most remarkable Test between the two countries took place during England's 1938–39 tour at a time when batting records were being broken everywhere. England had won the third Test by an innings and 13 runs. Paynter scored 243 and shared a partnership of 242 with Hammond (120) in England's total of 469 for four declared. The final Test at Durban was played on a timeless basis and was finally left as a draw at the end of the 10th day. South Africa opened with a score of 530 with centuries by Van der Byl (125) and Dudley Nourse (103). By the middle of the fifth day England were all out for 316 and South Africa made 481 in their second innings, Melville scoring 103. England needed 696 to win in four days before their ship left. With rain washing out the eighth, they were still 42 runs

130

short when they had to make a dash for the boat. Edrich hit 219, Hammond 140—his 21st Test century—and Gibb 120.

England's next tour in 1948–49 brought one of the most exciting finishes witnessed in Test history. England had been left to score 128 to win the first Test in 135 minutes on a poor wicket at Durban. Against some fine fast bowling by McCarthy they lost wickets steadily in keeping up with the clock, and when their number 10 batsman Gladwin entered only seven minutes remained. When the last over started eight runs were wanted. Gladwin struck four, Bedser one and the rest came from leg-byes, including the winning run off the game's very last ball.

South Africa had to wait until 1965 for the next win in a series against England, when Graeme Pollock swept them to victory at Nottingham with a century in two hours, but they had given England trouble both in 1955 and in 1956–57 when off-spinner Tayfield headed the wicket-takers in both series, supported by the fast bowling of Heine and Adcock.

Tayfield also posed many problems for the Australian batsmen while taking 30 wickets on the 1952–53 tour under Cheetham. That was a young and inexperienced South African side and few people had given them any chance when they landed, but they put their critics to flight by sharing the series 2–2. In the previous 29 Tests between the two countries South Africa had won only one.

This effort was the turning point in the cricket between the two countries. When Australia went to South Africa in 1966–67 they were defeated in a series for the first time by South Africa, losing 3–1. They were beaten by the pace attack of Procter, Peter Pollock, Barlow and Goddard, the sparkling batting of Graeme Pollock, who scored 537 runs, and Lindsay, who totalled 606 and took 24 catches as wicket-keeper. South Africa's new power was even more clearly demonstrated when Australia returned in 1969–70 for a four-match tour and were beaten in every game, destroyed by the Procter-Pollock-Barlow bowling combination and the batting strength of Graeme Pollock and Barry Richards. Sadly, it was to be South Africa's last appearance in Test cricket for a number of years as a result of their government's apartheid policy.

That 1952–53 tour by South Africa captured the imagination of the Australian public who admired the spirited manner in which the young Springboks rose to the challenge. But nothing could compare with the cricket fever that swept through the country in 1960–61 when Frank Worrell led his West Indies team through one sparkling display after another.

Their enthusiastic batting, the clever spin bowling of Ramadhin and Valentine and their general sporting approach had already made them favourites before the first Test started. The match ended in a tie and cricket swept all other news off the front pages. With Sobers scoring a century, Worrell, Solomon and Alexander all reaching the 60s and Hall making a half century, the West Indies scored 453 in their first innings. In reply Australia gained a lead of 52. O'Neill was the chief scorer with 181 and Simpson made 92. A further 284 by the West Indies left Australia needing 233 to win at the rate of 45 an hour.

They made a bad start against the pace of Hall and lost six wickets for 92 before Benaud joined Davidson in a flourishing partnership for the seventh wicket, which added 134 and took Australia to within seven runs of victory. Davidson was then run out. Hall started the last over with six runs wanted and three wickets left. Grout took a leg-bye off the first and Benaud was caught behind off the second. The fourth produced a bye, the fifth another run, but off the sixth Grout was run out, going for the third run that would have given Australia victory. Last man Kline entered with the scores level and two balls to go. They tried to take a run when Kline turned it to square-leg, but Solomon threw down the wicket with only the width of one stump as his target to run out Meckiff who had backed up well, and the match was tied!

The rest of the series swung one way and then the other. Australia won the second Test, West Indies the third, the fourth was drawn when the last Australian pair, Kline and Mackay, batted through the final 110 minutes with the victory well out of their reach. Australia won the fifth to take the series, but for the next six years the West Indies ruled the world.

They visited England in 1963 and took the series 3–1, adding to their series success in 1934–35, 1947–48 and 1950. Ramadhin had given away to Gibbs and Hall had been joined in the pace attack by Griffith. The only drawn Test was at Lord's in another dramatic finish which matched the Brisbane tie for excitement. England had to make 234 to win but lost Edrich, Stewart and Dexter for 31, and Cowdrey had to retire with the score at 72 when a rising delivery from Hall broke his left arm. Close then took over, desperately defending his wicket against Hall and Griffith by taking the ball on his body if he could not connect with the bat. When he was out 19 minutes were left with 15 runs wanted. Shackleton and Allen were together when Hall started his last over with eight runs needed and two wickets left. Singles came off the second and third balls then Shackleton was run out so Cowdrey resumed with his broken arm, intending to play left-handed if he had to face a delivery. Allen, however, played out the last two balls in grim light and the match was drawn.

Griffith, with 32 wickets, Sobers, Hall and Gibbs between them took all but three of the England wickets to fall during the summer and again dominated the bowling scene in 1966 when the West Indies returned for another 3–1 series win, this time with Sobers in command. Between these tours they had beaten Australia 2–1 in a home series in 1964–65, a rubber from which Lawry and Simpson extracted some satisfaction for Australia by opening with a partnership of 382 in the Bridgetown Test, both scoring double centuries.

When England went to the West Indies in 1967–68 Hall and Griffith were on the decline. England won the series 1–0 and West Indies were beaten 3–1 when they returned to Australia in 1968–69. They came back to England in 1969—this time without Hall and Griffith—and were defeated 2–0 in a three-match series.

But a 2–0 series win in England four years later, skippered by Rohan Kanhai, announced the revival of West Indies' fortunes. Armed with an array of exuberant batting and a powerful pace attack, they ended the lean years in style. They dominated a drawn series with England in 1973–74, opener Lawrence Rowe capturing the attention of the cricketing world with one triple-century, two centuries and a Test average of 88. By the mid-1970s, now led by Clive Lloyd, West Indies had become the world's strongest team. They possessed an outstanding stroke maker in Viv Richards and a superb fast bowling attack of Michael Holding, Joel Garner, Andy Roberts, Colin Croft and Malcom Marshall.

The West Indies had made their weight felt in Test cricket as the 1950s approached, particularly through the batting of Weekes. On their first tour of India in 1948–49 he scored four centuries in successive Tests and in England in 1950 he scored four double centuries, one triple century and two centuries in first-class matches though only one of the three-figure scores was made in a Test. In New Zealand in 1955–56 his first five innings were all centuries, three in consecutive Test innings.

In view of the quality of the batsmen in the first 90 years of Test cricket and the remarkable scoring records achieved, it is a little surprising that international cricket had to wait until 1968–69 for the first player to score a double century and a century in the same Test. This feat has been repeated three times since.

The first was by Walters (who had also scored 155 on his Test debut against England in 1965–66) when he made 242 and 103 in the Sydney Test during the West Indies tour of 1968–69. In 1970–71 Indian opening batsman Gavaskar scored 124 and 220 against West Indies at Port of Spain and the following winter during the tour by New Zealand, Lawrence Rowe, the Jamaican batsman, marked his Test debut on his home Kingston wicket by scoring 214 and 100 not out. In a high-scoring series on unresponsive wickets and weak fast-bowling attacks, the tour was remarkable for the scoring efforts of New Zealand's opening batsman Turner who replied to Rowe's double century in the West Indies' first innings of the first Test by carrying his bat for 223 not out after New Zealand had lost five for 108. In the fourth Test in Georgetown Turner scored 259 and Jarvis helped him in an opening stand of 387. This was the second highest opening stand in history and the highest for any wicket by New Zealand in Tests. The fourth batsman was Greg Chappell who scored 247 not out and 123 for Australia v. New Zealand, Wellington, 1974.

The Ashes

The story of the Ashes dates back to the Oval in 1882 when Australia won the only Test of the series by seven runs, their first victory on English soil. The Australian team of the time was one of the finest they have produced, containing great batsmen of the calibre of W. L Murdoch, their captain, A. Bannerman, all-rounder G. Giffen, master wicket-keeper J. McBlackham and the menacing fast bowler F. Spofforth.

It proved a low-scoring match. Australia were dismissed for 63, England made 101 and when Australia scored 122 in their second innings England were left needing 85 to win. It seemed a formality until Spofforth struck again. He followed his first innings seven for 46 with seven for 44 and England lost by seven runs. The following morning the old *Sporting Times* published a mock Memoriam in heavy black edging which read:

In affectionate remembrance of English cricket which died at The Oval, 29th August, 1882. Deeply lamented by a large circle of sorrowing friends and acquaintances, R.I.P. 'N.B. the body will be cremated and the ashes taken to Australia.'

The following winter England played in Australia under the Hon. Ivo Bligh, later Lord Darnley. After the third Test of a shared four-match series some ladies burnt a bail, put the ashes in a wooden urn wrapped in a velvet bag and presented them to Bligh. He bequeathed the urn to MCC on his death in 1927 and the urn remains on display in the Cricket Memorial Gallery building at Lord's.

Personalities of the Game

Barnes, Sydney: Right-arm bowler of Warwickshire, Lancashire, Staffordshire and England. Employing his long, powerful fingers and a superb action, he could swing and spin the ball with exceptional control. He played only 27 times for England but took an amazing 189 wickets at 16 apiece. He had taken only 13 first-class wickets when chosen for A. C. MacLaren's 1901–2 tour of Australia. He proved devastating until a twisted knee put him out of the series, but his greatest moment was 'Down Under' 10 years later. At Melbourne, and at a cost of one run, he dismissed the mass of Australia's batting strength—Bardsley, Kellaway, Hill and Armstrong. When he had Minnett caught after lunch his figures were 11–7–6–5.

Barrington, Ken: Sturdy right-handed batsman with a square-on stance who scored 6806 in 82 Test matches for England at an average of 58·67. In 1964 he hit 256 against Australia at Manchester, the highest of his 20 Test centuries. In a career lasting from 1953 to 1963 he hit 31,714 runs, completing 1000 in a season on 15 occasions for Surrey. His professionalism and integrity led to invitations to manage England teams abroad and he also served on the selection committee for home Test matches.

Bedi, Bishen Singh: One of the most popular and successful players to represent India. His classical left-arm bowling with its command of every aspect of the spinner's art earned him 1547 wickets during a career stretching from 1961–1981. He made his first-class debut for Northern Punjab in the Ranji Trophy in 1961–62 and the first of his 67 Test appearances in 1966–67, captaining his country in twenty-two matches. He played for Northamptonshire from 1972–1977 and twice took 100 wickets in an English season. His most successful Test series was as captain in Australia in 1977–78 when he captured 31 wickets, including 10 for 194 at Perth.

Bedser, Alec: Right-arm medium-pace bowler of Surrey, and England's leading bowler in the immediate post-war period. Joined Surrey staff with twin-brother Eric in 1938, but because of the war did not take his first-class wicket until 1946. Against India at Lord's in the first post-war Test that year he took seven for 49 and four for 96. Tall and powerfully built, his inswingers and leg-cutters took 236 Test wickets, and were a large factor in Surrey's seven consecutive championship wins in the 1950s.

Benaud, Richie: Right-handed wrist-spinner and batsman. Accomplished all-rounder who was the first Test cricketer to score 2000 runs and take 200 wickets, and an astute captain who led Australia 28 times. Appointed skipper in 1958–59 against England, he captained his country to a 4–0 win to regain the Ashes. These he successfully defended in England in 1961, as much with his mixture of leg-spin as with his inspiring attacking leadership.

Bradman, Don: Right-handed batsman of New South Wales, South Australia and Australia. The most clinically efficient run-getter in cricket history. He finished with a first-class batting average of 95·14, and would have been the only Test cricketer with an average of 100 had he scored just four runs, instead of a duck, in his last innings for Australia at the Oval in 1948. In 52 Tests he scored 6996 runs, including a record 29 hundreds, for an average of 99·94. He scored a record 37 double-hundreds, six treble-hundreds.

Compton, Denis: Right-handed batsman and slow left-arm bowler of Middlesex and England. His improvised strokes made him one of the most entertaining cricketers in the post-war era. Played eight times for England before the war but was at his prime in 1947 when he scored a record 3816 runs (average 90·85), including 18 hundreds during the summer. Despite the handicap of a knee injury received while playing football, he played many entertaining and invaluable innings for England, such as his 184 and 145 not out (with bloody bandages around his temple) against Australia in 1948.

Congdon, Bevan Ernest: He played in more Tests, 61, and scored more runs for his country, 3,448 including seven centuries, than any other New Zealand player. He led New Zealand to their first victory over Australia, at Christchurch, in March 1974, and was in the team which defeated England for the first time in 1978. In addition to being a sound captain and determined batsman, Bev Congdon was a useful medium-paced bowler who took 59 Test wickets. In a first-class career from 1960–78 he scored 13,101 runs (23 centuries), captured 204 wickets and held 201 catches.

Constantine, Learie: Right-handed batsmen and fast bowler. A fierce hitting, unorthodox batsman and a bowler who ranked among the fastest of his time, he will largely be remembered for his superb fielding and his gay, enthusiastic approach to the game. His Test record is no more than average, with 635 runs in 33 innings, a highest score of 90 against England in 1934–35 and 58 wickets. Test cricket, however, was too slow for his nature. Yet he was at his best in league cricket in Lancashire where he set record after record with his fast scoring. He was knighted in 1962 and created a life peer in 1969.

Cowdrey, Colin: Right-handed batsman. Took part in 114 Tests and scored more Test runs than any other England batsman except Boycott, totalling 7624 (av. 44·06). One of the most naturally gifted players cricket has produced, he has also taken more Test catches than any other player. He made six tours of Australia, captained England 27 times and, with May, shares the Test record fourth-wicket partnership of 411 against West Indies at Edgbaston in 1957. He scored 22 centuries in Test cricket and 107 centuries in first-class matches.

Evans, Godfrey: Wicket-keeper/batsman of Kent and England. His aggressive athleticism was one of the more eye-catching features of the England side through 91 Tests. Following in the footsteps of a long line of famous Kent stumpers—Huish, Wood, Hubble, Ames and Levett—he just had time to make his first appearance for the county before the outbreak of war. When cricket restarted, his position as England's No. 1 wicket-keeper was never seriously challenged until 1959—then, only to help build a younger team.

Faulkner, George Aubrey: Right-handed batsman and googly bowler. Until the emergence of Procter in the 1960s he was regarded as South Africa's greatest all-rounder, scoring 1754 runs in 25 Tests and taking 82 wickets. His best Test return was seven for 84 at the Oval in 1912, but his outstanding bowling performance was six for 17 in 11 overs at Headingley in 1907. Neither could save South Africa from defeat. He was the first South African to score a double century in Test cricket—an innings of 204 at Melbourne.

Fazal Mahmood: Right-arm medium-fast bowler. One of the finest opening bowlers in Pakistan's history. He had been sounded as to his availability to go with India to Australia in 1947–48 when the terms of partition were announced and he moved to Pakistan. He took 139 wickets in 34 Tests, with a leg-cutter his speciality, particularly on matting wickets. He will always be remembered for his performance of 12 for 99 which took Pakistan to victory over England at the Oval in 1954. Also obtained 12 wickets in a match against India and West Indies and 13 in a Test against Australia.

Grace, William Gilbert: Right-handed all-rounder of Gloucestershire and England. A master batsman on the bad wickets of his time, he scored a previously unapproached 2739 runs in 1871. 'The Doctor' was the first to score 200, the first to score 300, the first to make two centuries in a match, the first to perform the cricketer's double of 1000 runs and 100 wickets, and the breaker of many other records. At the age of 47 he scored his 100th century, and in the same season became the first man to score 1000 runs in May. Apart from his 54,896 runs he claimed 2876 wickets and made 871 catches. He captained England in 13 Tests between 1880 and 1899.

Grimmett, Clarrie: Right-arm leg-spinner of Victoria, South Australia and Australia. A New Zealander who became Australia's most consistent bowler between the wars with 216 wickets. Though 13 years older than O'Reilly, he is best remembered for his bowling partnership with the New South Welshman in the 1930s. He made his Test debut against England in 1924–25 and in the last match of that series he carried Australia to victory with five for 45 and six for 37.

Gupte, Subhas Pandhrinath: Leg-break and googly bowler. Regarded as the leading bowler of his type in the world during the 1950s when he played most of his Test cricket for India. Altogether he took 149 wickets in 36 Tests. In most series he was the leading India bowler, taking 27 wickets against the West Indies in 1952–53 and 22 in 1958–59 when he returned his best Test-match figures of nine for 102.

Hall, Wes: Right-arm fast bowler. With Charlie Griffith, he formed one of the finest Test fast-bowling attacks of all time and made West Indies the outstanding side of the early 1960s. With his long rhythmic approach to the wicket he was a menacing sight for any batsman to face, yet had great stamina, as he showed when bowling unchanged for 40 overs against England at Lord's in 1963. A knee injury received in a car accident limited his effectiveness towards the end of his career, otherwise he would undoubtedly have gained the extra eight wickets he needed to complete 200 in 48 Tests.

Hammond, Walter: Right-handed batsman and medium pace bowler of Gloucestershire and England. England's dominant batsman between the wars, he also claimed 83 Test wickets and was one of the finest slip fielders of all time. Though qualified to play for Kent he chose to maintain Gloucestershire's line of great all-rounders, started by Edward and W. G. Grace and continued by Gilbert Jessop. He was at his peak with Percy Chapman's MCC touring side in Australia in 1928–29 when he scored 905 runs, still a record for an English player in a Test series home or away. He survived the war to captain England in Australia.

Hanif, Mohammed: Right-handed batsman. An opening batsman with remarkable powers of concentration, stamina and sound defensive technique and an appetite for runs. He had the opportunity to display them all as Pakistan's leading batsman at a time when their batting was below strength. He holds the record for the largest first-class score of 499 for Karachi against Bahawalpur in 1958–59 when he was run out going for his 500th run, and the longest innings of 970 minutes while scoring 337 against West Indies in 1957–58.

Harvey, Neil: Left-handed batsman with Test aggregate of 6149. Small, neat and quick moving, with great power in his wrists, he was a member of Bradman's all-conquering 1948 team to England when they won four and drew one of the five Test matches. Played for Victoria and New South Wales and scored 67 hundreds, six of them against England. Brilliant fieldsman, notably in the deep where his length of throw and accuracy always delighted colleagues and onlookers.

Hassett, Lindsay: Right-handed batsman who succeeded Don Bradman as Australia's captain in 1949, retiring in 1953 after his third tour of England. Played for Victoria and hit 10 centuries in 43 Test matches, sharing a third wicket partnership of 276 with Bradman against England at Brisbane in 1946–47, which remains a record. Small, neat and technically correct batsman who scored 3073 runs in Tests.

Headley, George: Right-handed batsman. A legend not only in West Indies' cricketing history but throughout the game, this remarkable batsman averaged more than 60 in his 22 Tests, with an aggregate of 2190 runs. These figures were achieved at a time when West Indies were only just becoming established as a Test-playing country. In his Test debut in 1930 he scored 176 in the second innings against England and a century in each innings of the final Test of that series. During the 1934–35 tour by England he scored 270 not out at Kingston, his highest Test score.

Hobbs, Jack: Right-handed opening batsman of Surrey and England. Popularly considered the greatest batsman of all time, he spanned the years between Grace and Bradman and scored more runs (61,237) and more centuries (197) than any other player. Turned down by Essex, he made his debut for Surrey against that county, scoring 155 and winning his county cap. He provided the dominant half of four great opening partnerships—with Hayward and Sandham for Surrey, and Rhodes and Sutcliffe for England. He was a classical batsman and a generous man.

Hutton, Len: Right-handed opening batsman of Yorkshire and England. One of the world's greatest leading batsmen for 15 years which unfortunately included the Second World War. Achieved immortality with one innings—his 364 against Australia in the Oval Test of 1938. Even more remarkable were his performances after the war, for an accident in an army gym resulted in his left arm being shorter and weaker than his right. He failed to score in his first Test in 1937, but when he completed his international career in 1955 he had scored 6971 runs in 79 Tests. As famous for his captaincy as his batsmanship, he led England's recapture of the Ashes in 1953, and defended them with astute leadership in 1954–55.

Laker, Jim: Gifted off-spin bowler and useful batsman who will be remembered for his remarkable achievement against Australia in the 1956 Test at Old Trafford where he returned figures of 19 for 90 (9 for 37 and 10 for 53). This followed 10 for 88 in innings for Surrey against the touring side earlier in the summer. Played an important part in Surrey's sequence of Championship-title successes during the 1950s.

Larwood, Harold: Right-arm fast bowler who with Nottinghamshire colleague Bill Voce caused world-wide controversy under Douglas Jardine's captaincy for employing a 'body-line' attack for England in Australia during the 1932–33 series. In that stormy season Larwood took 33 wickets in the five Tests. He was only of average height but at the peak of his career linked immense speed to superb control and direction. 'Lol' as he was known, took 78 wickets in 21 Tests and completed 100 wickets in a season eight times. He and 'Patsy' Hendren created an eighth wicket record of 124 for England against Australia at Brisbane in 1928–29.

Lindwall, Ray: Right-arm fast bowler of New South Wales, Queensland and Australia. With Miller he formed Australia's lethal fast-bowling partnership after the Second World War. He played in 61 Tests, taking 228 wickets. His menacing rhythmic approach to the wicket gave him exceptional pace and he also had the ability to swing the ball to an alarming degree, which enabled him to play Test cricket until he was 38, when the edge had gone off his pace. Probably at his peak during the first of his three visits to England in 1948.

Lock, Tony: Slow left-arm bowler who formed a deadly spin partnership with Jim Laker for Surrey and England in the 1950s. In the 1958 series against New Zealand he took 34 wickets for 7·47 in the five Tests. Subsequently his bowling action came under suspicion and with characteristic courage he remodelled it, winning back his England place. He played for Western Australia for a period; then returned to play for Leicestershire. Twice he took 200 wickets in a season and was one of the greatest of all short-leg fieldsmen, holding 830 catches. He played in 49 Tests.

Macartney, Charlie: Right-handed batsman and occasional leg-break bowler of New South Wales and Australia. Rated with Trumper and Bradman as one of the finest batsmen to represent his country. Toured England in 1909, 1912 and 1921, but it was on his fourth visit in 1926 at the age of 40 that the records tumbled. He scored seven hundreds and took 49 wickets on the tour. Three centuries came in successive Tests—133 not out at Lord's, 151 at Leeds, and 109 at Old Trafford. His Headingley hundred was only the second Test century before lunch on the opening day.

McDonald, Ted: Right-arm fast bowler of Victoria, Lancashire and Australia. A wonderfully rhythmic fast bowler, he partnered Jack Gregory in the destruction of England's batting in the 1920–21 and 1921 Anglo–Australian Tests, the second series taking 27 wickets. The First World War delayed his rise to world fame, and he was 28 before he made his Test debut in 1920. But such was the effortless approach of this double-jointed athlete that he was still bowling magnificently 10 years later when he bowled Bradman for nine after the 'Don' had scored 236, 185 not out and 78 in the opening matches of the Australian tour. That was after McDonald had left Australia to play for Lancashire.

Mankad, Mulvantrai: Right-handed batsman and slow left-arm bowler. Known throughout cricket as 'Vinoo', he remains the outstanding all-rounder to represent India since the Second World War and probably in their history. He needed only 23 Tests to complete the Test 'double' of 1000 runs and 100 wickets which still stands as a record. For India in Tests he took 162 in his 44 matches, as well as scoring 2109 runs. In 1946 he completed the 'double' in England.

May, Peter: Right-handed batsman of Surrey, and England's leading batsman in the 1950s, he captained the country in a record 41 Tests before illness and the strain of captaincy led to his premature retirement. He played his first Test in 1951 just one year after making his county debut, and scored 138 against South Africa at Leeds. He played many other splendid innings for his country. In the first Test against the West Indies in 1957 he scored a career best 285 not out, and figured in a 4th-wicket stand of 411 with Cowdrey. For Surrey, he captained the side to two championship wins.

Miller, Keith: Right-handed all-rounder of Victoria, New South Wales and Australia. The more volatile of the Lindwall-Miller pace partnership that gave Australia such an advantage in the immediate post-war Tests. He took 170 wickets in 55 Tests and his 2958 runs, including seven centuries, place him comfortably among the greatest all-rounders in cricket history. He was also a slip fielder of the highest quality. A cricketer of mood and moment. He preferred batting to bowling, but even at the crease occasionally threw his wicket away on impulse.

Mitchell, Bruce: Right-handed batsman who opened the South African innings for 20 years, though he first toured England as a number seven order batsman and leg-break bowler. He was promoted to start the innings for the first Test and he and Bob Catterall shared century partnerships in each innings. In 1930–31 he shared a first wicket record stand of 260 with I. J Siedle against England at Cape Town and in 1947 he and L. Tuckett added an unbroken 109 for the eighth wicket at The Oval, which is also a record Test stand for South Africa against England. Powerful off-driver and fine slip.

Nourse, Dudley: Right-handed batsman. The son of Dave Nourse who is regarded as the first of South Africa's great batsmen, Dudley exceeded his father's Test aggregate of runs, although playing 11 fewer Tests. His final tally was 2960 from 34 matches. He started his Test career in England in 1935 and finished it in England in 1951 when leading South Africa and becoming the first South African batsman to score a double century against England, making 208 at Nottingham despite a broken thumb. In his first home Test series in 1935–36 he made his Test highest score of 231 against Australia.

Oldfield, Bert: Wicket-keeper and right-handed batsman of New South Wales and Australia. Widely regarded as the finest wicket-keeper of all time, he first modelled himself on—then perfected—the modern crouching style of Herbert Strudwick, his great friend and opposite number in the England side. He kept wicket with natural ease through 54 Tests between 1924 and 1937, and his 52 stumpings out of 130 Test dismissals is a Test record. Renowned for his courage, he kept in two Tests with ribs broken by fast bowler Jack Gregory, and was knocked unconscious while batting against Larwood in the 'Bodyline' series of 1932–33.

Kapil Dev (batting), Northamptonshire and India, and Ian Botham, Somerset and England

right:
Keith Miller
(batting),
Victoria, New
South Wales and
Australia, and
Godfrey Evans,
Kent and
England

far right:
Jack Hobbs,
Surrey and
England

right:
Len Hutton,
Yorkshire and
England

far right:
Wes Hall,
Barbados,
Trinidad and
West Indies

right:
Frank Worrell,
Barbados,
Jamaica and
West Indies

far right:
Bob Willis,
Warwickshire
and England

right:
Don Bradman,
New South
Wales, South
Australia and
Australia

far right:
Denis Compton,
Middlesex and
England

right:
Gary Sobers,
Barbados, South
Australia,
Nottinghamshire
and West Indies

far right:
Fred Trueman,
Yorkshire,
Derbyshire and
England

right:
Dennis Lillee,
Western
Australia and
Australia

far right:
Clive Lloyd,
Lancashire and
West Indies

right:
David Gower,
Leicestershire
and England

far right:
Imran Khan,
Sussex and
Pakistan

O'Reilly, Bill: Right-arm spin bowler of New South Wales and Australia. Nicknamed 'Tiger', he bowled off-breaks, leg-breaks and googlies off a long run and was largely responsible for Australia's Ashes supremacy in the 1930s when he took 102 England wickets in 19 Tests between 1932 and 1938. His 27 in 1932–33 series were overshadowed by the 'Bodyline' controversy, but in England in 1934 he formed a devastating partnership with Grimmett, and claimed 28 Test wickets. Four years later he ensured that Australia retained the Ashes with five for 66 and five for 56 at Headingley.

Ramadhin, Sonny: Off-break bowler. With two first-class trial matches behind him and only just 20, he became an overnight sensation on the West Indies' tour of England in 1950, thus starting a 43-match Test career that was to gain him 158 wickets. Twenty-six of them came in that first tour when West Indies gained a series victory in England for the first time. Although essentially an off-break bowler, he could turn the ball both ways.

Reid, John: Right-handed batsman and medium-paced bowler. New Zealand's captain from 1956 until 1965. Scored more than 3000 runs in Test cricket during a career of 58 matches. On his first tour of England in 1949 he doubled as reserve wicket-keeper, but later became a more than useful medium-paced bowler with 85 wickets to his credit. The majority of his Test innings were played when New Zealand were in trouble, but he never allowed the situation to cramp his natural, aggressive style. He holds the record for sixes scored in an innings, hitting 15 when making 296 for Wellington against Northern Districts.

Rhodes, Wilfred: Slow left-arm bowler and right-handed batsman of Yorkshire and England. The heaviest wicket-taker in cricket history (4187), he rose from No. 11 to become an accomplished opening batsman, finishing with a career aggregate of 39,802 runs. He performed the cricketer's double of 1000 runs and 100 wickets in a season, a record 16 times. He collected 100 wickets per season for 23 seasons. After a five-year break from international cricket he was recalled for the historic Oval Test of 1926 at the age of 48, and played in the last of his 58 Tests when 52.

Sobers, Sir Garfield: Left-handed batsman and capable of virtually every type of left-arm bowling, from fast to slow spin. Until the strain of playing cricket 12 months of the year caught up with him in 1971 he was the undisputed number one player in the world, and arguably the best all-rounder cricket has seen. He has scored more runs in Test cricket than any other batsman except Boycott—8032 in 93 Tests, and taken 235 wickets. He holds the world record Test score of 365 not out, made against Pakistan in Kingston, 1957–58, and in 1968 became the only player to hit six sixes in a six-ball over while playing for Nottinghamshire against Glamorgan.

Spofforth, Frederick: Right-arm fast bowler. Nicknamed the 'Demon' because of his pace and control, he was largely resposible for the introduction of the 'Ashes' in 1882 when England, needing 85 to win at the Oval, were destroyed by his bowling. They had reached 51 for two when Spofforth started his second spell in which he took five for 12 in 11 overs to sweep Australia to victory. His match total was 14 for 90. In 1878 at Lord's against MCC he took Australia to a nine-wicket win inside a day with 11 for 20 in the match. He was considered the greatest fast bowler of his time.

Sutcliffe, Herbert: Right-handed opening batsman of Yorkshire and England. With Hobbs he provided perhaps England's finest opening partnership. His alliance with Percy Holmes for Yorkshire was hardly less celebrated, and this pair's 555 at Leyton in 1932 stands as the second highest first-wicket partnership. Basic ability coupled with dour application made him one of the most successful batsmen of his time. He appeared regularly in first-class cricket from 1919 until 1939, and played one match for Yorkshire after the Second World War at the age of 51.

Sutcliffe, Bert: Left-handed batsman, one of the most gifted to grace the international cricket scene. Twice he scored over 300 runs in an innings, his 385 for Otago against Canterbury in 1952–53 being a world record for a left-hander. In Tests he scored 2727 runs in 42 matches—including an innings of 230 not out against India in 1955–56 which stood for 12 years as New Zealand's record individual Test score. In all he scored six double centuries, two triple centuries and 36 other innings of three figures in a career of 17,196 runs.

Trueman, Fred: Right-arm fast bowler of Yorkshire and England. Among the most successful Test bowlers with 307 wickets in 67 appearances. This colourful character was probably the most controversial cricketer of his period, as well known for his blunt Yorkshire wit as his fiery performances. He burst into the Test cricket scene in 1952 when he took 29 Indian wickets at 13·31 each—including a devastating eight for 31 at Old Trafford. A surprising omission from Hutton's MCC side in Australia 1954–55, he was to couple high speed with stamina which few fast bowlers have managed.

Trumper, Victor: Right-handed batsman. Other Australian batsmen of his time made more runs in Test cricket, but none could match the effortless ease with which Trumper scored his runs, and his name is still mentioned with deep respect in cricket circles. In his second Test match in 1899 he scored 135 not out at Lord's, but his most memorable summer in England was in 1902 when he scored 11 centuries (in all matches), amounting to 2570 runs. This total included the first instance of a Test century before lunch on the first day and that on a wet wicket at Old Trafford.

Verity, Hedley: Slow left-arm spinner who succeeded Wilfred Rhodes for Yorkshire and England. Killed leading troops in Sicily during the Second World War of 1939–45, he had already taken 1956 wickets at an average of almost 200 a year between 1930 and 1939. Took 15 Australian wickets for 104 in 1934 Lord's Test and all 10 Nottinghamshire wickets in an innings for only 10 runs in 1932.

Weekes, Everton: Right-handed batsman. The first West Indies batsman to score 4000 runs in Test cricket, he was the heaviest-scoring batsman in the famous 'Three W's' trio with Walcott and Worrell of the 1950s. A fine player of top-class bowling and savage against anything less. In one 10-month period in 1948–49 he scored five Test centuries in successive innings, starting with the final Test against England of the 1947–48 tour and in the first three Tests of the West Indies tour of India, 1948–49. In the next Test innings he was run out for 90.

Woolley, Frank: Left-handed batsman and slow left-arm spinner of Kent and England. One of the most powerful and graceful players in the game's long history, his 58,969 runs, 2068 wickets and 1018 catches establish him as one of the great all-rounders. All this after he made a duck and conceded 103 runs for one wicket during his debut for Kent at Old Trafford in 1906! He played 64 times for England, including 52 consecutive matches between 1909 and 1926. Never the most consistent Test performer, he is still responsible for some of the game's most memorable innings, such as his 95 and 93 at Lord's in 1921.

Worrell, Frank: Right-handed batsman and left-arm medium-paced bowler. Acclaimed for his leadership qualities in the outstanding West Indies side of the early 1950s, he was also a magnificent batsman whose Test aggregate of 3860 runs was compiled in only 51 Tests. He also obtained 69 Test wickets, twice taking seven wickets in an innings. He twice shared fourth-wicket partnerships exceeding 500 for Barbados—the first while only 19 when his share was 308 not out—and in 1957 against England at Nottingham he carried his bat for 191.

Records Section

Compiled by Irving Rosenwater, updated by Geoffrey Copinger

All facts and figures in this book are correct to the end of the 1982 cricket season in England.

Abbreviations

Countries etc.

Australia	A. or Aus.	dismissals	dis.
Australians	Ausns.	drawn	D.
England	E. or Eng.	hours	hrs.
India	I. or Ind.	highest score	H.S.
New South Wales	N.S.W.	innings	I. or inns.
New Zealand	N.Z.	lost	L.
Pakistan	P. or Pak.	maidens	mdns.
Queensland	Qld.	matches	M.
South Australia	S.Aus.	minutes	mins.
South Africa	S.A.	not out	N.O.
Sri Lanka	SL		*(quoted after
Victoria	Vic.		score)
West Australia	W.Aus.	played	Pl.
West Indies	W.I. or W.Ind.	south	S.
		stumped	st.
General		tied	T.
average	Av.	wickets	wkts.
caught	ct.	won	W.
declared	dec.		

Test Match Results and Records

England v Australia

Season	Country	Pl.	W. by E.	W. by A.	D.
1876–77	Aus.	2	1	1	0
1878–79	Aus.	1	0	1	0
1880	Eng.	1	1	0	0
1881–82	Aus.	4	0	2	2
1882	Eng.	1	0	1	0
1882–83	Aus.	4	2	2	0
1884	Eng	3	1	0	2
1884–85	Aus.	5	3	2	0
1886	Eng.	3	3	0	0
1886–87	Aus.	2	2	0	0
1887–88	Aus.	1	1	0	0
1888	Eng.	3	2	1	0
1890	Eng.	2	2	0	0
1891–92	Aus.	3	1	2	0
1893	Eng.	3	1	0	2
1894–95	Aus.	5	3	2	0
1896	Eng.	3	2	1	0
1897–98	Aus.	5	1	4	0
1899	Eng.	5	0	1	4
1901–2	Aus.	5	1	4	0
1902	Eng.	5	1	2	2
1903–4	Aus.	5	3	2	0

Season	Country	Pl.	W. by E.	W. by A.	D.
1905	Eng.	5	2	0	3
1907–8	Aus.	5	1	4	0
1909	Eng.	5	1	2	2
1911–12	Aus.	5	4	1	0
1912	Eng.	3	1	0	2
1920–21	Aus.	5	0	5	0
1921	Eng.	5	0	3	2
1924–25	Aus.	5	1	4	0
1926	Eng.	5	1	0	4
1928–29	Aus.	5	4	1	0
1930	Eng.	5	1	2	2
1932–33	Aus.	5	4	1	0
1934	Eng.	5	1	2	2
1936–37	Aus.	5	2	3	0
1938	Eng.	4	1	1	2
1946–47	Aus.	5	0	3	2
1948	Eng.	5	0	4	1
1950–51	Aus.	5	1	4	0
1953	Eng.	5	1	0	4
1954–55	Aus.	5	3	1	1
1956	Eng.	5	2	1	2
1958–59	Aus.	5	0	4	1
1961	Eng.	5	1	2	2
1962–63	Aus.	5	1	1	3
1964	Eng.	5	0	1	4
1965–66	Aus.	5	1	1	3
1968	Eng.	5	1	1	3
1970–71	Aus.	6	2	0	4
1972	Eng.	5	2	2	1
1974–75	Aus.	6	1	4	1
1975	Eng.	4	0	1	3
1976–77	Aus.	1	0	1	0
1977	Eng.	5	3	0	2
1978–79	Aus.	6	5	1	0
1979–80	Aus.	3	0	3	0
1980	Eng.	1	0	0	1
1981	Eng.	6	3	1	2
In England		117	34	29	54
In Australia		129	48	64	17
		246	82	93	71

England v. South Africa

Season	Country	Pl.	W. by E.	W. by S.A.	D.
1888–89	S.A.	2	2	0	0
1891–92	S.A.	1	1	0	0
1895–96	S.A.	3	3	0	0
1898–99	S.A.	2	2	0	0
1905–6	S.A.	5	1	4	0
1907	Eng.	3	1	0	2
1909–10	S.A.	5	2	3	0
1912	Eng.	3	3	0	0
1913–14	S.A.	5	4	0	1
1922–23	S.A.	5	2	1	2
1924	Eng.	5	3	0	2

Season	Country	Pl.	W. by E.	W. by S.A.	D.
1927–28	S.A.	5	2	2	1
1929	Eng.	5	2	0	3
1930–31	S.A.	5	0	1	4
1935	Eng.	5	0	1	4
1938–39	S.A.	5	1	0	4
1947	Eng.	5	3	0	2
1948–49	S.A.	5	2	0	3
1951	Eng.	5	3	1	1
1955	Eng.	5	3	2	0
1956–57	S.A.	5	2	2	1
1960	Eng.	5	3	0	2
1964-65	S.A.	5	1	0	4
1965	Eng.	3	0	1	2
In England		44	21	5	18
In S.Africa		58	25	13	20
		102	46	18	38

England v West Indies

Season	Country	Pl.	W. by E.	W. by W.I.	D.
1928	Eng.	3	3	0	0
1929–30	W.Ind.	4	1	1	2
1933	Eng.	3	2	0	1
1934–35	W.Ind.	4	1	2	1
1939	Eng.	3	1	0	2
1947–48	W.Ind.	4	0	2	2
1950	Eng.	4	1	3	0
1953–54	W.Ind.	5	2	2	1
1957	Eng.	5	3	0	2
1959–60	W. Ind.	5	1	0	4
1963	Eng.	5	1	3	1
1966	Eng.	5	1	3	1
1967–68	W. Ind.	5	1	0	4
1969	Eng.	3	2	0	1
1973	Eng.	3	0	2	1
1973–74	W. Ind.	5	1	1	3
1976	Eng.	5	0	3	2
1980	Eng.	5	0	1	4
1980–81	W. Ind.	4	0	2	2
In England		44	14	15	15
In W. Indies		36	7	10	19
		80	21	25	34

England v New Zealand

Season	Country	Pl.	W. by E.	W. by N.Z.	D.
1929–30	N.Z.	4	1	0	3
1931	Eng.	3	1	0	2
1932–33	N.Z.	2	0	0	2
1937	Eng.	3	1	0	2
1946–47	N.Z.	1	0	0	1
1949	Eng.	4	0	0	4

Season	Country	Pl.	W. by E.	W. by N.Z.	D.
1950–51	N.Z.	2	1	0	1
1954–55	N.Z.	2	2	0	0
1958	Eng.	5	4	0	1
1958–59	N.Z.	2	1	0	1
1962–63	N.Z.	3	3	0	0
1965	Eng.	3	3	0	0
1965–66	N.Z.	3	0	0	3
1969	Eng.	3	2	0	1
1970–71	N.Z.	2	1	0	1
1973	Eng.	3	2	0	1
1974–75	N.Z.	2	1	0	1
1977–78	N.Z.	3	1	1	1
1978	Eng.	3	3	0	0
In England		27	16	0	11
In N. Zealand		26	11	1	14
		53	27	1	25

England v India

Season	Country	Pl.	W. by E.	W. by I.	D.
1932	Eng.	1	1	0	0
1933–34	Ind.	3	2	0	1
1936	Eng.	3	2	0	1
1946	Eng.	3	1	0	2
1951–52	Ind.	5	1	1	3
1952	Eng.	4	3	0	1
1959	Eng.	5	5	0	0
1961–62	Ind.	5	0	2	3
1963–64	Ind.	5	0	0	5
1967	Eng.	3	3	0	0
1971	Eng.	3	0	1	2
1972–73	Ind.	5	1	2	2
1974	Eng.	3	3	0	0
1976–77	Ind.	5	3	1	1
1979	Eng.	4	1	0	3
1979–80	Ind.	1	1	0	0
1981–82	Ind.	6	0	1	5
1982	Eng.	3	1	0	2
In England		32	20	1	11
In India		35	8	7	20
		67	28	8	31

England v Pakistan

Season	Country	Pl.	W. by E.	W. by P.	D.
1954	Eng.	4	1	1	2
1961–62	Pak.	3	1	0	2
1962	Eng.	5	4	0	1
1967	Eng.	3	2	0	1
1968–69	Pak.	3	0	0	3
1971	Eng.	3	1	0	2
1972–73	Pak.	3	0	0	3
1974	Eng.	3	0	0	3

Season	Country	Pl.	W. by E.	W. by P.	D.
1977–78	Pak.	3	0	0	3
1978	Eng.	3	2	0	1
1982	Eng.	3	2	1	0
In England		24	12	2	10
In Pakistan		12	1	0	11
		36	13	2	21

England v Sri Lanka

Season	Country	Pl.	W. by E.	W. by S.L.	D.
1981–82	S.L.	1	1	0	0

Australia v South Africa

Season	Country	Pl.	W. by A.	W. by S.A.	D.
1902–3	S.A.	3	2	0	1
1910–11	Aus.	5	4	1	0
1912	Eng.	3	2	0	1
1921–22	S.A.	3	1	0	2
1931–32	Aus.	5	5	0	0
1935–36	S.A.	5	4	0	1
1949–50	S.A.	5	4	0	1
1952–53	Aus.	5	2	2	1
1957–58	S.A.	5	3	0	2
1963–64	Aus.	5	1	1	3
1966–67	S.A.	5	1	3	1
1969–70	S.A.	4	0	4	0
In Australia		20	12	4	4
In S. Africa		30	15	7	8
In England		3	2	0	1
		53	29	11	13

Australia v West Indies

Season	Country	Pl.	W. by A.	W. by W.I.	D.	T.
1930–31	Aus.	5	4	1	0	0
1951–52	Aus.	5	4	1	0	0
1954–55	W. Ind.	5	3	0	2	0
1960–61	Aus.	5	2	1	1	1
1964–65	W. Ind.	5	1	2	2	0
1968–69	Aus.	5	3	1	1	0
1972–73	W. Ind.	5	2	0	3	0
1975–76	Aus.	6	5	1	0	0
1977–78	W. Ind.	5	1	3	1	0
1979–80	Aus.	3	0	2	1	0
1981–82	Aus.	3	1	1	1	0
In Australia		32	19	8	4	1
In W. Indies		20	7	5	8	0
		52	26	13	12	1

Australia v New Zealand

Season	Country	Pl.	W. by A.	W. by N.Z.	D.
1945–46	N.Z.	1	1	0	0
1973–74	Aus.	3	2	0	1
1973–74	N.Z.	3	1	1	1
1976–77	N.Z.	2	1	0	1
1980–81	Aus.	3	2	0	1
1981–82	N.Z.	3	1	1	1
In Australia		6	4	0	2
In N. Zealand		9	4	2	3
		15	8	2	5

Australia v India

Season	Country	Pl.	W. by A.	W. by I.	D.
1947–48	Aus.	5	4	0	1
1956–57	Ind.	3	2	0	1
1959–60	Ind.	5	2	1	2
1964–65	Ind.	3	1	1	1
1967–68	Aus.	4	4	0	0
1969–70	Ind.	5	3	1	1
1977–78	Aus.	5	3	2	0
1979–80	Ind.	6	0	2	4
1980–81	Aus.	3	1	1	1
In Australia		17	12	3	2
In India		22	8	5	9
		39	20	8	11

Australia v Pakistan

Season	Country	Pl.	W. by A.	W. by P.	D.
1956–57	Pak.	1	0	1	0
1959–60	Pak.	3	2	0	1
1964–65	Pak.	1	0	0	1
1964–65	Aus.	1	0	0	1
1972–73	Aus.	3	3	0	0
1976–77	Aus.	3	1	1	1
1978–79	Aus.	2	1	1	0
1979–80	Pak.	3	0	1	2
1981–82	Aus.	3	2	1	0
In Australia		12	7	3	2
In Pakistan		8	2	2	4
		20	9	5	6

South Africa v New Zealand

Season	Country	Pl.	W. by S.A.	W. by N.Z.	D.
1931–32	N.Z.	2	2	0	0
1952–53	N.Z.	2	1	0	1
1953–54	S.A.	5	4	0	1
1961–62	S.A.	5	2	2	1
1963–64	N.Z.	3	0	0	3
In S. Africa		10	6	2	2
In N. Zealand		7	3	0	4
		17	9	2	6

West Indies v New Zealand

Season	Country	Pl.	W. by W.I.	W. by N.Z.	D.
1951–52	N.Z.	2	1	0	1
1955–56	N.Z.	4	3	1	0
1968–69	N.Z.	3	1	1	1
1971–72	W. Ind.	5	0	0	5
1979–80	N.Z.	3	0	1	2
In W. Indies		5	0	0	5
In N. Zealand		12	5	3	4
		17	5	3	9

West Indies v India

Season	Country	Pl.	W. by W.I.	W. by I.	D.
1948–49	Ind.	5	1	0	4
1952–53	W. Ind	5	1	0	4
1958–59	Ind.	5	3	0	2
1961–62	W. Ind.	5	5	0	0
1966–67	Ind.	3	2	0	1
1970–71	W. Ind.	5	0	1	4
1974–75	Ind.	5	3	2	0
1975–76	W. Ind.	4	2	1	1
1978–79	Ind.	6	0	1	5
In W. Indies		19	8	2	9
In India		24	9	3	12
		43	17	5	21

West Indies v Pakistan

Season	Country	Pl.	W. by W.I.	W. by P.	D.
1957–58	W. Ind.	5	3	1	1
1958–59	Pak.	3	1	2	0
1974–75	Pak.	2	0	0	2

Season	Country	Pl.	W. by W.I.	W. by P.	D.
1976–77	W. Ind.	5	2	1	2
1980–81	Pak.	3	1	0	2
In W. Indies		10	5	2	3
In Pakistan		8	2	2	4
		18	7	4	7

New Zealand v India

Season	Country	Pl.	W. by N.Z.	W. by I.	D.
1955–56	Ind.	5	0	2	3
1964–65	Ind.	4	0	1	3
1967–68	N.Z.	4	1	3	0
1969–70	Ind.	3	1	1	1
1975–76	N.Z.	3	1	1	1
1976–77	Ind.	3	0	2	1
1980–81	N.Z.	3	1	0	2
In N. Zealand		10	3	4	3
In India		15	1	6	8
		25	4	10	11

New Zealand v Pakistan

Season	Country	Pl.	W. by N.Z.	W. by P.	D.
1955–56	Pak.	3	0	2	1
1964–65	N.Z.	3	0	0	3
1964–65	Pak.	3	0	2	1
1969–70	Pak.	3	1	0	2
1972–73	N.Z.	3	0	1	2
1976–77	Pak.	3	0	2	1
1978–79	N.Z.	3	0	1	2
In N. Zealand		9	0	2	7
In Pakistan		12	1	6	5
		21	1	8	12

India v Pakistan

Season	Country	Pl.	W. by I.	W. by P.	D.
1952–53	Ind.	5	2	1	2
1954–55	Pak.	5	0	0	5
1960–61	Ind.	5	0	0	5
1978–79	Pak.	3	0	2	1
1979–80	Ind.	6	2	0	4
In India		16	4	1	11
In Pakistan		8	0	2	6
		24	4	3	17

Pantag{Pakistan v Sri Lanka}

Pakistan v Sri Lanka

Season	Country	Pl.	W. by P.	W. by S.L.	D.
1981–82	Pak.	3	2	0	1

Summary of Test Match Results

	Pl.	W.	L.	D.	T.
England	585	218	147	220	0
Australia	425	185	121	118	1
S. Africa	172	38	77	57	0
W. Indies	210	67	59	83	1
N. Zealand	148	13	67	68	0
India	198	35	72	91	0
Pakistan	122	24	34	64	0
Sri Lanka	4	0	3	1	0
	1864	580	580	702	2

Highest Innings Totals

903–7 (dec)	Eng. v Aus. (Oval)	1938
849	Eng. v W. Ind. (Kingston)	1929–30
790–3 (dec)	W. Ind. v Pak. (Kingston)	1957–58
758–8 (dec)	Aus. v W. Ind. (Kingston)	1954–55
729–6 (dec)	Aus. v Eng. (Lord's)	1930
701	Aus. v Eng. (Oval)	1934
695	Aus. v Eng. (Oval)	1930
687–8 (dec)	W. Ind. v Eng. (Oval)	1976
681–8 (dec)	W. Ind. v Eng. (Port of Spain)	1953–54
674	Aus. v Ind. (Adelaide)	1947–48
668	Aus. v W. Ind. (Bridgetown)	1954–55
659–8 (dec)	Aus. v Eng. (Sydney)	1946–47
658–8 (dec)	Eng. v Aus. (Nottingham)	1938
657–8 (dec)	Pak. v W. Ind. (Bridgetown)	1957–58
656–8 (dec)	Aus. v Eng. (Manchester)	1964
654–5	Eng. v S. Africa (Durban)	1938–39
652–8 (dec)	W. Ind. v Eng. (Lord's)	1973
650–6 (dec)	Aus. v W. Ind. (Bridgetown)	1964–65
645	Aus. v Eng. (Brisbane)	1946–47
644–7 (dec)	Ind. v W. Ind. (Kanpur)	1978–79
644–8 (dec)	W. Ind. v Ind. (New Delhi)	1958–59
636	Eng. v Aus. (Sydney)	1928–29
633–5 (dec)	Eng. v Ind. (Birmingham)	1979
631–8 (dec)	W. Ind. v Ind. (Kingston)	1961–62
631	W. Ind. v Ind. (New Delhi)	1948–49
629–6 (dec)	W. Ind. v Ind. (Bombay)	1948–49
629	Eng. v Ind. (Lord's)	1974
627–9 (dec)	Eng. v Aus. (Manchester)	1934
622–9 (dec)	S. Africa v Aus. (Durban)	1969–70
620	S. Africa v Aus. (Johannesburg)	1966–67
619–6 (dec)	Eng. v W. Ind. (Nottingham)	1957
619	Aus. v W. Ind. (Sydney)	1968–69
617	Aus. v Pak. (Faisalabad)	1979–80
616	W. Ind. v Aus. (Adelaide)	1968–69

614–5 (dec)	W. Ind. v Ind. (Calcutta)	1958–59
611	Eng. v Aus. (Manchester)	1964
608–7 (dec)	Pak. v Eng. (Birmingham)	1971
608	Eng. v S. Africa (Johannesburg)	1948–49
604–6 (dec)	W. Ind. v Ind. (Bombay)	1974–75
604	Aus. v Eng. (Melbourne)	1936–37
601–8 (dec)	Aus. v Eng. (Brisbane)	1954–55
600–7 (dec)	Pak. v Eng. (Oval)	1974
600–9 (dec)	Aus. v W. Ind. (Port of Spain)	1954–55
600	Aus. v Eng. (Melbourne)	1924–25

The highest innings totals by other countries are:

551–9 (dec)	N. Zealand v Eng. (Lord's)	1973

Lowest Innings Totals

26	N. Zealand v Eng. (Auckland)	1954–55
30	S. Africa v Eng. (Port Elizabeth)	1895–96
30	S. Africa v Eng. (Birmingham)	1924
35	S. Africa v Eng. (Cape Town)	1898–99
36	Aus. v Eng. (Birmingham)	1902
36	S. Africa v Aus. (Melbourne)	1931–32
42	Aus. v Eng. (Sydney)	1887–88
42	N. Zealand v Aus. (Wellington)	1945–46
42	Ind. v Eng. (Lord's)	1974
43	S. Africa v Eng. (Cape Town)	1888–89
44	Aus. v Eng. (Oval)	1896
45	Eng. v Aus. (Sydney)	1886–87
45	S. Africa v Aus. (Melbourne)	1931–32
47	S. Africa v Eng. (Cape Town)	1888–89
47	N. Zealand v Eng. (Lord's)	1958
52	Eng. v Aus. (Oval)	1948
53	Eng. v Aus. (Lord's)	1888
53	Aus. v Eng. (Lord's)	1896
54	N. Zealand v Aus. (Wellington)	1945–46
58	S. Africa v Eng. (Lord's)	1912
58	Aus. v Eng. (Brisbane)	1936–37
58	Ind. v Aus. (Brisbane)	1947–48
58	Ind. v Eng. (Manchester)	1952
60	Aus. v Eng. (Lord's)	1888

The lowest innings totals by other countries are:

76	W. Ind. v Pak. (Dacca)	1958–59
87	Pak. v Eng. (Lord's)	1954

The following innings closed at a low total:

32–7 (dec)	Aus. v Eng. (Brisbane)	1950–51
35–8	Aus. v Eng. (Manchester)	1953
48–8	N. Zealand v Eng. (Christchurch)	1965–66
51–6 (dec)	W. Indies v Eng. (Bridgetown)	1934–35

In the following matches, one side was dismissed twice for an aggregate of less than 100:

81 (36 & 45)	S. Africa v Aus. (Melbourne)	1931–32
90 (47 & 43)	S. Africa v Eng. (Cape Town)	1888–89
96 (42 & 54)	N. Zealand v Aus. (Wellington)	1945–46

Highest Match Aggregates

1981 for 35 wkts	S. Africa v Eng. (Durban)		1938–39
1815 „ 34 „	W. Indies v Eng. (Kingston)		1929–30
1764 „ 39 „	Aus. v W. Indies (Adelaide)		1968–69
1753 „ 40 „	Aus. v Eng. (Adelaide)		1920–21
1723 „ 31 „	Eng. v Aus. (Leeds)		1948
1661 „ 36 „	W. Indies v Aus. (Bridgetown)		1954–55
1646 „ 40 „	Aus. v S. Africa (Adelaide)		1910–11
1644 „ 38 „	Aus. v W. Indies (Sydney)		1968–69
1640 „ 24 „	W. Indies v Aus. (Bridgetown)		1964–65
1640 „ 33 „	Aus. v Pak. (Melbourne)		1972–73
1619 „ 40 „	Aus. v Eng. (Melbourne)		1924–25
1611 „ 40 „	Aus. v Eng. (Sydney)		1924–25
1601 „ 29 „	Eng. v Aus. (Lord's)		1930

Lowest Match Aggregates
(completed matches)

234 for 29 wkts	Aus. v S. Africa (Melbourne)		1931–32
291 „ 40 „	Eng. v Aus. (Lord's)		1888
295 „ 28 „	N. Zealand v Aus. (Wellington)		1945–46
309 „ 40 „	W. Indies v Eng. (Bridgetown)		1934–35
323 „ 30 „	Eng. v Aus. (Manchester)		1888
363 „ 40 „	Eng. v Aus. (Oval)		1882
374 „ 40 „	Aus. v Eng. (Sydney)		1887–88
378 „ 30 „	Eng. v S. Africa (Oval)		1912
382 „ 30 „	S. Africa v Eng. (Cape Town)		1888–89
389 „ 38 „	Eng. v Aus. (Oval)		1890
390 „ 30 „	Eng. v N. Zealand (Lord's)		1958
392 „ 40 „	Eng. v Aus. (Oval)		1896

Biggest Victories

Inns. & 579 runs	Eng. v Aus. (Oval)	1938
„ „ 336 „	W. Indies v India (Calcutta)	1958–59
„ „ 332 „	Aus. v Eng. (Brisbane)	1946–47
„ „ 285 „	Eng. v Ind. (Lord's)	1974
„ „ 259 „	Aus. v S. Africa (Port Elizabeth)	1949–50
„ „ 237 „	Eng. v W. Indies (Oval)	1957
„ „ 230 „	Eng. v Aus. (Adelaide)	1891–92
„ „ 226 „	Aus. v India (Brisbane)	1947–48
„ „ 226 „	W. Indies v Eng. (Lord's)	1973
„ „ 225 „	Eng. v Aus. (Melbourne)	1911–12
„ „ 217 „	Eng. v Aus. (Oval)	1886
„ „ 217 „	Aus. v W. Indies (Brisbane)	1930–31
„ „ 215 „	Eng. v N. Zealand (Auckland)	1962–63
„ „ 207 „	Eng. v India (Manchester)	1952
„ „ 202 „	Eng. v S. Africa (Cape Town)	1888–89
„ „ 200 „	Aus. v Eng. (Melbourne)	1936–37
675 runs	Eng. v Aus. (Brisbane)	1928–29
562 „	Aus. v Eng. (Oval)	1934
530 „	Aus. v S. Africa (Melbourne)	1910–11
425 „	W. Indies v Eng. (Manchester)	1976

409	„	Aus. v Eng. (Lord's)	1948
408	„	W. Indies v Aus. (Adelaide)	1979–80
382	„	Aus. v Eng. (Adelaide)	1894–95
382	„	Aus. v W. Indies (Sydney)	1968–69
377	„	Aus. v Eng. (Sydney)	1920–21
365	„	Aus. v Eng. (Melbourne)	1936–37

Closest Finishes

Tie		Aus. v W. Indies (Brisbane)	1960–61
3 runs		Aus. v Eng. (Manchester)	1902
6	„	Aus. v Eng. (Sydney)	1884–85
7	„	Aus. v Eng. (Oval)	1882
1 wicket		Eng. v Aus. (Oval)	1902
1	„	S. Africa v Eng. (Johannesburg)	1905–6
1	„	Eng. v Aus. (Melbourne)	1907–8
1	„	Eng. v S. Africa (Cape Town)	1922–23
1	„	Aus. v W. Indies (Melbourne)	1951–52
1	„	N. Zealand v W. Indies (Dunedin)	1979–80

India, set 361 to win, scored 355–8 v W. Indies (Bombay) 1948–49.
England, set 234 to win, scored 228–9 v W. Indies (Lord's) 1963.
Australia, set 246 to win, scored 238–8 v England (Melbourne) 1974–75.
England beat S. Africa by two wickets at Durban, 1948–49, by scoring a leg-bye off the
last possible ball.
W. Indies beat England by 217 runs at Port of Spain, 1934–35, by taking the last wicket
with the fifth ball of the last possible over.

Longest Matches

| 10 days | | S. Africa v Eng. (Durban) | 1938–39 |
| 9 | „ | W. Indies v Eng. (Kingston) | 1929–30 |

In both matches, it had been arranged to play to a finish, but the match was left drawn
when the English team had to catch the boat home.

Winning Every Match in a Series

Five matches	Aus. v Eng. in Aus.	1920–21
	Aus. v S. Africa in Aus.	1931–32
	Eng. v India in Eng.	1959
	W. Indies v India in W. Indies	1961–62
Four matches	Aus. v India in Aus.	1967–68
	S. Africa v Aus. in S. Africa	1969–70

Most Consecutive Victories

8	Aus.: Sydney 1920–21 to Leeds 1921
7	Eng.: Melbourne 1884–85 to Sydney 1887–88
7	Eng.: Lord's 1928 to Adelaide 1928–29

Most Consecutive Defeats

8	S. Africa:	Port Elizabeth 1888–89 to Cape Town 1898–99
8	Eng.:	Sydney 1920–21 to Leeds 1921
7	Aus.:	Melbourne 1884–85 to Sydney 1887–88
7	Eng.:	Lord's 1950 to Adelaide 1950–51
7	India:	Leeds 1967 to Sydney 1967–68

Most Consecutive Matches Without Defeat

26	Eng.: Lord's 1968 to Manchester 1971
25	Aus.: Wellington 1945–46 to Adelaide 1950–51

Most Consecutive Matches Without Victory

44	N. Zealand: Christchurch 1929–30 to Wellington 1955–56
28	S. Africa: Leeds 1935 to Port Elizabeth 1949–50

Highest Individual Scores

365*	G. S. Sobers: W. Ind. v Pak. (Kingston)	1957–58
364	L. Hutton: Eng. v Aus. (Oval)	1938
337	Hanif Mohammad: Pak. v W. Indies (Bridgetown)	1957–58
336*	W. R. Hammond: Eng. v N. Zealand (Auckland)	1932–33
334	D. G. Bradman: Aus. v Eng. (Leeds)	1930
325	A. Sandham: Eng. v W. Indies (Kingston)	1929–30
311	R. B. Simpson: Aus. v Eng. (Manchester)	1964
310*	J. H. Edrich: Eng. v N. Zealand (Leeds)	1965
307	R. M. Cowper: Aus. v Eng. (Melbourne)	1965–66
304	D. G. Bradman: Aus. v Eng. (Leeds)	1934
302	L. G. Rowe: W. Ind. v Eng. (Bridgetown)	1973–74
299*	D. G. Bradman: Aus. v S. Africa (Adelaide)	1931–32
291	I. V. A. Richards: W. Ind. v Eng. (Oval)	1976
287	R. E. Foster: Eng. v Aus. (Sydney)	1903–4
285*	P. B. H. May: Eng. v W. Indies (Birmingham)	1957
278	D. C. S. Compton: Eng. v Pak. (Nottingham)	1954
274	R. G. Pollock: S. Africa v Aus. (Durban)	1969–70
274	Zaheer Abbas: Pak. v Eng. (Birmingham)	1971
270*	G. A. Headley: W. Indies v Eng. (Kingston)	1934–35
270	D. G. Bradman: Aus. v Eng. (Melbourne)	1936–37
266	W. H. Ponsford: Aus. v Eng. (Oval)	1934
262*	D. L. Amiss: Eng. v W. Ind. (Kingston)	1973–74
261	F. M. Worrell: W. Indies v Eng. (Nottingham)	1950
260	C. C. Hunte: W. Indies v Pak. (Kingston)	1957–58
259	G. M. Turner: N. Zealand v W. Indies (Georgetown)	1971–72
258	T. W. Graveney: Eng. v W. Indies (Nottingham)	1957
258	S. M. Nurse: W. Indies v N. Zealand (Christchurch)	1968–69
256	R. B. Kanhai: W. Indies v India (Calcutta)	1958–59
256	K. F. Barrington: Eng. v Aus. (Manchester)	1964
255*	D. J. McGlew: S. Africa v N. Zealand (Wellington)	1952–53
254	D. G. Bradman: Aus. v Eng. (Lord's)	1930

251	W. R. Hammond: Eng. v Aus. (Sydney)	1928–29
250	K. D. Walters: Aus. v N. Zealand (Christchurch)	1976–77
250	S. F. A. F. Bacchus: W. Indies v India (Kanpur)	1978–79

The highest individual score for India is:

| 231 | V. Mankad: India v N. Zealand (Madras) | 1955–56 |

Most Runs In A Series

			M.	I.	N.O.	Runs	H.S.	Av.	100s	50s
D.G. Bradman	A. v E.	1930	5	7	0	974	334	139·14	4	0
W.R. Hammond	E. v A.	1928–29	5	9	1	905	251	113·12	4	0
R.N. Harvey	A. v S.A.	1952–53	5	9	0	834	205	92·66	4	3
I.V.A. Richards	W.I. v E.	1976	4	7	0	829	291	118·42	3	2
C.L. Walcott	W.I. v A.	1954–55	5	10	0	827	155	82·70	5	2
G.S. Sobers	W.I. v P.	1957–58	5	8	2	824	365*	137·33	3	3
D.G. Bradman	A. v E.	1936–37	5	9	0	810	270	90·00	3	1
D.G. Bradman	A. v S.A.	1931–32	5	5	1	806	299*	201·50	4	0
E.D. Weekes	W.I. v I.	1948–49	5	7	0	779	194	111·28	4	2
S.M. Gavaskar	I. v W.I.	1970–71	4	8	3	774	220	154·80	4	3
D.G. Bradman	A. v E.	1934	5	8	0	758	304	94·75	2	1
D.C.S. Compton	E. v S.A.	1947	5	8	0	753	208	94·12	4	2
H. Sutcliffe	E. v A.	1924–25	5	9	0	734	176	81·55	4	2
G.A. Faulkner	S.A. v A.	1910–11	5	10	0	732	204	73·20	2	5
S.M. Gavaskar	I. v W.I.	1978–79	6	9	1	732	205	91·50	4	1
G.S. Sobers	W.I. v E.	1966	5	8	1	722	174	103·14	3	2
E.D. Weekes	W.I. v I.	1952–53	5	8	1	716	207	102·28	3	2
D.G. Bradman	A. v I.	1947–48	5	6	2	715	201	178·75	4	1
G.S. Sobers	W.I. v E.	1959–60	5	8	1	709	226	101·28	3	1
G.A. Headley	W.I. v E.	1929–30	4	8	0	703	223	87·87	4	0
G.S. Chappell	A. v W.I.	1975–76	6	11	5	702	182*	117·00	3	3

The most for other countries are:

| G.M. Turner | N.Z. v W.I. | 1971–72 | 5 | 8 | 1 | 672 | 259 | 96·00 | 2 | 2 |
| Hanif Mohammed | P. v W.I. | 1957–58 | 5 | 9 | 0 | 628 | 337 | 69·77 | 1 | 3 |

Highest Run Aggregates

		Tests	Inns	N.O.	Runs	H.S.	Av.	100s	50s
G. Boycott	E.	108	193	23	8114	246*	47·72	22	42
G.S. Sobers	W.I.	93	160	21	8032	365*	57·78	26	30
M.C. Cowdrey	E.	114	188	15	7624	182	44·06	22	38
W.R. Hammond	E.	85	140	16	7249	336*	58·45	22	24
D.G. Bradman	A.	52	80	10	6996	334	99·94	29	13
L. Hutton	E.	79	138	15	6971	364	56·67	19	33
K.F. Barrington	E.	82	131	15	6806	256	58·67	20	35
S.M. Gavaskar	I.	78	137	9	6792	221	53·06	24	30
G.S. Chappell	A.	76	134	16	6291	247*	53·31	20	29
R.B. Kanhai	W.I.	79	137	6	6227	256	47·23	15	28
R.N. Harvey	A.	79	137	10	6149	205	48·42	21	24
G.R. Viswanath	I.	84	145	10	5935	222	43·96	14	34
C.H. Lloyd	W.I.	85	143	10	5831	242*	43·84	14	30
D.C.S. Compton	E.	78	131	15	5807	278	50·06	17	28

		Tests	Inns	N.O.	Runs	H.S.	Av.	100s	50s
J.B. Hobbs	E.	61	102	7	5410	211	56·94	15	28
K.D. Walters	A.	74	125	14	5357	250	48·26	15	30
I.M. Chappell	A.	75	136	10	5345	196	42·42	14	25
W.M. Lawry	A.	67	123	12	5234	210	47·15	13	27
J.H. Edrich	E.	77	127	9	5138	310*	43·54	12	24
T.W. Graveney	E.	79	123	13	4882	258	44·38	11	20
R.B. Simpson	A.	62	111	7	4869	311	46·81	10	27
I.R. Redpath	A.	66	120	11	4737	171	43·45	8	31
H. Sutcliffe	E.	54	84	9	4555	194	60·73	16	23
P.B.H. May	E.	66	106	9	4537	285*	46·77	13	22
E.R. Dexter	E.	62	102	8	4502	205	47·89	9	27
E.D. Weekes	W.I.	48	81	5	4455	207	58·61	15	19
A.I. Kallicharran	W.I.	66	109	10	4399	187	44·43	12	21
A.P.E. Knott	E.	95	149	15	4389	135	32·75	5	30
R.C. Fredericks	W.I.	59	109	7	4334	169	42·49	8	26
I.V.A. Richards	W.I.	47	74	4	4129	291	58·98	13	17
Majid Khan	P.	62	105	5	3931	167	39·31	8	19

The highest for other countries are:

		Tests	Inns	N.O.	Runs	H.S.	Av.	100s	50s
B. Mitchell	S.A.	42	80	9	3471	189*	48·88	8	21
B.E. Congdon	N.Z.	61	114	7	3448	176	32·22	7	19

Most Centuries

D.G. Bradman	A.	29
G.S. Sobers	W.I.	26
S.M. Gavaskar	I.	24
G. Boycott	E.	22
M.C. Cowdrey	E.	22
W.R. Hammond	E.	22
R.N. Harvey	A.	21
K.F. Barrington	E.	20
G.S. Chappell	A.	20

Record Wicket Partnerships

1st	413	V. Mankad (231) & P. Roy (173): Ind. v N. Zealand (Madras)	1955–56
2nd	451	W.H. Ponsford (266) & D.G. Bradman (244): Aus. v Eng. (Oval)	1934
3rd	370	W.J. Edrich (189) & D.C.S. Compton (208): Eng. v S. Africa (Lord's)	1947
4th	411	P.B.H. May (285*) & M.C. Cowdrey (154): Eng. v W. Indies (Birmingham)	1957
5th	405	S.G. Barnes (234) & D.G. Bradman (234): Aus. v Eng. (Sydney)	1946–47
6th	346	J.H. Fingleton (136) & D.G. Bradman (270): Aus. v Eng. (Melbourne)	1936–37
7th	347	D. Atkinson (219) & C.C. Depeiaza (122): W. Ind. v Aus. (Bridgetown)	1954–55
8th	246	L.E.G. Ames (137) & G.O. Allen (122): Eng. v N. Zealand (Lord's)	1931
9th	190	Asif Iqbal (146) & Intikhab Alam (51): Pak. v Eng. (Oval)	1967
10th	151	B.F. Hastings (110) & R.O. Collinge (68*): N. Zealand v Pak. (Auckland)	1972–73

Century on Test Debut

118	L. Amarnath	Ind. v Eng. (Bombay)	1933–34
124	S. Amarnath	Ind. v N.Z. (Auckland)	1975–76
105*	L. Baichan	W. Ind. v Pak. (Lahore)	1974–75
112	A.A. Baig	Ind. v Eng. (Manchester)	1959
165*	C. Bannerman,	Aus. v Eng. (Melbourne)	1876–77
101*	J.W. Burke	Aus. v Eng. (Adelaide)	1950–51
108	G.S. Chappell	Aus. v Eng. (Perth)	1970–71
104	H.L. Collins	Aus. v Eng. (Sydney)	1920–21
109	G.J. Cosier	Aus. v W. Ind. (Melbourne)	1975–76
104	R.A. Duff	Aus. v Eng. (Melbourne)	1901–2
287	R.E. Foster	Eng. v Aus. (Sydney)	1903–4
112	A.G. Ganteaume	W. Ind. v Eng. (Port of Spain)	1947–48
106	P.A. Gibb	Eng. v S. Africa (Johannesburg)	1938–39
152	W.G. Grace	Eng. v Aus. (Oval)	1880
107	H. Graham	Aus. v Eng. (Lord's)	1893
107	C.G. Greenidge	W. Ind. v Ind. (Bangalore)	1974–75
140	S.C. Griffith	Eng. v W. Ind. (Port of Spain)	1947–48
119	G. Gunn	Eng. v Aus. (Sydney)	1907–8
107	J.H. Hampshire	Eng. v W. Ind. (Lord's)	1969
105	Hanumant Singh	Ind. v Eng. (New Delhi)	1963–64
116	R.J. Hartigan	Aus. v Eng. (Adelaide)	1907–8
106*	F.C. Hayes	Eng. v W. Ind. (Oval)	1973
176	G.A. Headley	W. Ind. v Eng. (Bridgetown)	1929–30
142	C.C. Hunte	W. Ind. v Pak. (Bridgetown)	1957–58
166	K. Ibadulla	Pak. v Aus. (Karachi)	1964–65
164	A. Jackson	Aus. v Eng. (Adelaide)	1928–29
163	Javed Miandad	Pak. v N.Z. (Lahore)	1976–77
100*	A.I. Kallicharran	W. Ind. v N.Z. (Georgetown)	1971–72
100*	A.G. Kripal Singh	Ind. v N. Zealand (Hyderabad)	1955–56
138	P.B.H. May	Eng. v S. Africa (Leeds)	1951
117	J.E. Mills	N. Zealand v Eng. (Wellington)	1929–30
104*	C.A. Milton	Eng. v N. Zealand (Leeds)	1958
115	B.H. Pairaudeau	W. Ind. v Ind. (Port of Spain)	1952–53
102	Nawab of Pataudi, sr.	Eng. v Aus. (Sydney)	1932–33
110	W.H. Ponsford	Aus. v Eng. (Sydney)	1924–25
154*	K.S. Ranjitsinhji	Eng. v Aus. (Manchester)	1896
107	R.E. Redmond	N.Z. v Pak. (Auckland)	1972–73
214 } 100* }	L.G. Rowe	W. Ind. v N. Zealand (Kingston)	1971–72
110	D.H. Shodhan	Ind. v Pak. (Calcutta)	1952–53
104	O.G. Smith	W. Indies v Aus. (Kingston)	1954–55
105	B.R. Taylor	N. Zealand v Ind. (Calcutta)	1964–65
136	B.H. Valentine	Eng. v Ind. (Bombay)	1933–34
137	G.R. Viswanath	Ind. v Aus. (Kanpur)	1969–70
155	K.D. Walters	Aus. v Eng. (Brisbane)	1965–66
132*	P.F. Warner	Eng v S. Africa (Johannesburg)	1898–99
103	D.M. Wellham	Aus. v Eng. (Oval)	1981
100	A.B. Williams	W. Ind. v Aus. (Georgetown)	1977–78

Century in Each Innings

136	130	W. Bardsley	Aus. v Eng. (Oval)	1909
150*	153	A.R. Border	Aus. v Pak. (Lahore)	1979–80
132	127*	D.G. Bradman	Aus. v Ind. (Melbourne)	1947–48
247*	133	G.S. Chappell	Aus. v N. Zealand (Wellington)	1973–74

123	109*	G. S. Chappell	Aus. v W. Ind. (Brisbane)	1976–77
145	121	I. M. Chappell	Aus. v N. Zealand (Wellington)	1973–74
147	103*	D. C. S. Compton	Eng. v Aus. (Adelaide)	1946–47
124	220	S. M. Gavaskar	Ind. v W. Ind. (Port of Spain)	1970–71
111	137	S. M. Gavaskar	Ind. v Pak. (Karachi)	1978–79
107	182*	S. M. Gavaskar	Ind. v W. Ind. (Calcutta)	1978–79
134	101	C. G. Greenridge	W. Ind. v Eng. (Manchester)	1976
119*	177	W. R. Hammond	Eng. v Aus. (Adelaide)	1928–29
111	104	Hanif Mohammad	Pak. v Eng. (Dacca)	1961–62
116	145	V. S. Hazare	Ind. v Aus. (Adelaide)	1947–48
114	112	G. A. Headley	W. Ind. v Eng. (Georgetown)	1929–30
106	107	G. A. Headley	W. Ind. v Eng. (Lord's)	1939
122	102	G. P. Howarth	N. Zealand v Eng. (Auckland)	1977–78
117	115	R. B. Kanhai	W. Ind. v Aus. (Adelaide)	1960–61
189	104*	A. Melville	S. Africa v Eng. (Nottingham)	1947
120	189*	B. Mitchell	S. Africa v Eng. (Oval)	1947
118	101*	J. A. R. Moroney	Aus. v S. Africa (Johannesburg)	1949–50
122	124*	A. R. Morris	Aus. v Eng. (Adelaide)	1946–47
117	100	E. Paynter	Eng. v S. Africa (Johannesburg)	1938–39
214	100*	L. G. Rowe	W. Ind. v N. Zealand (Kingston)	1971–72
140	111	A. C. Russell	Eng. v S. Africa (Durban)	1922–23
153	115	R. B. Simpson	Aus. v Pak. (Karachi)	1964–65
125	109*	G. S. Sobers	W. Ind. v Pak. (Georgetown)	1957–58
176	127	H. Sutcliffe	Eng. v Aus. (Melbourne)	1924–25
104	109*	H. Sutcliffe	Eng. v S. Africa (Oval)	1929
101	110*	G. M. Turner	N. Zealand v Aus. (Christchurch)	1973–74
126	110	C. L. Walcott	W. Ind. v Aus. (Port of Spain)	1954–55
155	110	C. L. Walcott	W. Ind. v Aus. (Kingston)	1954–55
242	103	K. D. Walters	Aus. v W. Ind. (Sydney)	1968–69
162	101	E. D. Weekes	W. Ind. v Ind. (Calcutta)	1948–49

Most Centuries in Succession

5	E. D. Weekes (W.I.)	141 v Eng. (Kingston)	1947–48
		128 v Ind. (New Delhi)	1948–49
		194 v Ind. (Bombay)	1948–49
		162 } 101 } v Ind. (Calcutta)	1948–49
4	J. H. Fingleton (Aus.)	112 v S. Africa (Cape Town)	1935–36
		108 v S. Africa (Johannesburg)	1935–36
		118 v S. Africa (Durban)	1935–36
		100 v Eng. (Brisbane)	1936–37
4	A. Melville (S.A.)	103 v Eng. (Durban)	1938–39
		189 } 104* } v Eng. (Nottingham)	1947
		117 v Eng. (Lord's)	1947

Century Before Lunch

On first day

V. T. Trumper	Aus. v Eng. (Manchester)	1902
C. G. Macartney	Aus. v Eng. (Leeds)	1926
D. G. Bradman	Aus. v Eng. (Leeds)	1930
Majid Khan	Pak. v N.Z. (Karachi)	1976–77

Fastest Fifties

28 mins	J. T. Brown	Eng. v Aus. (Melbourne)	1894–95
29 ,,	S. A. Durani	Ind. v Eng. (Kanpur)	1963–64
30 ,,	E. A. V. Williams	W. Ind. v Eng. (Bridgetown)	1947–48
30 ,,	B. R. Taylor	N. Zealand v W. Ind. (Auckland)	1968–69

Fastest Centuries

70 mins	J. M. Gregory	Aus. v S. Africa (Johannesburg)	1921–22
75 ,,	G. L. Jessop	Eng. v Aus. (Oval)	1902
78 ,,	R. Benaud	Aus. v W. Ind. (Kingston)	1954–55
80 ,,	J. H. Sinclair	S. Africa v Aus. (Cape Town)	1902–3
86 ,,	B. R. Taylor	N. Zealand v W. Ind. (Auckland)	1968–69

Fastest Double Centuries

214 mins	D. G. Bradman	Aus. v Eng. (Leeds)	1930
223 ,,	S. J. McCabe	Aus. v Eng. (Nottingham)	1938
226 ,,	V. T. Trumper	Aus. v S. Africa (Adelaide)	1910–11
234 ,,	D. G. Bradman	Aus. v Eng. (Lord's)	1930
240 ,,	W. R. Hammond	Eng. v N. Zealand (Auckland)	1932–33

Most Centuries in a Series

5	C. L. Walcott		W. Ind. v Aus.	1954–55
4	D. G. Bradman	(3)	Aus. v Eng.	1930
			Aus. v S. Africa	1931–32
			Aus. v Ind.	1947–48
4	R. N. Harvey	(2)	Aus. v S. Africa	1949–50
			Aus. v S. Africa	1952–53
4	H. Sutcliffe	(2)	Eng. v Aus.	1924–25
			Eng. v S. Africa	1929
4	D. C. S. Compton		Eng. v S. Africa	1947
4	W. R. Hammond		Eng. v Aus.	1928–29
4	S. M. Gavaskar		Ind. v W. Ind.	1970–71
4	S. M. Gavaskar		Ind. v W. Ind.	1978–79
4	G. A. Headley		W. Ind. v Eng.	1929–30
4	K. D. Walters		Aus. v W. Ind.	1968–69
4	E. D. Weekes		W. Ind. v. Ind.	1948–49

Hundred and Ten Wickets in a Test Match

I. T. Botham	114 & 13–106	Eng. v Ind. (Bombay)	1979–80

Highest Wicket Aggregates

		Tests	Balls	Mdns.	Runs.	Wkts.	Av.	5w inns	10w match
D. K. Lillie	A.	63	16,478	569	7568	328	23·07	22	7
L. R. Gibbs	W.I.	79	27,115	1313	8989	309	29·09	18	2
F. S. Trueman	E.	67	15,178	522	6625	307	21·57	17	3
D. L. Underwood	E.	86	21,862	1239	7674	297	25·83	17	6
R. G. D. Willis	E.	74	14,302	440	6712	267	25·13	14	0
B. S. Bedi	I.	67	21,364	1096	7637	266	28·71	14	1
J. B. Statham	E.	70	16,056	595	6261	252	24·84	9	1
I. T. Botham	E.	54	12,767	504	5807	249	23·32	20	4
R. Benaud	A.	63	19,108	805	6704	248	27·03	16	1
G. D. McKenzie	A.	60	17,681	547	7328	246	29·78	16	3
B. S. Chandrasekhar	I.	58	15,963	585	7199	242	29·74	16	2
A. V. Bedser	E.	51	15,913	574	5876	236	24·89	15	5
G. S. Sobers	W.I.	93	21,599	974	7999	235	34·03	6	0
R. R. Lindwall	A.	61	13,650	419	5251	228	23·03	12	0
C. V. Grimmett	A.	37	14,513	735	5231	216	24·21	21	7
J. A. Snow	E.	49	12,021	415	5387	202	26·16	8	1
J. C. Laker	E.	46	12,027	674	4101	193	21·24	9	3
W. W. Hall	W.I.	48	10,421	312	5066	192	26·38	9	1
S. F. Barnes	E.	27	7,873	356	3106	189	16·43	24	7
E. A. S. Prasanna	I.	49	14,353	602	5742	189	30·38	10	2
A. K. Davidson	A.	44	11,587	431	3819	186	20·53	14	2
Imran Khan	P.	40	10,592	359	4587	179	25·62	12	2
G. A. R. Lock	E.	49	13,147	819	4451	174	25·58	9	3
A. M. E. Roberts	W.I.	40	9,674	332	4481	173	25·90	10	2
J. R. Thomson	A.	42	8,959	247	4620	172	26·86	5	0
K. R. Miller	A.	55	10,461	337	3906	170	22·97	7	1
H. J. Tayfield	S.A.	37	13,568	602	4405	170	25·91	14	2
R. J. Hadlee	N.Z.	38	9,498	271	4464	169	26·41	13	3
V. Mankad	I.	44	14,685	777	5236	162	32·32	8	2
W. A. Johnston	A.	40	11,048	372	3826	160	23·91	7	0
S. Ramadhin	W.I.	43	13,939	813	4579	158	28·98	10	1
Kapil Dev	I.	41	9,139	324	4620	157	29·42	11	1
M. W. Tate	E.	39	12,523	581	4055	155	26·16	7	1
F. J. Titmus	E.	53	15,118	777	4931	153	32·22	7	0

Most Wickets in a Series

			Tests	Balls	Mdns.	Runs	Wkts.	Av.	5w inns	10w match
S. F. Barnes	E. v S.A.	1913–14	4	1356	56	536	49	10·93	7	3
J. C. Laker	E. v A.	1956	5	1703	127	442	46	9·60	4	2
C. V. Grimmett	A. v S.A.	1935–36	5	2077	140	642	44	14·59	5	3
T. M. Alderman	A. v. Eng.	1981	6	1950	76	893	42	21·26	4	0
R. M. Hogg	A. v. E.	1978–79	6	1306	60	527	41	12·85	4	2
A. V. Bedser	E. v A.	1953	5	1591	58	682	39	17·48	5	1
D. K. Lillie	A. v E.	1981	6	1870	81	870	39	22·30	2	1
M. W. Tate	E. v A.	1924–25	5	2528	62	881	38	23·18	5	1
W. J. Whitty	A. v S.A.	1910–11	5	1395	55	632	37	17·08	2	0
H. J. Tayfield	S.A. v E.	1956–57	5	2280	105	636	37	17·18	4	1
A. E. E. Vogler	S.A. v E.	1909–10	5	1349	33	783	36	21·75	4	1
A. A. Mailey	A. v E.	1920–21	5	1465	27	946	36	26·27	4	2
G. A. Lohmann	E. v S.A.	1895–96	3	520	38	203	35	5·80	4	2
B. S. Chandrasekhar	I. v E.	1972–73	5	1747	83	662	35	18·91	4	0

Most Wickets in a Match

19–90	J. C. Laker	Eng. v Aus. (Manchester)	1956
17–159	S. F. Barnes	Eng. v S. Africa (Johannesburg)	1913–14
16–137	R. A. L. Massie	Aus. v Eng. (Lord's)	1972
15–28	J. Briggs	Eng. v S. Africa (Cape Town)	1888–89
15–45	G. A. Lohmann	Eng. v S. Africa (Port Elizabeth)	1895–96
15–99	C. Blythe	Eng. v S. Africa (Leeds)	1907
15–104	H. Verity	Eng. v Aus. (Lord's)	1934
15–124	W. Rhodes	Eng. v Aus. (Melbourne)	1903–4
14–90	F. R. Spofforth	Aus. v Eng. (Oval)	1882
14–99	A. V. Bedser	Eng. v Aus. (Nottingham)	1953
14–102	W. Bates	Eng. v Aus. (Melbourne)	1882–83
14–124	J. M. Patel	Ind. v Aus. (Kanpur)	1959–60
14–144	S. F. Barnes	Eng. v S. Africa (Durban)	1913–14
14–149	M. A. Holding	W. Ind. v Eng. (Oval)	1976
14–199	C. V. Grimmett	Aus. v S. Africa (Adelaide)	1931–32

The most for other countries are:
S. Africa—13 by H. J. Tayfield (twice); Pakistan—13 by Fazal Mahmood; N. Zealand—11 by R. J. Hadlee

Most Wickets in an Innings

10–53	J. C. Laker	Eng. v Aus. (Manchester) (2nd inns.)	1956
9–28	G. A. Lohmann	Eng. v S. Africa (Johannesburg)	1895–96
9–37	J. C. Laker	Eng. v Aus. (Manchester) (1st inns.)	1956
9–69	J. M. Patel	Ind. v Aus. (Kanpur)	1959–60
9–86	Sarfraz Nawaz	Pak. v. Aus. (Melbourne)	1978–79
9–95	J. Noreiga	W. Ind. v Ind. (Port of Spain)	1970–71
9–102	S. P. Gupte	Ind. v W. Ind. (Kanpur)	1958–59
9–103	S. F. Barnes	Eng. v S. Africa (Johannesburg)	1913–14
9–113	H. J. Tayfield	S. Africa v Eng. (Johannesburg)	1956–57
9–121	A. A. Mailey	Aus. v Eng. (Melbourne)	1920–21

The most for New Zealand are: 7 by B. R. Taylor and R. J. Hadlee.

Hat-Tricks

*M. J. C. Allom	Eng. v N. Zealand (Christchurch)	1929–30
W. Bates	Eng. v Aus. (Melbourne)	1882–83
J. Briggs	Eng. v Aus. (Sydney)	1891–92
L. R. Gibbs	W. Ind. v Aus. (Adelaide)	1960–61
T. W. J. Goddard	Eng. v S. Africa (Johannesburg)	1938–39
G. M. Griffin	S. Africa v Eng. (Lord's)	1960
W. W. Hall	W. Ind. v Pak. (Lahore)	1958–59
J. T. Hearne	Eng. v Aus. (Leeds)	1899
L. F. Kline	Aus. v S. Africa (Cape Town)	1957–58
P. J. Loader	Eng. v W. Ind. (Leeds)	1957

G. A. Lohmann	Eng. v S. Africa (Port Elizabeth)	1895–96
T. J. Matthews	Aus. v S. Africa (Manchester) (1st inns)	1912
T. J. Matthews	Aus. v S. Africa (Manchester) (2nd inns)	1912
P. J. Petherick	N. Zealand v Pak. (Lahore)	1976–77
F. R. Spofforth	Aus. v Eng. (Melbourne)	1878–79
H. Trumble	Aus. v Eng. (Melbourne)	1901–2
H. Trumble	Aus. v Eng. (Melbourne)	1903–4

*Allom took four wickets with five consecutive balls.
Note: K. Cranston (Eng. v S. Africa 1947) and F. J. Titmus (Eng. v N. Zealand 1965), both at Leeds and C. M. Old (Eng. v Pak., Birmingham, 1978) took four wickets in a six-ball over, but none did the hat-trick.

Most Wickets on Test Debut

16–137	R. A. L. Massie	Aus. v Eng. (Lord's)	1972
12–102	F. Martin	Eng. v Aus. (Oval)	1890
11–82	C. V. Grimmett	Aus. v Eng. (Sydney)	1924–25
11–96	C. S. Marriott	Eng. v Ind. (Oval)	1933
11–112	A. E. Hall	S. Africa v Eng. (Cape Town)	1922–23
11–145	A. V. Bedser	Eng. v India (Lord's)	1946
11–196	S. F. Burke	S. Africa v N. Zealand (Cape Town)	1961–62
11–204	A. L. Valentine	W. Ind. v Eng. (Manchester)	1950
10–96	H. H. H. Johnson	W. Ind. v Eng. (Kingston)	1947–48
10–156	T. Richardson	Eng. v Aus. (Manchester)	1893
10–179	K. Farnes	Eng. v Aus. (Nottingham)	1934

A Wicket With First Ball

E. G. Arnold	Eng. v Aus. (Sydney)	1903–4
A. Coningham	Aus. v Eng. (Melbourne)	1894–95
M. Henderson	N. Zealand v Eng. (Christchurch)	1929–30
R. Howorth	Eng. v S. Africa (Oval)	1947
Intikhab Alam	Pak. v Aus. (Karachi)	1959–60
T. Johnson	W. Ind. v Eng. (Oval)	1939
G. G. Macaulay	Eng. v S. Africa (Cape Town)	1922–23
H. D. Smith	N. Zealand v Eng. (Christchurch)	1932–33
M. W. Tate	Eng. v S. Africa (Birmingham)	1924

1000 Runs and 100 Wickets

		Tests	Runs	Wkts
England	T. E. Bailey	61	2290	132
	I. T. Botham	54	2996	249
	A. W. Greig	58	3599	141
	R. Illingworth	61	1836	122
	W. Rhodes	58	2325	127
	M. W. Tate	39	1198	155
	F. J. Titmus	53	1449	153
Australia	R. Benaud	63	2201	248
	A. K. Davidson	44	1328	186
	G. Giffen	31	1238	103
	I. W. Johnson	45	1000	109
	R. R. Lindwall	61	1502	228
	K. R. Miller	55	2958	170
	M. A. Noble	42	1997	121

		Tests	Runs	Wkts
South Africa	T. L. Goddard	41	2516	123
West Indies	G. S. Sobers	93	8032	235
New Zealand	R. J. Hadlee	38	1241	169
India	Kapil Dev	41	1760	157
	V. Mankad	44	2109	162
Pakistan	Imran Khan	40	1542	179
	Intikhab Alam	47	1493	125

Most Dismissals by a Wicket-Keeper

		Tests	Dis.	Ct.	St.
R. W. Marsh	A.	83	302	291	11
A. P. E. Knott	E.	95	269	250	19
T. G. Evans	E.	91	219	173	46
D. L. Murray	W.I.	62	189	181	8
A. T. W. Grout	A.	51	187	163	24
Wasim Bari	P.	64	173	153	20
J. H. B. Waite	S.A.	50	141	124	17
R. W. Taylor	E.	42	138	131	7
S. M. H. Kirmani	I.	57	136	106	30
W. A. S. Oldfield	A.	54	130	78	52
J. M. Parks	E.	46	114	103	11

Note: J. M. Parks' catches include 2 when not keeping wicket.

Most Dismissals by a Wicket-Keeper in a Match

10 (10 ct.)	R. W. Taylor	Eng. v Ind. (Bombay)	1979–80
9 (8 ct., 1 st.)	G. R. A. Langley	Aus. v Eng. (Lord's)	1956
8 (6 ct., 2 st.)	L. E. G. Ames	Eng. v W. Ind. (Oval)	1933
8 (6 ct., 2 st.)	A. T. W. Grout	Aus. v Pak. (Lahore)	1959–60
8 (8 ct.)	A. T. W. Grout	Aus. v Eng. (Lord's)	1961
8 (8 ct.)	J. J. Kelly	Aus. v Eng. (Sydney)	1901–2
8 (8 ct.)	G. R. A. Langley	Aus. v W. Ind. (Kingston)	1954–55
8 (8 ct.)	D. T. Lindsay	S. Africa v Aus. (Johannesburg)	1966–67
8 (8 ct.)	J. M. Parks	Eng. v N. Zealand (Christchurch)	1965–66
8 (7 ct., 1 st.)	H. B. Taber	Aus. v S. Africa (Johannesburg)	1966–67
8 (8 ct.)	Wasim Bari	Pak. v Eng. (Leeds)	1971
8 (8 ct.)	R. W. Marsh	Aus. v W. Ind. (Melbourne)	1975–76
8 (8 ct.)	R. W. Marsh	Aus. v N. Zealand (Christchurch)	1976–77

Most Dismissals by a Wicket-keeper in an Innings

7 (7 ct.)	Wasim Bari	Pak. v N.Z. (Auckland)	1978–79
7 (7 ct.)	R. W. Taylor	Eng. v Ind. (Bombay)	1979–80
6 (6 ct.)	A. T. W. Grout	Aus. v S. Africa (Johannesburg)	1957–58
6 (6 ct.)	D. T. Lindsay	S. Africa v Aus. (Johannesburg)	1966–67
6 (6 ct.)	J. T. Murray	Eng. v Ind. (Lord's)	1967
6 (5 ct. 1 st.)	S. M. H. Kirmani	Ind. v N. Zealand (Christchurch)	1975–76

Most Dismissals by a Wicket-keeper in a Series

26 (26 ct.)	R. W. Marsh	Aus. v W. Indies	1975–76
26 (23 ct., 3 st.)	J. H. B. Waite	S. Africa v N. Zealand	1961–62
24 (24 ct.)	D. T. Lindsay	S. Africa v Aus.	1966–67
24 (22 ct., 2 st.)	D. L. Murray	W. Ind. v Eng.	1963
24 (21 ct., 3 st.)	A. P. E. Knott	Eng. v Aus.	1970–71
23 (22 ct., 1 st.)	F. C. M. Alexander	W. Ind. v Eng.	1959–60
23 (20 ct., 3 st.)	A. E. Dick	N. Zealand v S. Africa	1961–62
23 (20 ct., 3 st.)	A. T. W. Grout	Aus. v W. Ind.	1960–61
23 (22 ct., 1 st.)	A. P. E. Knott	Eng. v Aus.	1974–75
23 (21 ct., 2 st.)	R. W. Marsh	Aus. v Eng.	1972
23 (16 ct., 7 st.)	J. H. B. Waite	S. Africa v N. Zealand	1953–54

Most Catches

		Tests	Catches
M. C. Cowdrey	E.	114	120
W. R. Hammond	E.	85	110
R. B. Simpson	A.	62	110
G. S. Sobers	W.I	93	109
G. S. Chappell	A.	76	106
I. M. Chappell	A.	75	105
A. W. Greig	E.	58	87
I. R. Redpath	A.	66	83
T. W. Graveney	E.	79	80
Majid Khan	P.	62	70
S. M. Gavaskar	I.	78	69
R. Benaud	A.	63	65
F. S. Trueman	E.	67	64
F. E. Woolley	E.	64	64
C. H. Lloyd	W.I.	85	63
R. N. Harvey	A.	79	62
R. C. Fredericks	W.I.	59	62
G. R. Viswanath	I.	84	61
I. T. Botham	E.	54	60
W. Rhodes	E.	58	60
G. A. R. Lock	E.	49	59
K. F. Barrington	E.	82	58
L. Hutton	E.	79	57
B. Mitchell	S.A.	42	56
K. W. R. Fletcher	E.	59	54
M. J. K. Smith	E.	50	53
E. D. Solkar	I.	27	53
L. R. Gibbs	W.I.	79	52
R. B. Kanhai	W.I.	79	50

Most for New Zealand:

B. E. Congdon	N.Z.	61	44

Note: The above include catches taken while keeping wicket by R. B. Kanhai (9), F. E. Woolley (1) and K. F. Barrington (1).

Most Catches in a Series

J. M. Gregory	15	Aus. v Eng.	1920–21
G. S. Chappell	14	Aus. v Eng.	1974–75
R. B. Simpson	13	Aus. v S. Africa	1957–58

R. B. Simpson	13	Aus. v W. Ind.	1960–61
L. C. Braund	12	Eng. v Aus.	1901–02
T. L. Goddard	12	S. Africa v Eng.	1956–57
A. W. Greig	12	Eng. v Aus.	1974–75
W. R. Hammond	12	Eng. v Aus.	1934
J. T. Ikin	12	Eng. v S. Africa	1951
B. Mitchell	12	S. Africa v Eng.	1930–31
G. S. Sobers	12	W. Ind. v Aus.	1960–61
E. D. Solkar	12	Ind. v Eng.	1972–73
A. E. E. Vogler	12	S. Africa v Eng.	1909–10
D. F. Whatmore	12	Aus. v Ind.	1979–80

Most Catches in a Match

G. S. Chappell	7	Aus. v Eng. (Perth)	1974–75
Yajurvindra Singh	7	Ind. v Eng. (Bangalore)	1976–77
I. M. Chappell	6	Aus. v N. Zealand (Adelaide)	1973–74
M. C. Cowdrey	6	Eng. v W. Ind. (Lord's)	1963
J. M. Gregory	6	Aus. v Eng. (Sydney)	1920–21
A. W. Greig	6	Eng. v Pak. (Leeds)	1974
R. N. Harvey	6	Aus. v Eng. (Sydney)	1962–63
B. Mitchell	6	S. Africa v Aus. (Melbourne)	1931–32
V. Y. Richardson	6	Aus. v S. Africa (Durban)	1935–36
A. Shrewsbury	6	Eng. v Aus. (Sydney)	1887–88
G. S. Sobers	6	W. Ind. v Eng. (Lord's)	1973
E. D. Solkar	6	Ind. v W. Ind. (Port of Spain)	1970–71
A. E. E. Vogler	6	S. Africa v Eng. (Durban)	1909–10
D. F. Whatmore	6	Aus. v Ind. (Kanpur)	1979–80
F. E. Woolley	6	Eng. v Aus. (Sydney)	1911–12

Most Catches in an Innings

| V. Y. Richardson | 5 | Aus. v S. Africa (Durban) | 1935–36 |
| Yajurvindra Singh | 5 | Ind. v Eng. (Bangalore) | 1976–77 |

Captain in Most Test Matches

C. H. Lloyd	W.I.	45	1974–75 to 1981–82
G. S. Chappell	A.	42	1975–76 to 1981–82
P. B. H. May	E.	41	1955 to 1961
Nawab of Pataudi, jun.	I.	40	1961–62 to 1974–75
R. B. Simpson	A.	39	1963–64 to 1977–78
G. S. Sobers	W.I.	39	1964–65 to 1971–72
J. R. Reid	N.Z.	34	1955–56 to 1965
S. M. Gavaskar	I.	33	1975–76 to 1982
J. M. Brearley	E.	31	1977 to 1981
R. Illingworth	E.	31	1969 to 1972
I. M. Chappell	A.	30	1970–71 to 1975
E. R. Dexter	E.	30	1961–62 to 1964
R. Benaud	A.	28	1958–59 to 1963–64
M. C. Cowdrey	E.	27	1959 to 1968–69
W. M. Lawry	A.	25	1967–68 to 1970–71
M. J. K. Smith	E.	25	1963–64 to 1966
W. M. Woodfull	A.	25	1930 to 1934
D. G. Bradman	A.	24	1936–37 to 1948
A. L. Hassett	A.	24	1949–50 to 1953

L. Hutton	E.	23	1952 to 1954–55
A. H. Kardar	P.	23	1952–53 to 1957–58
B. S. Bedi	I.	22	1975–76 to 1978–79
J. D. C. Goddard	W.I.	22	1947–48 to 1957
A. C. MacLaren	E.	22	1897–98 to 1909
J. Darling	A.	21	1899 to 1905
W. R. Hammond	E.	20	1938 to 1946–47

Most for South Africa is 18 by H. W. Taylor (1913–14 to 1924).

Captain in Most Consecutive Test Matches

G.S. Sobers	W.I.	39	1964–65 to 1971–72
P.B.H. May	E.	35	1955 to 1959
J.R. Reid	N.Z.	34	1955–56 to 1965
I.M. Chappell	A.	30	1970–71 to 1975
C.H. Lloyd	W.I.	29	1974–75 to 1977–78
R. Illingworth	E.	25	1969 to 1972
W.M. Woodfull	A.	25	1930 to 1934
A.H. Kardar	P.	23	1952–53 to 1957–58
B. S. Bedi	I.	22	1975–76 to 1978–79
Nawab of Pataudi, jun.	I.	21	1961–62 to 1967–68
W.M. Lawry	A.	20	1968 to 1970–71
M.J.K. Smith	E.	20	1964–65 to 1966
R. Benaud	A.	19	1958–59 to 1961
W.R. Hammond	E.	19	1938 to 1946–47
R.B. Simpson	A.	19	1963–64 to 1964–65
G.T. Dowling	N.Z.	19	1967–68 to 1971–72
F.C.M. Alexander	W.I.	18	1957–58 to 1959–60
H.W. Taylor	S.A.	18	1913–14 to 1924

Captains Who Won the Toss in all Five Tests of a Series

M.C. Cowdrey	Eng. v S. Africa	1960
H.G. Deane	S. Africa v Eng.	1927–28
J.D.C. Goddard	W. Ind. v Ind.	1948–49
A.L. Hassett	Aus. v Eng.	1953
Hon. F.S. Jackson	Eng. v Aus.	1905
M.A. Noble	Aus. v Eng.	1909
Nawab of Pataudi, jun.	Ind. v Eng.	1963–64
G.S. Sobers	W. Ind. v Eng.	1966
G.S. Sobers	W. Ind. v N. Zealand	1971–72

Note: England won the toss in all five Tests v W. Indies in 1959–60; P. B. H. May (3) and M.C. Cowdrey (2) were the captains.

Most Test Appearances

England

M.C. Cowdrey	114	W.R. Hammond	85
G.Boycott	108	K.F. Barrington	82
A.P.E. Knott	95	T.W. Graveney	79
T.G. Evans	91	L. Hutton	79
D.L. Underwood	86	D.C.S. Compton	78

Australia			South Africa	
R.W. Marsh	83		J.H.B. Waite	50
R.N. Harvey	79		A.D. Nourse, snr.	45
G.S. Chappell	76		B. Mitchell	42
I.M. Chappell	75		H.W. Taylor	42
K.D. Walters	74		T.L. Goddard	41
W.M. Lawry	67		R.A. McLean	40
I.R. Redpath	66		H.J. Tayfield	37
R. Benaud	63		D.J. McGlew	34
D.K. Lillee	63		A.D. Nourse Jnr.	34
R.B. Simpson	62		E.J. Barlow	30

West Indies			India	
G.S. Sobers	93		G.R. Viswanath	84
C.H. Lloyd	85		S.M. Gavaskar	78
L.R. Gibbs	79		B.S. Bedi	67
R.B. Kanhai	79		P.R. Umrigar	59
A.I. Kallicharran	66		B.S. Chandrasekhar	58
D.L. Murray	62		S.M.H. Kirmani	57
R.C. Fredericks	59		C.G. Borde	55
F.M. Worrell	51		V.L. Manjrekar	55
W.W. Hall	48		D.B. Vengsarkar	51
E.D. Weekes	48		S. Venkataraghavan	50

New Zealand			Pakistan	
B.E. Congdon	61		Wasim Bari	64
J.R. Reid	58		Majid Khan	62
M.G. Burgess	50		Asif Iqbal	58
B. Sutcliffe	42		Mushtaq Mohammad	57
G.T. Dowling	39		Hanif Mohammad	55
G.M. Turner	39		Zaheer Abbas	49
R.J. Hadlee	38		Intikhab Alam	47
J.M. Parker	36		Wasim Raja	44
R.O. Collinge	35		Javed Miandad	43
R.C. Motz	32		Sarfraz Nawaz	43
V. Pollard	32			

Most Consecutive Test Appearances

G.S. Sobers	W.I.	85	1954–55 to 1971–72
G.R. Viswanath	I.	80	1970–71 to 1982
I.M. Chappell	A.	71	1965–66 to 1975–76
A.P.E. Knott	E.	65	1970–71 to 1977
S.M. Gavaskar	I.	62	1974–75 to 1982
R.B. Kanhai	W.I.	61	1957 to 1968–69
J.R. Reid	N.Z.	58	1949 to 1965
A.W. Greig	E.	58	1972 to 1977
F.E. Woolley	E.	52	1909 to 1926
P.B.H. May	E.	52	1953 to 1959
R.W. Marsh	A.	51	1970–71 to 1977
G.S. Chappell	A.	51	1970–71 to 1977

Most for other countries are:

A.D. Nourse, Sen.	S.A.	45	1902–03 to 1924
Asif Iqbal	P.	45	1964–65 to 1976–77

Most Test Matches as Umpire

F. Chester	48	1924 to 1955	Eng.
C.S. Elliott	42	1957 to 1974	Eng. (41)
			N. Zealand (1)

J.S. Buller	33	1956 to 1969			Eng.
R.W. Crockett	32	1901–02 to 1924–25			Aus.
C.J. Egar	29	1960–61 to 1968–69			Aus.
F.S. Lee	29	1949 to 1962			Eng.
J. Phillips	29	1884–85 to 1905–06			Eng. (11)
					Aus. (13)
					S. Africa (5)
D. Sang Hue	31	1961–62 to 1980–81			W.Ind.
Shuja-Ud-Din	26	1954–55 to 1978–79			Ind.
L.P. Rowan	25	1962–63 to 1970–71			Aus.

Note: C.J. Egar and L.P. Rowan officiated together in 19 Test matches.

First-Class Records
Most Runs in Career

		Inns.	N.O.	Runs	H.S.	Av.
J.B. Hobbs	Surrey	1315	106	61,237	316*	50·65
F.E. Woolley	Kent	1532	85	58,969	305*	40·75
E.H. Hendren	Middx	1300	166	57,611	301*	50·80
C.P. Mead	Hants	1340	185	55,061	280*	47·67
W.G. Grace	Glos	1493	105	54,896	344	39·55
W.R. Hammond	Glos	1005	104	50,551	336*	56·10
H. Sutcliffe	Yorks	1088	123	50,138	313	51·95
T.W. Graveney	Glos & Worcs	1223	159	47,793	258	44·91
T.W. Hayward	Surrey	1138	96	43,551	315*	41·79
M.C. Cowdrey	Kent	1130	134	42,719	307	42·89
G. Boycott	Yorks	871	129	41,568	261*	56·02
A. Sandham	Surrey	1000	79	41,284	325	44·82
L. Hutton	Yorks	814	91	40,140	364	55·51
M.J.K. Smith	Leics & Warws	1091	139	39,832	204	41·84
W. Rhodes	Yorks	1528	237	39,802	267*	30·83
J.H. Edrich	Surrey	979	104	39,790	310*	45·47
R.E.S. Wyatt	Warws & Worcs	1141	157	39,404	232	40·04
D.C.S. Compton	Middx	839	88	38,942	300	51·85
E. Tyldesley	Lancs	961	106	38,874	256*	45·46
J.T. Tyldesley	Lancs	994	62	37,897	295*	40·66
J.W. Hearne	Middx	1025	116	37,252	285*	40·98
L.E.G. Ames	Kent	951	95	37,248	295	43·51
D. Kenyon	Worcs	1159	59	37,002	259	33·63
W.J. Edrich	Middx	964	92	36,965	267*	42·39
J.M. Parks	Sussex & Som	1227	172	36,673	205*	34·76
D. Denton	Yorks	1163	70	36,479	221	33·37
G.H. Hirst	Yorks	1215	151	36,323	341	34·13
W.G. Quaife	Warws	1203	186	36,012	255*	35·38
R.E. Marshall	Hants	1053	59	35,725	228*	35·94
G. Gunn	Notts	1061	82	35,208	220	35·96
D.L. Amiss	Warws	911	98	35,158	262*	43·24

In addition to the above, the following have also exceeded 30,000 runs: A. Jones (Glam) 34,987; D.B. Close (Yorks & Som) 34,833; John Langridge (Sussex) 34,380; G.M. Turner (Worcs. & New Zealand) 34,213; C. Washbrook (Lancs) 34,101; M. Leyland (Yorks) 33,659; H.T.W. Hardinge (Kent) 33,519; R. Abel (Surrey) 33,124; K.W.R. Fletcher (Essex) 32,299; C.A. Milton (Glos) 32,150; J.D.B. Robertson (Middx) 31,914; J. Hardstaff, jnr. (Notts) 31,847; James Langridge (Sussex) 31,716; K.F. Barrington (Surrey) 31,714; C.B. Fry (Sussex & Hants) 30,886; D. Brookes (Northants) 30,874; Mushtaq Mohammad (Pakistan & Northants) 30,777; P. Holmes (Yorks) 30,574; R.T. Simpson (Notts) 30,546; L.G. Berry (Leics) 30,225; K.G. Suttle (Sussex) 30,225; Zaheer Abbas (Pakistan & Glos.) 30,069.

175

Most Runs in a Season

		Inns.	N.O.	Runs	H.S.	Av.
D.C.S. Compton	1947	50	8	3816	246	90·85
W.J. Edrich	1947	52	8	3539	267*	80·43
T.W. Hayward	1906	61	8	3518	219	66·37
L. Hutton	1949	56	6	3429	269*	68·58
F.E. Woolley	1928	59	4	3352	198	60·94
H. Sutcliffe	1932	52	7	3336	313	74·13
W.R. Hammond	1933	54	5	3323	264	67·81
E.H. Hendren	1928	54	7	3311	209*	70·44
R. Abel	1901	68	8	3309	247	55·15
W.R. Hammond	1937	55	5	3252	217	65·04
M.J.K. Smith	1959	67	11	3245	200*	57·94
E.H. Hendren	1933	65	9	3186	301*	56·89
C.P. Mead	1921	52	6	3179	280*	69·10
T.W. Hayward	1904	63	5	3170	203	54·65
K.S. Ranjitsinhji	1899	58	8	3159	197	63·18
C.B. Fry	1901	43	3	3147	244	78·67
K.S. Ranjitsinhji	1900	40	5	3065	275	87·57
L.E.G. Ames	1933	57	5	3058	295	58·80
J.T. Tyldesley	1901	60	5	3041	221	55·29
C.P. Mead	1928	50	10	3027	180	75·67
J.B. Hobbs	1925	48	5	3024	266*	70·32
E. Tyldesley	1928	48	10	3024	242	79·57
W.E. Alley	1961	64	11	3019	221*	56·96
W.R. Hammond	1938	42	2	3011	271	75·27
E.H. Hendren	1923	51	12	3010	200*	77·17
H. Sutcliffe	1931	42	11	3006	230	96·96
J.H. Parks	1937	63	4	3003	168	50·89
H. Sutcliffe	1928	44	5	3002	228	76·97

Best Batting Average in Season

		Inns.	N.O.	Runs	H.S.	Av.
D.G. Bradman	1938	26	5	2429	278	115·66
G. Boycott	1979	20	5	1538	175*	102·53
W.A. Johnston	1953	17	16	102	28*	102·00
G. Boycott	1971	30	5	2503	233	100·12
D.G. Bradman	1930	36	6	2960	334	98·66
H. Sutcliffe	1931	42	11	3006	230	96·96
R.M. Poore	1899	21	4	1551	304	91·23
D.R. Jardine	1927	14	3	1002	147	91·09
D.C.S. Compton	1947	50	8	3816	246	90·85
G.M. Turner	1982	16	3	1171	311*	90·07
D.G. Bradman	1948	31	4	2428	187	89·92
Zaheer Abbas	1981	36	10	2306	215*	88·69
K.S. Ranjitsinhji	1900	40	5	3065	275	87·57
D.R. Jardine	1928	17	4	1133	193	87·15

Highest Individual Innings in First-Class Cricket

499	Hanif Mohammad	Karachi v Bahawalpur, Karachi	1958–59
452*	D.G. Bradman	N.S.W. v Qld., Sydney	1929–30
443*	B.B. Nimbalkar	Maharashtra v Kathiawar, Poona	1948–49
437	W.H. Ponsford	Vic. v Qld., Melbourne	1927–28
429	W.H. Ponsford	Vic. v Tas., Melbourne	1922–23

428	Aftab Baloch	Sind v Baluchistan, Karachi	1973–74
424	A.C. MacLaren	Lancs v Som., Taunton	1895
385	B. Sutcliffe	Otago v Canterbury, Christchurch	1952–53
383	C.W. Gregory	N.S.W. v Qld., Brisbane	1906–7
369	D.G. Bradman	S. Aus. v Tas., Adelaide	1935–36
365*	C. Hill	S. Aus. v N.S.W., Adelaide	1900–1
365*	G.S. Sobers	W. Indies v Pak., Kingston	1957–58
364	L. Hutton	Eng. v Aus., Oval	1938
359*	V.M. Merchant	Bombay v Maharashtra, Bombay	1943–44
359	R.B. Simpson	N.S.W. v Qld., Brisbane	1963–64
357*	R. Abel	Surrey v Som., Oval	1899
357	D.G. Bradman	S. Aus. v Vic., Melbourne	1935–36
356	B.A. Richards	S. Aus. v W. Aus., Perth	1970–71
355	B. Sutcliffe	Otago v Auckland, Dunedin	1949–50
352	W.H. Ponsford	Vic. v N.S.W., Melbourne	1926–27
350	Rashid Israr	Habib Bank v National Bank, Lahore	1976–77

The highest innings in first-class cricket in S. Africa is 306* by E.A.B. Rowan for Transvaal v Natal, Johannesburg, 1939–40.

Altogether there have been 92 instances of an innings of 300 or more in first-class cricket, scored as follows:

In England	42 inns.	In New Zealand	4 inns.
„ Australia	19 „	„ India	7 „
„ South Africa	3 „	„ Pakistan	8 „
„ West Indies	9 „		

Most Runs in a Day by an Individual

345	(0–345)	C.G. Macartney 345	Ausns. v Notts, Nottingham	1921
334	(0–334*)	W.H. Ponsford 352	Vic. v N.S.W., Melbourne	1926–27
333	(0–333)	K.S. Duleepsinhji 333	Sussex v Northants, Hove	1930
331	(0–331*)	J.D. Robertson 331*	Middx v Worcs, Worcester	1949
325	(0–325*)	B.A. Richards 356	S. Aus. v W. Aus., Perth	1970–71
322	(0–322)	E. Paynter 322	Lancs v Sussex, Hove	1937
318	(48*–366*)	C.W. Gregory 383	N.S.W. v Qld., Brisbane	1906–7
316	(0–316)	R.H. Moore 316	Hants v Warws, Bournemouth	1937
315	(0–315*)	R.C. Blunt 338*	Otago v Cant., Christchurch	1931–32
312	(0–312*)	J.M. Brearley 312*	M.C.C. v N. Zone, Peshawar	1966–67
311	(0–311*)	G.M. Turner 311*	Worcs v Warws Worcester	1982
309	(0–309*)	D.G. Bradman 334	Aus. v Eng., Leeds	1930
307	(0–307*)	W.H. Ashdown 332	Kent v Essex, Brentwood	1934
306	(0–306*)	A.N. Ducat 306*	Surrey v Oxford Univ., Oval	1919
305	(0–305*)	F.R. Foster 305*	Warws v Worcs, Dudley	1914

The innings of E. Paynter and R.H. Moore (above) were both scored on the same day— July 28, 1937.

(The figure after the name indicates the batsman's final score.)

Most Runs in a Calendar Month

			Inns.	N.O.	Runs	H.S.	Av.
June	1949	L. Hutton (Yorks)	16	2	1294	201	92·42
August	1936	W.R. Hammond (Glos)	16	3	1281	317	98·53
August	1876	W.G. Grace (Glos)	11	1	1278	344	127·80
July	1959	M.J.K. Smith (Warws)	15	2	1209	200*	93·00

The greatest number of runs in a calendar month abroad is 1146 by W.H. Ponsford (Vic.) in December, 1927. He scored the runs in 5 innings and his average for the month was 229·20.

Most Centuries in Career

197	J.B. Hobbs (Surrey)		117	D.G. Bradman (N.S.W.& S. Aus)
170	E.H. Hendren (Middx)		107	A. Sandham (Surrey)
167	W.R. Hammond (Glos)		107	M.C. Cowdrey (Kent)
153	C.P. Mead (Hants)		104	T.W. Hayward (Surrey)
149	H. Sutcliffe (Yorks)		103	J.H. Edrich (Surrey)
145	F.E. Woolley (Kent)		103	G.M. Turner (New Z. & Worcs)
130	G. Boycott (Yorks)		102	E. Tyldesley (Lancs)
129	L. Hutton (Yorks)		102	L.E.G. Ames (Kent)
126	W.G. Grace (Glos)		96	J.W. Hearne (Middx)
123	D.C.S. Compton (Middx)		95	Zaheer Abbas (Pak. & Glos)
122	T.W. Graveney (Glos & Worcs)		94	C.B. Fry (Sussex & Hants)

Most Centuries in a Season

18	D.C.S. Compton (Middx)	in 1947
16	J.B. Hobbs (Surrey)	„ 1925
15	W.R. Hammond (Glos)	„ 1938
14	H. Sutcliffe (Yorks)	„ 1932
13	C.B. Fry (Sussex)	„ 1901
13	T.W. Hayward (Surrey)	„ 1906
13	E.H. Hendren (Middx)	„ 1923
13	E.H. Hendren (Middx)	„ 1927
13	E.H. Hendren (Middx)	„ 1928
13	C.P. Mead (Hants)	„ 1928
13	H. Sutcliffe (Yorks)	„ 1928
13	H. Sutcliffe (Yorks)	„ 1931
13	W.R. Hammond (Glos)	„ 1933
13	W.R. Hammond (Glos)	„ 1937
13	D.G. Bradman (Ausns.)	„ 1938
13	G. Boycott (Yorks)	„ 1971

The greatest number of centuries in an overseas season is 8—by D.G. Bradman (in Aus., 1947–48), D.C.S. Compton (in S. Africa, 1948–49), R.N. Harvey (in S. Africa, 1949–50) and A.R. Morris (in S. Africa 1949–50).

The greatest number of centuries in a season in the County Championship is 13—by W.R. Hammond (Glos) in 1938.

Most Double-Centuries in Career

37	D.G. Bradman (N.S.W. & S. Aus.)		13	W.G. Grace (Glos)
36	W.R. Hammond (Glos)		13	J.T. Tyldesley (Lancs)
22	E.H. Hendren (Middx)		13	C.P. Mead (Hants)
17	H. Sutcliffe (Yorks)		13	W.H. Ponsford (Vic.)
16	C.B. Fry (Sussex & Hants)		12	P. Holmes (Yorks)
16	J.B. Hobbs (Surrey)		12	R.B. Simpson (N.S.W. & W. Aus.)
14	K.S. Ranjitsinhji (Sussex)			

Most Double-Centuries in a Season

6	D.G. Bradman (Ausns.)	in 1930
5	K.S. Ranjitsinhji (Sussex)	„ 1900
5	E.D. Weekes (W. Indians)	„ 1950
4	C.B. Fry (Sussex)	„ 1901
4	E.H. Hendren (M.C.C.)	„ 1929–30
4	W.R. Hammond (Glos)	„ 1933
4	W.R. Hammond (Glos)	„ 1934

| 4 | V.M. Merchant (Bombay) | „ 1944–45 |
| 4 | G.M. Turner (N. Zealanders) | „ 1971–72 |

The greatest number of double-centuries in a season in the County Championship is 4—by K.S. Ranjitsinhji (Sussex) in 1900, and by W.R. Hammond (Glos) in 1934.

Two Centuries in Same Match

8 times	Zaheer Abbas (Pak. v Glos.)
7 „	W.R. Hammond (Glos)
7 „	G.M. Turner (New Z. v Glos.)
6 „	J.B. Hobbs (Surrey)
5 „	C.B. Fry (Sussex)
4 „	D.G. Bradman (N.S.W. & S. Aus.)
4 „	G.S. Chappell (S. Aus. & Qld.)
4 „	J.H. Edrich (Surrey)
4 „	L.B. Fishlock (Surrey)
4 „	T.W. Graveney (Glos & Worcs)
4 „	H.T.W. Hardinge (Kent)
4 „	E.H. Hendren (Middx)
4 „	G.L. Jessop (Glos)
4 „	P.A. Perrin (Essex)
4 „	B. Sutcliffe (Otago & Auckland)
4 „	H. Sutcliffe (Yorks)

In addition to his five instances above, C.B. Fry missed the feat by a single run on three occasions.

Two Double-Centuries in Same Match

| 244 & 202* | A.E. Fagg | Kent v Essex, Colchester | 1938 |

Most Centuries in Consecutive Innings

6	C.B. Fry (Sussex)	in 1901	106, 209, 149, 105, 140, 105
6	D.G. Bradman (S. Aus.)	„ 1938–39	118, 143, 225, 107, 186, 135*
6	M.J. Procter (Rhodesia)	„ 1970–71	119, 129, 107, 174, 106, 254
5	E.D. Weekes (W. Indians)	„ 1955–56	156, 148, 123, 119*, 103

E.D. Weekes (above) scored his 5 consecutive centuries while on tour in N. Zealand—the record for a touring batsman.

Apart from the above feats D. G. Bradman, W. R. Hammond, J. B. Hobbs and H. Sutcliffe have each *twice* scored four centuries in consecutive innings.

1000 Runs in a Season Most Times

W.G. Grace	Glos	28 times	between	1869 and 1902
F.E. Woolley	Kent	28 „	„	1907 and 1938
C.P. Mead	Hants	27 „	„	1906 and 1936
M.C. Cowdrey	Kent	27 „	„	1951 and 1974
J.B. Hobbs	Surrey	26 „	„	1905 and 1933
E.H. Hendren	Middx	25 „	„	1911 and 1937
W.G. Quaife	Warws	24 „	„	1896 and 1926
H. Sutcliffe	Yorks	24 „	„	1919 and 1939

F.E Woolley (Kent) scored 1000 or more runs in 28 successive seasons, and C. P. Mead (Hants) did so in 27 successive seasons.

Highest Innings on First-Class Debut

240	W.F.E. Marx	Transvaal v Griqualand West,	
		Johannesburg	1920–21
232*	S.J.E. Loxton	Vic. v Qld., Melbourne	1946–47
230	G.R. Viswanath	Mysore v Andhra, Vijayawada	1967–68
215*	G.H.G. Doggart	Cambridge Univ. v Lancs, Cambridge	1948
207	N.F. Callaway	N.S.W. v Qld., Sydney	1914–15
202	J. Hallebone	Vic. v Tasmania, Melbourne	1951–52
200*	A. Maynard	Trinidad v M.C.C., Port of Spain	1934–35

Fastest Centuries

35 mins	P.G.H Fender (113*)	Surrey v Northants	N'ampton	1920
37 „	C.M. Old (107)	Yorks v Warws	Birmingham	1977
40 „	G.L. Jessop (101)	Glos v Yorks	Harrogate	1897
42 „	G.L. Jessop (191)	Gents of S. v Players of S.	Hastings	1907
43 „	A.H. Hornby (106)	Lancs v Somerset	Manchester	1905
44 „	R.N.S. Hobbs (100)	Essex v Ausns.	Chelmsford	1975
45 „	E.M. Sprot (125*)	Hants v Glos	Bristol	1911
45 „	W. Voce (129)	Notts v Glamorgan	Nottingham	1931
48 „	A.W. Carr (124)	Notts v Sussex	Hove	1925
50 „	K.L. Hutchings (100)	Kent v Glos	Catford	1909
50 „	D.R.A. Gehrs (119)	S. Aus. v W. Aus.	Adelaide	1912–13

Most Sixes in an Innings

Sixes		Score			
15	J.R. Reid	296	Wellington v N. Districts	Wellington	1962–63
13	Majid Jehangir				
	Khan	147*	Pakistanis v Glam	Swansea	1967
13	C.G. Greenidge	273*	D.H. Robins' XI v Pakistanis	Eastbourne	1974
13	C.G. Greenidge	259	Hants v Sussex	Southampton	1975
12	Gulfraz Khan	207	Pak. Rlwys. v Pak. Univs.	Lahore	1976–77
11	C.K. Nayudu	153	Hindus v M.C.C.	Bombay	1926–27
11	C.J. Barnett	194	Glos v Somerset	Bath	1934
11	R. Benaud	135	Ausns. v T.N. Pearce's XI	Scarborough	1953
10	H.L. Simms	126	Sussex v Notts	Hove	1912
10	A.M. Crawley	204	Oxford Univ. v Northants	W'borough	1929
10	W.R. Hammond	336*	Eng. v N. Zealand	Auckland	1932–33
10	H. Sutcliffe	113	Yorks v Northants	Kettering	1933
10	W.J. Stewart	155	Warws v Lancs	Blackpool	1959
10	H.R. Lance	122	Transvaal v Eastern	Johannes-	
			Province	burg	1966–67
10	I.T. Botham	228	Somerset v Glos.	Taunton	1980

The greatest number of sixes scored by a player in a match is 17, by W.J. Stewart (Warws) in innings of 155 (10 sixes) and 125 (7 sixes) v Lancs, Blackpool, 1959.

Most Sixes in a Season

72 sixes	A.W. Wellard	in 1935	(68 for Somerset; 4 for others)
57 „	A.W. Wellard	„ 1936	(50 „ Somerset; 7 for others)
57 „	A.W. Wellard	„ 1938	(50 „ Somerset; 7 for others)
51 „	A.W. Wellard	„ 1933	(51 „ Somerset; 0 for others)

Most Runs in an Over

36	(666666)	G.S. Sobers	off M.A. Nash	Notts v Glam	Swansea	1968
*34	(46604446)	E.B. Alletson	„ E.H. Killick	Notts v Sussex	Hove	1911
†34	(40446664)	R.M. Edwards	„ M.C. Carew	Gov.-Gen. XI v		
				W. Indians	Auckland	1968–69
34	(646666)	F.C. Hayes	„ M.A. Nash	Lancs v Glam	Swansea	1977
32	(664664)	C.C. Smart	„ G. Hill	Glam v Hants	Cardiff	1935
32	(466664)	C.C. Inman	„ N. Hill	Leics v Notts	N'ham	1965
32	(666644)	I.R. Redpath	„ N. Rosen-	Ausns v		
			dorff	O.F.S.	B'fontein	1969–70

*Two no-balls were included in the over.
†8-ball over.

Longest Individual Innings

The longest innings in point of time have been:

16 hrs 10 mins.	Hanif Mohammad	337	Pak. v W. Ind., Bridgetown	1957–58
13 „ 17 „	L. Hutton	364	Eng. v Aus., Oval	1938
12 „ 42 „	R.B. Simpson	311	Aus. v Eng., Manchester	1964
12 „ 30 „	Rashid Israr	350	Habib Bank v National Bank, Lahore	1976–77
12 „ 7 „	R.M. Cowper	307	Aus. v Eng., Melbourne	1965–66
12 „ 0 „	Zakir Butt	290	Railways v N.W.F.P., Peshawar	1972–73
11 „ 48 „	L. Wight	262*	Br. Guiana v Barbados, Georgetown	1951–52
11 hrs 44 mins	G.M. Turner	259	N. Zealand v W. Ind., Georgetown	1971–72
11 „ 23 „	K.F. Barrington	256	Eng. v Aus., Manchester	1964
11 „ 22 „	F.M. Worrell	197*	W. Ind. v Eng., Bridgetown	1959–60

The longest innings in a first-class inter-county match is 10 hrs. 15 mins. by A. Shrewsbury (267) for Notts v Middx., Nottingham, 1887.

Most Wickets in Career

		Runs	Wkts.	Av.
W. Rhodes	Yorks	69,993	4187	16·71
A.P. Freeman	Kent	69,577	3776	18·42
C.W.L. Parker	Glos	63,821	3278	19·46
J.T. Hearne	Middx	54,342	3061	17·75
T.W. Goddard	Glos	59,116	2979	19·84
W.G. Grace	Glos	51,545	2876	17·92
A.S. Kennedy	Hants	61,044	2874	21·24
D. Shackleton	Hants	53,303	2857	18·65
G.A.R. Lock	Surrey and Leics	54,710	2844	19·23
F.J. Titmus	Middx and Surrey	63,313	2830	22·37
M.W. Tate	Sussex	50,567	2784	18·16
G.H. Hirst	Yorks	51,300	2739	18·72
C. Blythe	Kent	42,136	2506	16·81
W.E. Astill	Leics	57,784	2431	23·76
J.C. White	Somerset	43,759	2356	18·57
W.E. Hollies	Warws	48,656	2323	20·94

		Runs	Wkts.	Av.
F.S. Trueman	Yorks	42,154	2304	18·29
J.B. Statham	Lancs	36,995	2260	16·36
R.T.D. Perks	Worcs	53,770	2233	24·07
J. Briggs	Lancs	35,390	2221	15·93
D.J. Shepherd	Glam	47,298	2218	22·32
G.E. Dennett	Glos	42,568	2147	19·82
T. Richardson	Surrey	38,794	2105	18·42
D.L. Underwood	Kent	41,186	2084	19·76
T.E. Bailey	Essex	48,170	2082	23·13
F.E. Woolley	Kent	41,058	2066	19·87
G. Geary	Leics	41,339	2063	20·03
D.V.P. Wright	Kent	49,305	2056	23·98
R. Illingworth	Yorks and Leics	41,072	2040	20·13
J.A. Newman	Hants	51,211	2032	25·20
A. Shaw	Notts and Sussex	24,496	2021	12·12
S. Haigh	Yorks	32,091	2012	15·94

Most Wickets in a Season

		Overs	Mdns.	Runs	Wkts.	Av.
A.P. Freeman	1928	1976·1	423	5489	304	18·05
A.P. Freeman	1933	2039	651	4549	298	15·26
T. Richardson	1895	1690·1	463	4170	290	14·37
C.T.B. Turner	1888	2427·2	1127	3307	283	11·68
A.P. Freeman	1931	1618	360	4307	276	15·60
A.P. Freeman	1930	1914·3	472	4632	275	16·84
T. Richardson	1897	1603·4	495	3945	273	14·45
A.P. Freeman	1929	1670·5	381	4879	267	18·27
W. Rhodes	1900	1553	455	3606	261	13·81
J.T. Hearne	1896	2003·1	818	3670	257	14·28
A.P. Freeman	1932	1565·5	404	4149	253	16·39
W. Rhodes	1901	1565	505	3797	251	15·12

The feat of taking 200 or more wickets in a season has been performed on 59 occasions (including the above). A. P. Freeman performed the feat the record number of 8 times (between 1928 and 1935) and C. W. L. Parker did so 5 times (between 1922 and 1931). Freeman's 8 performances were in successive seasons.

The last occasion on which 200 or more wickets were taken in a season was in 1957 by G. A. R. Lock (212 wkts., av. 12·02).

100 or More Wickets in a Season Most Times

W. Rhodes	Yorks	23	times	between	1898 & 1929
D. Shackleton	Hants	20	„	„	1949 „ 1968
A.P. Freeman	Kent	17	„	„	1920 „ 1936
C.W.L. Parker	Glos	16	„	„	1920 „ 1935
T.W. Goddard	Glos	16	„	„	1929 „ 1950
R.T.D. Perks	Worcs	16	„	„	1934 „ 1955
F.J. Titmus	Middx	16	„	„	1953 „ 1971
J.T. Hearne	Middx	15	„	„	1891 „ 1911
G.H. Hirst	Yorks	15	„	„	1895 „ 1913
A.S. Kennedy	Hants	15	„	„	1912 „ 1932

D. Shackleton (Hants) took 100 or more wickets in 20 successive seasons, and A.P. Freeman (Kent) did so in 17 successive seasons.

Most Wickets in a Match

19–90	J.C. Laker	Eng. v Aus.	Manchester	1956
17–48	C. Blythe	Kent v Northants	Northampton	1907
17–50	C.T.B. Turner	Ausns. v An Eng. XI	Hastings	1888
17–54	W.P. Howell	Ausns. v Western Prov.	Cape Town	1902–3
17–56	C.W.L. Parker	Glos v Essex	Gloucester	1925
17–67	A.P. Freeman	Kent v Sussex	Hove	1922
17–89	W.G. Grace	Glos v Notts	Cheltenham	1877
17–89	F.C.L. Matthews	Notts v Northants	Nottingham	1923
17–91	H. Dean	Lancs v Yorks	Liverpool	1913
17–91	H. Verity	Yorks v Essex	Leyton	1933
17–92	A.P. Freeman	Kent v Warws	Folkestone	1932
17–103	W. Mycroft	Derby v Hants	Southampton	1876
17–106	G.R. Cox	Sussex v Warws	Horsham	1926
17–106	T.W. Goddard	Glos v Kent	Bristol	1939
17–119	W. Mead	Essex v Hants	Southampton	1895
17–137	W. Brearley	Lancs v Somerset	Manchester	1905
17–159	S.F. Barnes	Eng. v S. Africa	Johannesburg	1913–14
17–201	G. Giffen	South Aus. v Vic.	Adelaide	1885–86
17–212	J.C. Clay	Glam v Worcs	Swansea	1937

A.P. Freeman (Kent) is the only bowler who has taken 17 wickets in a match on more than one occasion, though W. Mead (Essex), apart from his one instance above, also took 17–205 for Essex v Ausns, Leyton, 1893, before Essex attained first-class status.
For Gentlemen of England v M.C.C., Lord's, 1818, R. Holden took 19 wickets. The arrangement was that Holden should bowl from **both** ends throughout the match.
In a 12-a-side match at Canterbury in 1861, H. Arkwright took 18–96 for Gentlemen of M.C.C. v Gentlemen of Kent.

Most Wickets in a Day

17	C. Blythe	Kent v Northants, Northampton	1907
17	H. Verity	Yorks v Essex, Leyton	1933
17	T.W. Goddard	Glos v Kent, Bristol	1939
16	T. Emmett	Yorks v Cambridgeshire, Hunslet	1869
16	J. Southerton	South v North, Lord's	1875
16	T.G. Wass	Notts v Lancs, Liverpool	1906
16	A.E.E. Vogler	Eastern Province v Griqualand West, Johannesburg	1906–7
16	T.G. Wass	Notts v Essex, Nottingham	1908
16	J.C. White	Somerset v Worcs, Bath	1919

Most Hat-tricks in Career

7	D.V.P. Wright (Kent)	4	T. Richardson (Surrey)
6	C.W.L. Parker (Glos)	4	J.T. Hearne (Middx)
6	T.W. Goddard (Glos)	4	T.J. Matthews (Vic.)
5	S. Haigh (Yorks)	4	G.G. Macaulay (Yorks)
5	F.A. Tarrant (Middx)	4	J.C. Laker (Surrey)
5	V.W.C. Jupp (Sussex & Northants)	4	F.S. Trueman (Yorks)
5	A.E.G. Rhodes (Derby)	4	G.A.R. Lock (Surrey & Leics)
4	R.G. Barlow (Lancs)	4	M.J. Procter (Glos. & S.A.)

In addition to his five hat-tricks above, A.E.G. Rhodes (Derby) also took three wickets with three successive balls he bowled in first-class cricket in 1952, the feat, however, being spread over two matches.

Most Runs Conceded in an Innings

runs	wkts.				
362	4	A.A. Mailey	N.S.W. v Vic.	Melbourne	1926–27
309	5	G. Giffen	S. Aus. v A.E. Stoddart's XI	Adelaide	1894–95
301	4	B.K. Garudacher	Mysore v Holkar	Indore	1945–46
298	1	L. O'B. Fleetwood–Smith	Aus. v Eng.	Oval	1938
295	3	Anwar	Dera Ismail Khan v Railways	Lahore	1964–65
287	8	G. Giffen	S. Aus. v N.S.W.	Adelaide	1899–1900
279	1	Anayat	Dera Ismail Khan v Railways	Lahore	1964–65
275	5	C.S. Nayudu	Holkar v Bombay	Bombay	1944–45

The instances recorded by Anwar and Anayat (above) were in the same innings.
    The greatest number of runs conceded in an innings in the County Championship is 231 (6 Wkts.) by C.W.L. Parker, Glos v Somerset, Bristol, 1923.

Most Runs Conceded in a Match

runs	wkts.				
428	11	C.S. Nayudu	Holkar v Bombay	Bombay	1944–45
394	10	C.V. Grimmett	S. Aus. v N.S.W.	Sydney	1925–26
374	9	O.C. Scott	W. Ind. v Eng.	Kingston	1929–30
362	4	A.A. Mailey	N.S.W. v Vic.	Melbourne	1926–27
359	7	D.G. Choudhari	Maharashtra v Bombay	Poona	1948–49
345	3	J.D. Scott	S. Aus. v N.S.W.	Sydney	1925–26
331	8	A.P. Freeman	Kent v M.C.C.	Folkestone	1934

The instances recorded by C.V. Grimmett and J.D. Scott (above) were in the same innings.
    The greatest number of runs conceded in a match in the County Championship is 306 (4 wkts.) by J. Briggs, Lancs v Sussex, Manchester, 1897.

Long Distance for a Bail

yd.	in.				
67	6	R.D. Burrows (Worcs)	bowling W. Huddleston (Lancs) Manchester		1911
66	0	H. Larwood (M.C.C.)	„ G.W. Martin (Tasmania) Launceston		1928–29
64	6	R.D. Burrows (Worcs)	„ A.C. MacLaren (Lancs) Manchester		1901
63	6	A. Mold (Lancs)	„ G.A. Lohmann (Surrey) Oval		1896
58	0	F.E. Field (Warws)	„ R.B. Rickman (Derby) Birmingham		1908

The record in minor cricket is 83 yd 1 ft 9 in. by A.O. Burrows in a club match in Tasmania—for New Town v North-West Hobart on the New Town ground, Hobart, November 21, 1925.

Highest Innings Totals

1107	Vic. v N.S.W.	Melbourne	1926–27
1059	Vic. v Tasmania	Melbourne	1922–23
951–7 (dec)	Sind v Baluchistan	Karachi	1973–74
918	N.S.W. v S. Aus.	Sydney	1900–1
912–8 (dec)	Holkar v Mysore	Indore	1945–46
910–6 (dec)	Railways v Dera Ismail Khan	Lahore	1964–65
903–7 (dec)	Eng. v Aus.	Oval	1938
887	Yorks v Warwicks	Birmingham	1896
849	Eng. v W. Ind.	Kingston	1929–30
843	Ausns v Oxford & Cambridge Univs. P. & P.	Portsmouth	1893
839	N.S.W. v Tasmania	Sydney	1898–99
826–4	Maharashtra v Kathiawar	Poona	1948–49
824	Lahore Greens v Bahawalpur	Lahore	1965–66
821–7 (dec)	S. Aus. v Qld.	Adelaide	1939–40
815	N.S.W. v Vic.	Sydney	1908–9
811	Surrey v Somerset	Oval	1899
807	N.S.W. v S. Aus	Adelaide	1899–1900
805	N.S.W. v Vic.	Melbourne	1905–6
803–4 (dec)	Kent v Essex	Brentwood	1934
803	Non-Smokers v Smokers	East Melbourne	1886–87
802	N.S.W. v S. Aus.	Sydney	1920–21
801	Lancs v Somerset	Taunton	1895

Lowest Innings Totals

*12	Oxford Univ. v M.C.C.	Oxford	1877
12	Northants v Glos	Gloucester	1907
13	Auckland v Canterbury	Auckland	1877–78
13	Notts v Yorks	Nottingham	1901
15	M.C.C. v Surrey	Lord's	1839
*15	Vic. v M.C.C.	Melbourne	1903–4
*15	Northants v Yorks	Northampton	1908
15	Hants v Warws	Birmingham	1922
16	M.C.C. v Surrey	Lord's	1872
16	Derby v Notts	Nottingham	1879
16	Surrey v Notts	Oval	1880
16	Warws v Kent	Tonbridge	1913
16	Trinidad v Barbados	Bridgetown	1941–42
16	Border v Natal	East London	1959–60

*Batted one man short.

Lowest Match Aggregate by a Side

34 (16 & 18)	Border v Natal	East London	1959–60
*42 (27 & 15)	Northants v Yorks	Northampton	1908

*Batted one man short in each innings.

Highest Match Aggregates

2376 for 37 wkts.		Bombay v Maharashtra	Poona	1948–49
2078	40 „	Bombay v Holkar	Bombay	1944–45
1981	35 „	S. Africa v Eng.	Durban	1938–39
1929	39 „	N.S.W. v S. Aus.	Sydney	1925–26
1911	34 „	N.S.W. v Vic.	Sydney	1908–9
1905	40 „	Otago v Wellington	Dunedin	1923–24
1815	34 „	W. Ind. v Eng.	Kingston	1929–30
1801	40 „	A.L. Hassett's XI v A.R. Morris's XI	Melbourne	1953–54
1764	39 „	Aus. v W. Ind.	Adelaide	1968–69
1753	40 „	Aus. v Eng.	Adelaide	1920–21
1752	34 „	N.S.W. v Qld.	Sydney	1926–27
1744	40 „	N.S.W. v S. Africans	Sydney	1910–11
1739	40 „	N.S.W. v A.E. Stoddart's XI	Sydney	1897–98
1723	31 „	Eng. v Aus.	Leeds	1948
1716	40 „	N.S.W. v S. Aus.	Sydney	1907–8
1704	39 „	J. Ryder's XI v W.M. Woodfull's XI	Sydney	1929–30

The highest aggregate in a first-class inter-county match is 1475 for 27 wickets (Northants v Surrey, Northampton, 1920).

Lowest Match Aggregates
(completed matches)

105 for 31 wkts.		M.C.C. v Ausns.	Lord's	1878
134	30 „	Eng. v The B's	Lord's	1831
147	40 „	Kent v Sussex	Sevenoaks	1828
149	30 „	Eng. v Kent	Lord's	1858
151	30 „	Canterbury v Otago	Christchurch	1866–67
153	37 „	M.C.C. v Sussex	Lord's	1843
153	31 „	Otago v Canterbury	Dunedin	1896–97
156	30 „	Nelson v Wellington	Nelson	1885–86
158	22 „	Surrey v Worcs	Oval	1954
159	31 „	Nelson v Wellington	Nelson	1887–88

Biggest Victories

Inns. & 851 runs	Railways v Dera Ismail Khan	Lahore	1964–65
„ „ 666 „	Vic. v Tasmania	Melbourne	1922–23
„ „ 656 „	Vic. v N.S.W.	Melbourne	1926–27
„ „ 605 „	N.S.W. v S. Aus.	Sydney	1900–1
„ „ 579 „	Eng. v Aus.	Oval	1938
„ „ 575 „	Sind v Baluchistan	Karachi	1973–74
„ „ 527 „	N.S.W. v S. Aus.	Adelaide	1908–9
„ „ 517 „	Ausns v Notts	Nottingham	1921
685 runs	N.S.W. v Qld.	Sydney	1929–30
675 „	Eng. v Aus.	Brisbane	1928–29
638 „	N.S.W. v S. Aus.	Adelaide	1920–21
625 „	Sargodha v Lahore Mun. Corp.	Faisalabad	1978–79
609 „	Muslim Comm. Bank v WAPDA	Lahore	1977–78
571 „	Vic. v S. Aus.	Adelaide	1926–27
562 „	Aus. v Eng.	Oval	1934
541 „	N.S.W. v S. Aus.	Sydney	1925–26
540 „	Bengal v Orissa	Cuttack	1953–54

The biggest victory in a first-class inter-county match is by an innings and 485 runs (Surrey v Sussex, Oval, 1888).

Wicket-Keeping
Most Dismissals in an Innings

8 (8 ct., 0 st.)	A.T.W. Grout	Qld. v W. Aus. (Brisbane)	1959–60
7 (4 ct., 3 st.)	E.J. Smith	Warws v Derby (Birmingham)	1926
7 (6 ct., 1 st.)	W.F. Farrimond	Lancs v Kent (Manchester)	1930
7 (7 ct., 0 st.)	W.F.F. Price	Middx v Yorks (Lord's)	1937
7 (3 ct., 4 st.)	D. Tallon	Qld. v Vic. (Brisbane)	1938–39
7 (7 ct., 0 st.)	R.A. Saggers	N.S.W. v Combined XI (Brisbane)	1940–41
7 (1 ct., 6 st.)	H. Yarnold	Worcs v Scotland (Broughty Ferry)	1951
7 (4 ct., 3 st.)	J.W. Brown	Scotland v Ireland (Dublin)	1957
7 (7 ct., 0 st.)	M.S. Smith	Natal v Border (East London)	1959–60
7 (6 ct., 1 st.)	N. Kirsten	Border v Rhodesia (East London)	1959–60
7 (7 ct., 0 st.)	K.V. Andrew	Northants v Lancs (Manchester)	1962
7 (7 ct., 0 st.)	A. Long	Surrey v Sussex (Hove)	1964
7 (7 ct., 0 st.)	R.M. Schofield	Central Districts v Wellington (Wellington)	1964–65
7 (7 ct., 0 st.)	R.W. Taylor	Derby v Glam (Derby)	1966
7 (6 ct., 1 st.)	H.B. Taber	N.S.W. v S. Aus. (Adelaide)	1968–69
7 (5 ct., 2 st.)	R.A. Pinnock	Jamaica v Trinidad (Port of Spain)	1969–70
7 (6 ct., 1 st.)	E.W. Jones	Glam v Cambridge Univ. (Cambridge)	1970
7 (6 ct., 1 st.)	S. Benjamin	Central Zone v North Zone (Bombay)	1973–74
7 (7 ct., 0 st.)	R.W. Taylor	Derby v Yorks (Chesterfield)	1975
7 (6 ct., 1 st.)	Shahid Israr	Karachi Whites v Quetta (Karachi)	1976–77
7 (7 ct., 0 st.)	J.A. Maclean	Qld. v Vic. (Melbourne)	1977–78
7 (5 ct., 2 st.)	Taslim Arif	Nat. Bank v Punjab (Lahore)	1978–79
7 (7 ct., 0 st.)	Wasim Bari	Pak. v N.Z. (Auckland)	1978–79
7 (7 ct., 0 st.)	R.W. Taylor	Eng. v Ind. (Bombay)	1979–80

Most Dismissals in a Match

12 (8 ct., 4 st.)	E. Pooley	Surrey v Sussex (Oval)	1868
12 (9 ct., 3 st.)	D. Tallon	Qld. v N.S.W. (Sydney)	1938–39
12 (9 ct., 3 st.)	H.B. Taber	N.S.W. v S. Aus. (Adelaide)	1968–69
11 (11 ct., 0 st.)	A. Long	Surrey v Sussex (Hove)	1964
11 (11 ct., 0 st.)	R.W. Marsh	W. Aus. v Vic. (Perth)	1975–76

Most Dismissals in a Season

127 (79 ct., 48 st.)	L.E.G. Ames (Kent)	in	1929
121 (69 ct., 52 st.)	L.E.G. Ames (Kent)	„	1928
110 (62 ct., 48 st.)	H. Yarnold (Worcs)	„	1949
107 (77 ct., 30 st.)	G. Duckworth (Lancs)	„	1928
107 (96 ct., 11 st.)	J.G. Binks (Yorks)	„	1960
104 (82 ct., 22 st.)	J.T. Murray (Middx)	„	1957
102 (70 ct., 32 st.)	F.H. Huish (Kent)	„	1913
102 (95 ct., 7 st.)	J.T. Murray (Middx)	„	1960
101 (85 ct., 16 st.)	R. Booth (Worcs)	„	1960
100 (62 ct., 38 st.)	F.H. Huish (Kent)	„	1911
100 (36 ct., 64 st.)	L.E.G. Ames (Kent)	„	1932
100 (91 ct., 9 st.)	R. Booth (Worcs)	„	1964

All-Rounders

The Double—1000 runs and 100 wickets in a Season

Most Doubles

16	W. Rhodes (Yorks)	8	M.S. Nichols (Essex)
14	G.H. Hirst (Yorks)	8	A.E. Relf (Sussex)
10	V.W.C. Jupp (Sussex & Northants)	8	F.A. Tarrant (Middx)
9	W.E. Astill (Leics)	8	M.W. Tate (Sussex)
8	T.E. Bailey (Essex)	8	F.J. Titmus (Middx)
8	W.G. Grace (Glos)	8	F.E. Woolley (Kent)

The double was last performed in first-class cricket in 1967, by F.J. Titmus (Middx).

2000 *Runs and* 200 *Wickets in Season*
G.H. Hirst (Yorks)   in 1906

3000 *Runs and* 100 *Wickets in Season*
J.H. Parks (Sussex)   in 1937

1000 *Runs and* 200 *Wickets in Season*
A.E. Trott (Middx)   in 1899, 1900
A.S. Kennedy (Hants)   in 1922
M.W. Tate (Sussex)   in 1923, 1924, 1925

200 *Runs and* 15 *Wickets in Match*
271 & 9–96 & 7–70   G. Giffen   S. Aus. v Vic. (Adelaide)   1891–92

County Championship

Although inter-county cricket had been played since the eighteenth century, and a form of 'merit table' existed from the mid 1860s, the first season in which county qualification rules were in operation was in 1873, a date conveniently and generally agreed as the start of the County Championship.

The winners have been:

1873 { Glos / Notts	1890 Surrey	1912 Yorks	1938 Yorks
1874 Glos	1891 Surrey	1913 Kent	1939 Yorks
1875 Notts	1892 Surrey	1914 Surrey	1946 Yorks
1876 Glos	1893 Yorks	1919 Yorks	1947 Middx
1877 Glos	1894 Surrey	1920 Middx	1948 Glam
1878 Undecided	1895 Surrey	1921 Middx	1949 { Middx / Yorks
1879 { Notts / Lancs	1896 Yorks	1922 Yorks	
1880 Notts	1897 Lancs	1923 Yorks	1950 { Lancs / Surrey
1881 Lancs	1898 Yorks	1924 Yorks	
1882 { Notts / Lancs	1899 Surrey	1925 Yorks	1951 Warws
1883 Notts	1900 Yorks	1926 Lancs	1952 Surrey
1884 Notts	1901 Yorks	1927 Lancs	1953 Surrey
1885 Notts	1902 Yorks	1928 Lancs	1954 Surrey
1886 Notts	1903 Middx	1929 Notts	1955 Surrey
1887 Surrey	1904 Lancs	1930 Lancs	1956 Surrey
1888 Surrey	1905 Yorks	1931 Yorks	1957 Surrey
1889 { Surrey / Lancs / Notts	1906 Kent	1932 Yorks	1958 Surrey
	1907 Notts	1933 Yorks	1959 Yorks
	1908 Yorks	1934 Lancs	1960 Yorks
	1909 Kent	1935 Yorks	1961 Hants
	1910 Kent	1936 Derbys	1962 Yorks
	1911 Warws	1937 Yorks	1963 Yorks

1964	Worcs	1969	Glam	1974	Worcs	1978	Kent
1965	Worcs	1970	Kent	1975	Leics	1979	Essex
1966	Yorks	1971	Surrey	1976	Middx	1980	Middx
1967	Yorks	1972	Warws	1977 { Middx	1981	Notts
1968	Yorks	1973	Hants	{ Kent	1982	Middx

Sheffield Shield

The Sheffield Shield was first competed for in 1892–93 and was named after the Earl of Sheffield, who took a team to Australia the previous season and left a sum of money (with which the Shield was purchased) for the furtherance of the game in Australia.

The original competitors were Victoria, New South Wales and South Australia. Queensland first competed in 1926–27 and Western Australia in 1947–48 (playing on a full home and away basis since 1956–57). Tasmania entered in 1977–78.

The winners have been:

Season	Winner	Season	Winner
1892–93	Vic.	1936–37	Vic.
1893–94	S. Aus.	1937–38	N.S.W.
1894–95	Vic.	1938–39	S. Aus.
1895–96	N.S.W.	1939–40	N.S.W.
1896–97	N.S.W.	1946–47	Vic.
1897–98	Vic.	1947–48	W. Aus.
1898–99	Vic.	1948–49	N.S.W.
1899–00	N.S.W.	1949–50	N.S.W.
1900–1	Vic.	1950–51	Vic.
1901–2	N.S.W.	1951–52	N.S.W.
1902–3	N.S.W.	1952–53	S. Aus.
1903–4	N.S.W.	1953–54	N.S.W.
1904–5	N.S.W.	1954–55	N.S.W.
1905–6	N.S.W.	1955–56	N.S.W.
1906–7	N.S.W.	1956–57	N.S.W.
1907–8	Vic.	1957–58	N.S.W.
1908–9	N.S.W.	1958–59	N.S.W.
1909–10	S. Aus.	1959–60	N.S.W.
1910–11	N.S.W.	1960–61	N.S.W.
1911–12	N.S.W.	1961–62	N.S.W.
1912–13	S. Aus.	1962–63	Vic.
1913–14	N.S.W.	1963–64	S. Aus.
1914–15	Vic.	1964–65	N.S.W.
1919–20	N.S.W.	1965–66	N.S.W.
1920–21	N.S.W.	1966–67	Vic.
1921–22	Vic.	1967–68	W. Aus.
1922–23	N.S.W.	1968–69	S. Aus.
1923–24	Vic.	1969–70	Vic.
1924–25	Vic.	1970–71	S. Aus.
1925–26	N.S.W.	1971–72	W. Aus.
1926–27	S. Aus.	1972–73	W. Aus.
1927–28	Vic.	1973–74	Vic.
1928–29	N.S.W.	1974–75	W. Aus.
1929–30	Vic.	1975–76	S. Aus.
1930–31	Vic.	1976–77	W. Aus.
1931–32	N.S.W.	1977–78	W. Aus.
1932–33	N.S.W.	1978–79	Vic
1933–34	Vic.	1979–80	Vic
1934–35	Vic.	1980–81	W. Aus.
1935–36	S. Aus.	1981–82	S. Aus.

Currie Cup

The Currie Cup was first presented for competition in 1888–89, but the first tournament was not played until April 1890. It was not competed for regularly, and normally there was no competition when a first-class touring side was in South Africa. Since 1965–66 it has been held annually, whether or not a touring side has been present.

The winners have been:

1889–90	Transvaal	1950–51	Transvaal
1890–91	Griqualand West	1951–52	Natal
1892–93	Western Province	1952–53	Western Province
1893–94	Western Province	1954–55	Natal
1894–95	Transvaal	1955–56	Western Province
1896–97	Western Province	1958–59	Transvaal
1897–98	Western Province	1959–60	Natal
1902–3	Transvaal	1960–61	Natal
1903–4	Transvaal	1962–63	Natal
1904–5	Transvaal	1963–64	Natal
1906–7	Transvaal	1965–66	Natal, Transvaal (tied)
1908–9	Western Province	1966–67	Natal
1910–11	Natal	1967–68	Natal
1912–13	Natal	1968–69	Transvaal
1920–21	Western Province	1969–70	Transvaal, Western Province (tied)
1921–22	Transvaal, Natal, Western Province (tied)	1970–71	Transvaal
1923–24	Transvaal	1971–72	Transvaal
1925–26	Transvaal	1972–73	Transvaal
1926–27	Transvaal	1973–74	Natal
1929–30	Transvaal	1974–75	Western Province
1931–32	Western Province	1975–76	Natal
1933–34	Natal	1976–77	Natal
1934–35	Transvaal	1977–78	Western Province
1936–37	Natal	1978–79	Transvaal
1937–38	Natal, Transvaal (tied)	1979–80	Transvaal
1946–47	Natal	1980–81	Natal
1947–48	Natal	1981–82	Western Province

Plunket Shield and Shell Trophy

The Plunket Shield was first awarded in 1906–7 to Canterbury as the side with the best record that season in first-class cricket in New Zealand. It was competed for on a challenge-match basis until 1921–22, since when a points system and an annual table has obtained.

The holders under the challenge match system were:

Canterbury	1906–7 to December 17, 1907
Auckland	December 17, 1907 to February 1, 1911
Canterbury	February 1, 1911 to February 12, 1912
Auckland	February 12, 1912 to January 31, 1913
Canterbury	January 31, 1913 to December 27, 1918
Wellington	December 27, 1918 to January 24, 1919
Canterbury	January 24, 1919 to January 4, 1920
Auckland	January 4, 1920 to January 10, 1921
Wellington	January 10, 1921 to end of challenge system.

The winners from 1921–22 were:

1921–22	Auckland	1923–24	Wellington
1922–23	Canterbury	1924–25	Otago

1925–26	Wellington		1953–54	Central Districts
1926–27	Auckland		1954–55	Wellington
1927–28	Wellington		1955–56	Canterbury
1928–29	Auckland		1956–57	Wellington
1929–30	Wellington		1957–58	Otago
1930–31	Canterbury		1958–59	Auckland
1931–32	Wellington		1959–60	Canterbury
1932–33	Otago		1960–61	Wellington
1933–34	Auckland		1961–62	Wellington
1934–35	Canterbury		1962–63	Northern Districts
1935–36	Wellington		1963–64	Auckland
1936–37	Auckland		1964–65	Canterbury
1937–38	Auckland		1965–66	Wellington
1938–39	Auckland		1966–67	Central Districts
1939–40	Auckland		1967–68	Central Districts
1945–46	Canterbury		1968–69	Auckland
1946–47	Auckland		1969–70	Otago
1947–48	Otago		1970–71	Central Districts
1948–49	Canterbury		1971–72	Otago
1949–50	Wellington		1972–73	Wellington
1950–51	Otago		1973–74	Wellington
1951–52	Canterbury		1974–75	Otago
1952–53	Otago			

In 1975–76 the Plunket Shield was replaced by a fresh first-class programme in New Zealand called the Shell Series, comprising an initial round of matches on a points system for the Shell Cup, after which the teams are divided into two divisions for the second round, with each team playing the other teams in their section, again for points. The two teams with the highest aggregate number of points in each section compete in a final for the Shell Trophy.

The winners of the Shell Trophy since 1975–76 have been:

1975–76	Canterbury
1976–77	Otago
1977–78	Auckland
1978–79	Otago
1979–80	Northern Districts
1980–81	Auckland
1981–82	Wellington

Ranji Trophy

The Ranji Trophy is played for the cricket championship of India and was presented by the Maharaja of Patiala to perpetuate the memory of K. S. Ranjitsinhji. It was first competed for in 1934–35 and was played on a knock-out basis until 1956–57, since when it has been staged as part league, part knock-out.

The winners have been:

1934–35	Bombay		1944–45	Bombay
1935–36	Bombay		1945–46	Holkar
1936–37	Nawanagar		1946–47	Baroda
1937–38	Hyderabad		1947–48	Holkar
1938–39	Bengal		1948–49	Bombay
1939–40	Maharashtra		1949–50	Baroda
1940–41	Maharashtra		1950–51	Holkar
1941–42	Bombay		1951–52	Bombay
1942–43	Baroda		1952–53	Holkar
1943–44	Western India States		1953–54	Bombay

1954–55	Madras	1968–69	Bombay
1955–56	Bombay	1969–70	Bombay
1956–57	Bombay	1970–71	Bombay
1957–58	Baroda	1971–72	Bombay
1958–59	Bombay	1972–73	Bombay
1959–60	Bombay	1973–74	Karnataka
1960–61	Bombay	1974–75	Bombay
1961–62	Bombay	1975–76	Bombay
1962–63	Bombay	1976–77	Bombay
1963–64	Bombay	1977–78	Karnataka
1964–65	Bombay	1978–79	Delhi
1965–66	Bombay	1979–80	Delhi
1966–67	Bombay	1980–81	Bombay
1967–68	Bombay	1981–82	Delhi

Quaid-E-Azam Trophy

The Quaid-E-Azam Trophy, first competed for in 1953–54, is the oldest surviving national first-class tournament of Pakistan. It is played under the aegis of the Board of Control for Cricket in Pakistan.
  The winners have been:

1953–54	Bahawalpur	1968–69	Lahore
1954–55	Karachi	1969–70	Pakistan International Airways
1955–56	No tournament	1970–71	Karachi Blues
1956–57	Punjab	1971–72	No tournament
1957–58	Bahawalpur	1972–73	Railways
1958–59	Karachi	1973–74	Railways
1959–60	Karachi	1974–75	Punjab 'A'
1960–61	No tournament	1975–76	National Bank
1961–62	Karachi Blues	1976–77	United Bank
1962–63	Karachi 'A'	1977–78	Habib Bank
1963–64	Karachi Blues	1978–79	National Bank
1964–65	Karachi Blues	1979–80	P.I.A.
1965–66	No tournament	1980–81	United Bank
1966–67	Karachi	1981–82	National Bank
1967–68	No tournament		

(*The final three matches of each of the tournaments of 1964–65 and 1966–67 were played in the respective following season.*)

Shell Shield

The Shell Shield, which takes its name from its sponsor, the Shell Oil Company, was first competed for in 1965–66. It is played under the aegis of the West Indies Board of Control.
  The winners have been:

1965–66	Barbados	1974–75	Guyana
1966–67	Barbados	1975–76	Barbados / Trinidad
1967–68	No tournament	1976–77	Barbados
1968–69	Jamaica	1977–78	Barbados
1969–70	Trinidad	1978–79	Barbados
1970–71	Trinidad	1979–80	Barbados
1971–72	Barbados	1980–81	Combined Islands
1972–73	Guyana	1981–82	Barbados
1973–74	Barbados		

192